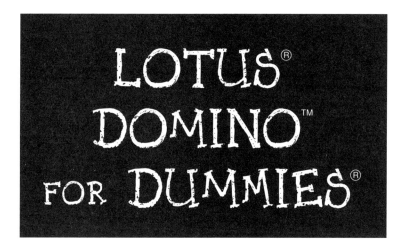

LOTUS® DOMINO™ FOR DUMMIES®

by Jon S. Stuart

IDG BOOKS WORLDWIDE

IDG Books Worldwide, Inc.
An International Data Group Company

Foster City, CA ♦ Chicago, IL ♦ Indianapolis, IN ♦ Southlake, TX

Lotus® Domino™ For Dummies®

Published by
IDG Books Worldwide, Inc.
An International Data Group Company
919 E. Hillsdale Blvd.
Suite 400
Foster City, CA 94404
http://www.idgbooks.com (IDG Books Worldwide Web site)
http://www.dummies.com (Dummies Press Web site)

Library of Congress Catalog Card No.: 97-71808

ISBN: 0-7645-0177-1

Printed in the United States of America

10 9 8 7 6 5 4 3 2 1

1O/QW/QW/ZX/IN

Distributed in the United States by IDG Books Worldwide, Inc.

Distributed by Macmillan Canada for Canada; by Transworld Publishers Limited in the United Kingdom; by IDG Norge Books for Norway; by IDG Sweden Books for Sweden; by Woodslane Pty. Ltd. for Australia; by Woodslane Enterprises Ltd. for New Zealand; by Longman Singapore Publishers Ltd. for Singapore, Malaysia, Thailand, and Indonesia; by Simron Pty. Ltd. for South Africa; by Toppan Company Ltd. for Japan; by Distribuidora Cuspide for Argentina; by Livraria Cultura for Brazil; by Ediciencia S.A. for Ecuador; by Addison-Wesley Publishing Company for Korea; by Ediciones ZETA S.C.R. Ltda. for Peru; by WS Computer Publishing Corporation, Inc., for the Philippines; by Unalis Corporation for Taiwan; by Contemporanea de Ediciones for Venezuela; by Computer Book & Magazine Store for Puerto Rico; by Express Computer Distributors for the Caribbean and West Indies. Authorized Sales Agent: Anthony Rudkin Associates for the Middle East and North Africa.

For general information on IDG Books Worldwide's books in the U.S., please call our Consumer Customer Service department at 800-762-2974. For reseller information, including discounts and premium sales, please call our Reseller Customer Service department at 800-434-3422.

For information on where to purchase IDG Books Worldwide's books outside the U.S., please contact our International Sales department at 415-655-3200 or fax 415-655-3295.

For information on foreign language translations, please contact our Foreign & Subsidiary Rights department at 415-655-3021 or fax 415-655-3281.

For sales inquiries and special prices for bulk quantities, please contact our Sales department at 415-655-3200 or write to the address above.

For information on using IDG Books Worldwide's books in the classroom or for ordering examination copies, please contact our Educational Sales department at 800-434-2086 or fax 817-251-8174.

For press review copies, author interviews, or other publicity information, please contact our Public Relations department at 415-655-3000 or fax 415-655-3299.

For authorization to photocopy items for corporate, personal, or educational use, please contact Copyright Clearance Center, 222 Rosewood Drive, Danvers, MA 01923, or fax 508-750-4470.

is a trademark under exclusive license to IDG Books Worldwide, Inc., from International Data Group, Inc.

About the Author

Jon Stuart and Kelly, his high school sweetheart and wife, live in the Boston area. After a number of years working for Lotus Development supporting and selling Notes, Jon started a small consulting company that specializes in Notes and Domino development, administration, and training. When he's not wearing his pocket protector he can be found trying to perfect his skiing technique on the moguls and hard packed snow (that's "ice" to non-New England skiers) of Vermont or working, often unsuccessfully, to keep his golf handicap down. Much to the relief of his golfing partners, however, he says he always drives past the red tees.

ABOUT IDG BOOKS WORLDWIDE

Welcome to the world of IDG Books Worldwide.

IDG Books Worldwide, Inc., is a subsidiary of International Data Group, the world's largest publisher of computer-related information and the leading global provider of information services on information technology. IDG was founded more than 25 years ago and now employs more than 8,500 people worldwide. IDG publishes more than 275 computer publications in over 75 countries (see listing below). More than 60 million people read one or more IDG publications each month.

Launched in 1990, IDG Books Worldwide is today the #1 publisher of best-selling computer books in the United States. We are proud to have received eight awards from the Computer Press Association in recognition of editorial excellence and three from *Computer Currents'* First Annual Readers' Choice Awards. Our best-selling *...For Dummies*® series has more than 30 million copies in print with translations in 30 languages. IDG Books Worldwide, through a joint venture with IDG's Hi-Tech Beijing, became the first U.S. publisher to publish a computer book in the People's Republic of China. In record time, IDG Books Worldwide has become the first choice for millions of readers around the world who want to learn how to better manage their businesses.

Our mission is simple: Every one of our books is designed to bring extra value and skill-building instructions to the reader. Our books are written by experts who understand and care about our readers. The knowledge base of our editorial staff comes from years of experience in publishing, education, and journalism — experience we use to produce books for the '90s. In short, we care about books, so we attract the best people. We devote special attention to details such as audience, interior design, use of icons, and illustrations. And because we use an efficient process of authoring, editing, and desktop publishing our books electronically, we can spend more time ensuring superior content and spend less time on the technicalities of making books.

You can count on our commitment to deliver high-quality books at competitive prices on topics you want to read about. At IDG Books Worldwide, we continue in the IDG tradition of delivering quality for more than 25 years. You'll find no better book on a subject than one from IDG Books Worldwide.

John Kilcullen
CEO
IDG Books Worldwide, Inc.

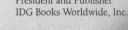

Steven Berkowitz
President and Publisher
IDG Books Worldwide, Inc.

*Eighth Annual
Computer Press
Awards ≥1992*

*Ninth Annual
Computer Press
Awards ≥1993*

*Tenth Annual
Computer Press
Awards ≥1994*

*Eleventh Annual
Computer Press
Awards ≥1995*

IDG Books Worldwide, Inc., is a subsidiary of International Data Group, the world's largest publisher of computer-related information and the leading global provider of information services on information technology. International Data Group publishes over 275 computer publications in over 75 countries. Sixty million people read one or more International Data Group publications each month. International Data Group's publications include: **ARGENTINA:** Buyer's Guide, Computerworld Argentina, PC World Argentina; **AUSTRALIA:** Australian Macworld, Australian PC World, Australian Reseller News, Computerworld, IT Casebook, Network World, Publish, Webmaster; **AUSTRIA:** Computerwelt Österreich, Networks Austria, PC Tip Austria; **BANGLADESH:** PC World Bangladesh; **BELARUS:** PC World Belarus; **BELGIUM:** Data News; **BRAZIL:** Annuário de Informática, Computerworld, Connections, Macworld, PC Player, PC World, Publish, Reseller News, Supergamepower; **BULGARIA:** Computerworld Bulgaria, Network World Bulgaria, PC & MacWorld Bulgaria; **CANADA:** CIO Canada, Client/Server World, ComputerWorld Canada, InfoWorld Canada, NetworkWorld Canada, WebWorld; **CHILE:** Computerworld Chile, PC World Chile; **COLOMBIA:** Computerworld Colombia, PC World Colombia; **COSTA RICA:** PC World Centro America; **THE CZECH AND SLOVAK REPUBLICS:** Computerworld Czechoslovakia, Macworld Czech Republic, PC World Czechoslovakia; **DENMARK:** Communications World Danmark, Computerworld Danmark, Macworld Danmark, PC World Danmark, Techworld Denmark; **DOMINICAN REPUBLIC:** PC World Republica Dominicana; **ECUADOR:** PC World Ecuador; **EGYPT:** Computerworld Middle East, PC World Middle East; **EL SALVADOR:** PC World Centro America; **FINLAND:** MikroPC, Tietoverkko, Tietoviikko; **FRANCE:** Distributique, Hebdo, Info PC, Le Monde Informatique, Macworld, Reseaux & Telecoms, WebMaster France; **GERMANY:** Computer Partner, Computerwoche, Computerwoche Extra, Computerwoche FOCUS, Global Online, Macwelt, PC Welt; **GREECE:** Amiga Computing, GamePro Greece, Multimedia World; **GUATEMALA:** PC World Centro America; **HONDURAS:** PC World Centro America; **HONG KONG:** Computerworld Hong Kong, PC World Hong Kong, Publish in Asia; **HUNGARY:** ABCD CD-ROM, Computerworld Szamitastechnika, Internetto online Magazine, PC World Hungary, PC-X Magazin Hungary; **ICELAND:** Tolvuheimur PC World Island; **INDIA:** Information Communications World, Information Systems Computerworld, PC World India, Publish in Asia; **INDONESIA:** InfoKomputer PC World, Komputek Computerworld, Publish in Asia; **IRELAND:** ComputerScope, PC Live!; **ISRAEL:** Macworld Israel, People & Computers/Computerworld; **ITALY:** Computerworld Italia, Macworld Italia, Networking Italia, PC World Italia; **JAPAN:** DTP World, Macworld Japan, Nikkei Personal Computing, OS/2 World Japan, SunWorld Japan, Windows NT World, Windows World Japan; **KENYA:** PC World East African; **KOREA:** Hi-Tech Information, Macworld Korea, PC World Korea; **MACEDONIA:** PC World Macedonia; **MALAYSIA:** Computerworld Malaysia, PC World Malaysia, Publish in Asia; **MALTA:** PC World Malta; **MEXICO:** Computerworld Mexico, PC World Mexico; **MYANMAR:** PC World Myanmar; **NETHERLANDS:** Computer! Totaal, LAN Internetworking Magazine, LAN World Buyers Guide, Macworld Netherlands, Net, WebWereld; **NEW ZEALAND:** Absolute Beginners Guide and Plain & Simple Series, Computer Buyer, Computer Industry Directory, Computerworld New Zealand, MTB, Network World, PC World New Zealand, Publish in Asia; **NICARAGUA:** PC World Centro America; **NORWAY:** Computerworld Norge, CW Rapport, Datamagasinet, Financial Rapport, Kursguide Norge, Macworld Norge, Multimediaworld Norge, PC World Ekspress Norge, PC World Nettverk, PC World Norge, PC World ProduktGuide Norge; **PAKISTAN:** Computerworld Pakistan; **PANAMA:** PC World Panama; **PEOPLE'S REPUBLIC OF CHINA:** China Computer Users, China Computerworld, China InfoWorld, China Telecom World Weekly, Computer & Communication, Electronic Design China, Electronics Today, Electronics Weekly, Game Software, PC World China, Popular Computer Week, Software Weekly, Software World, Telecom World; **PERU:** Computerworld Peru, PC World Profesional Peru, PC World SoHo Peru; **PHILIPPINES:** Click!, Computerworld Philippines, PC World Philippines, Publish in Asia; **POLAND:** Computerworld Poland, Computerworld Special Report Poland, Cyber, Macworld Poland, Networld Poland, PC World Komputer; **PORTUGAL:** Cerebro/PC World, Computerworld/Correio Informático, Dealer World Portugal, Mac*In/PC*In Portugal, Multimedia World; **PUERTO RICO:** PC World Puerto Rico; **ROMANIA:** Computerworld Romania, PC World Romania, Telecom Romania; **RUSSIA:** Computerworld Russia, Mir PK, Publish, Seti; **SINGAPORE:** Computerworld Singapore, PC World Singapore, Publish in Asia; **SLOVENIA:** Monitor; **SOUTH AFRICA:** Computing SA, Network World SA, Software World SA; **SPAIN:** Communicaciones World España, Computerworld España, Dealer World España, Macworld España, PC World España; **SRI LANKA:** Infolink PC World; **SWEDEN:** CAP&Design, Computer Sweden, Corporate Computing Sweden, Internetworld Sweden, it.branschen, Macworld Sweden, MaxiData Sweden, MikroDatorn, Nätverk & Kommunikation, PC World Sweden, PCaktiv, Windows World Sweden; **SWITZERLAND:** Computerworld Schweiz, Macworld Schweiz, PCtip; **TAIWAN:** Computerworld Taiwan, Macworld Taiwan, NEW ViSiON/Publish, PC World Taiwan, Windows World Taiwan; **THAILAND:** Publish in Asia, Thai Computerworld; **TURKEY:** Computerworld Turkiye, Macworld Turkiye, Network World Turkiye, PC World Turkiye; **UKRAINE:** Computerworld Kiev, Multimedia World Ukraine, PC World Ukraine; **UNITED KINGDOM:** Acorn User UK, Amiga Action UK, Amiga Computing UK, Apple Talk UK, Computing, Macworld, Parents and Computers UK, PC Advisor, PC Home, PSX Pro, The WEB; **UNITED STATES:** Cable in the Classroom, CIO Magazine, Computerworld, DOS World, Federal Computer Week, GamePro Magazine, InfoWorld, I-Way, Macworld, Network World, PC Games, PC World, Publish, Video Event, THE WEB Magazine, and WebMaster; online webzines: JavaWorld, NetscapeWorld, and SunWorld Online; **URUGUAY:** InfoWorld Uruguay; **VENEZUELA:** Computerworld Venezuela, PC World Venezuela; and **VIETNAM:** PC World Vietnam. 3/24/97

Dedication

This book is dedicated to the love of my life — my wife, Kelly Stuart — and to those who bestowed my life — my parents, Bill and Jean Stuart.

Acknowledgments

I want to thank Lisa Buttiglieri, who is one of the great minds at Lotus Development, for doing a technical edit of the entire book in such a superb fashion. I also want to thank Robert Wallace, my project editor at IDG Books Worldwide, Inc., for all his expertise and patience.

My thanks also go to Phil Worthington, my copy editor; Gareth Hancock, an acquisitions editor at IDG; Pat Freeland, a friend and author without whom this book would not have been possible; Matt Wagner, my agent; and Rich Davis, an HTML guru.

Publisher's Acknowledgments

We're proud of this book; please send us your comments about it by using the IDG Books Worldwide Registration Card at the back of the book or by e-mailing us at feedback/dummies@idgbooks.com. Some of the people who helped bring this book to market include the following:

Acquisitions, Development, and Editorial

Project Editors: Leah P. Cameron, Robert H. Wallace

Acquisitions Editor: Gareth Hancock

Product Development Director: Mary Bednarek

Copy Editors: Gwenette Gaddis, Phil A. Worthington

Technical Editor: Lisa A. Buttiglieri

Editorial Manager: Leah P. Cameron

Editorial Assistant: Chris H. Collins

Production

Project Coordinator: Valery Bourke

Layout and Graphics: Lou Boudreau, Linda M. Boyer, Maridee V. Ennis, Todd Klemme, Theresa Sánchez-Baker, Brent Savage, Michael A. Sullivan

Proofreaders: Arielle Carole Mennelle, Christine D. Berman, Nancy Price, Robert Springer, Ethel M. Winslow

Indexer: Ty Koontz

General and Administrative

IDG Books Worldwide, Inc.: John Kilcullen, CEO; Steven Berkowitz, President and Publisher

IDG Books Technology Publishing: Brenda McLaughlin, Senior Vice President and Group Publisher

Dummies Technology Press and Dummies Editorial: Diane Graves Steele, Vice President and Associate Publisher; Judith A. Taylor, Product Manager; Kristin A. Cocks, Editorial Director

Dummies Trade Press: Kathleen A. Welton, Vice President and Publisher; Stacy S. Collins, Marketing Manager

IDG Books Production for Dummies Press: Beth Jenkins, Production Director; Cindy L. Phipps, Supervisor of Project Coordination, Production Proofreading, and Indexing; Kathie S. Schutte, Supervisor of Page Layout; Shelley Lea, Supervisor of Graphics and Design; Debbie J. Gates, Production Systems Specialist; Tony Augsburger, Supervisor of Reprints and Bluelines; Leslie Popplewell, Media Archive Coordinator

Dummies Packaging and Book Design: Patti Sandez, Packaging Specialist; Lance Kayser, Packaging Assistant; Kavish + Kavish, Cover Design

♦

The publisher would like to give special thanks to Patrick J. McGovern, without whom this book would not have been possible.

♦

Contents at a Glance

Cartoons at a Glance

By Rich Tennant • Fax: 508-546-7747 • E-mail: the5wave@tiac.net

page 5

page 207

page 307

page 87

page 343

Table of Contents

Introduction

· ·

Welcome to *Lotus Domino For Dummies!* This book is your hand-held personal guru for getting your Domino Web site up and running. In these pages I try to inform and entertain you by offering down-to-earth information about Lotus Domino and how it works. Though this is an honest-to-gosh computer book, it's not a technical manual. The computer-nerd quotient is very low; you don't have to be an expert programmer to understand what is contained within. All the whys and wherefores of Domino are explained in easy-to-understand language.

About This Book

You're not meant to read this book from cover to cover, though you can. Instead, this book is a reference explaining how to use Domino in creating a powerful and user-friendly Web site. Each chapter is a self-contained unit covering a specific topic in Lotus Domino, and each section within the chapter describes a basic element of the topic. Sample sections you encounter in this book include

- ✔ Getting the gist of Domino lingo
- ✔ Creating a home page
- ✔ Making your Web site secure
- ✔ Incorporating HTML code into your Web pages
- ✔ Troubleshooting error messages

What you *won't* find in the book are complex technical notions, lots of information that must be memorized, or pages of horrifying codes to key in. All terminology in these pages is defined on the spot or is cross-referenced to more complete information. Really technical information is clearly marked so that you can avoid it if you want. Nothing threatening here.

How to Use This Book

If you really *want* to, you can read this book from this Introduction to the Index, but I don't recommend it. Use this book as a reference; just look for the part or chapter that deals with the Domino-related problem you're facing and read only what you need. (If you get really hard up for information, look in the Index — but that's like cheating and reading the assembly instructions, isn't it?)

I do recommend that you read this Introduction first, just to understand some of the conventions I use. For example, when you see "Press Ctrl+S to save the file," don't try to hold down the Ctrl key, the shift key, the plus key, and the S key all at the same time. *Ctrl+S* is my shorthand for "hold down the Ctrl key and press S."

I also use some shorthand for menu commands: "File⇨New" means for you to choose File from the main menu and then choose New from the pop-up menu that appears. The lines under *F* and *N* show you that you can perform the same function by holding down Alt and pressing F, and then holding down Alt and pressing N.

Occasionally I have to put in some code — yeah, I know, code is scary, but this *is* a computer book — and to set it off from the rest of the text, it looks like this:

```
[<img src = "/corporatelogo.gif">]
```

If you need to type something into a text field, the text is set in **bold type.** Screens, dialog boxes, and other software elements' names are in regular type, but I use the proper name of the element in each reference; for example, I refer occasionally to the Properties for Text InfoBox because the box's name is Properties for Text.

Rash Assumptions

I make a few assumptions about you as the reader. First, I assume that you're thinking about developing a Web site for use as a company intranet and as a tool for doing business on the Internet. You may be the developer who's responsible for building the site or a business manager who wants to know how the site can be used to further the company's goals.

If you're a developer, this book is a great tool for setting up your Domino Web server, creating the Web pages, and integrating the necessary security protocols and utilities that make up a good corporate Web site. By using Domino and Lotus Notes, you put your company information within easy reach of those outside the office building who need it. Business managers can read this book to investigate the possibility of a Web presence without hiring a $125-per-hour consultant for six weeks to create a site that doesn't provide a good return on that investment. You'll just love how this book puts the technology in terms the average person can understand.

How This Book Is Organized

This book contains five parts, each of which is divided into more chapters. The chapters are divided into even more sections, and each section contains all the information you need to understand the topic being discussed (or contains cross-references to other sections or chapters that fill in the blanks). You can pick up this book, open it to any page, and start reading without necessarily knowing what was covered before that page.

So without further ado, here's what each part covers:

Part I: Before You Charge into Developing

Most of the chapters in this part deal with the basics of the Internet, the World Wide Web, and Lotus Domino itself. You find out about how the Internet came to be, what the Web means to businesses in general, and how Domino can use these networks to strengthen communication within your company and with your customers. I also define the terminology commonly associated with the Web and with Domino.

Part II: Start Your Engines

This part covers the nuts and bolts that make up Lotus Domino. Chapters include information on how you set up your Domino Web server, create complex structures such as forms and actions without going crazy, and use Domino's powerful management tools to your best advantage. You also see lots of step-by-step instructions that have real-world value. No useless information in *this* book!

Part III: How to Win Accolades and Influence People

Some of the more complex features of Lotus Domino get dissected in this part. Using these features makes your Domino Web site super-useful to people inside and outside your organization — and that means *you* get recognized for making it happen, right? Even complex issues such as setting up security protocols are presented to you in easy-to-understand language.

Part IV: Enhancing with Other Tools

Many pages of text by the computer-publishing industry have been devoted to new Web-based technologies such as Java and HTML. Chapters in this part tell you how Lotus Domino can use these Johnny-come-latelies and make your Web site shine. As a bonus, you also get acquainted with some of the neat built-in features of Domino.

Part V: The Part of Tens

This is the signature *...For Dummies* part. I include such tasty tidbits as "Ten Error Messages and How to Troubleshoot Them" and "Ten Great Domino Web Sites." All this in one book? Talk about *convenience!*

Icons Used in This Book

For your convenience, I use the following icons in this book to denote certain passages of text:

This icon flags useful, helpful tips or shortcuts. Paying attention to the paragraphs marked by the bull's-eye can bring only good karma.

Always read text marked with this icon, because the Warning icon means "Watch out! Something bad can happen if you don't read me!"

I try to avoid putting in chapters any information that you must keep in mind, but sometimes I have to. The Remember icon highlights those important passages.

This icon is the red flag meaning "Nerdy stuff coming through." Treat text so marked as optional reading or as a good cure for insomnia.

Where to Go from Here

You know what the book is supposed to tell you, how it's organized, and what stuff you should and shouldn't read. So now what? Well, if you ask me, I suggest that you grab hold of your server workstation, gather up all the CD-ROMs, diskettes, and other digital minutia you need, tuck this beautiful yellow-and-black book under your favorite arm, and start making Domino magic!

Part I
Before You Charge into Developing

The 5th Wave   By Rich Tennant

"We pulled from several outside sources to build our Web site – Lotus, Andersen Consulting, the Seventh Cavalry..."

In this part . . .

Lotus Domino makes developing Web sites easy, but that doesn't mean you can hop right into creating a site with Domino. You need to know a few things about how Domino works before you start using it. Consider these next few chapters as an introduction to the powerful Domino Web server application.

This part of the book puts Domino in the proper frame of reference. You find answers to questions such as: How does Domino relate to Lotus Notes? What does Domino do that other server software doesn't do? What parts make up Domino? And can I get one with anchovies and green olives? (Woops. How'd that question get in here?)

Chapter 1

The Pieces to the Domino Puzzle

. . . .

. . . .

*B*efore you dive into the Lotus Domino Web server, you should get a brief introduction to some of the pieces that make up the Domino puzzle — if I may be so bold as to use the word *puzzle*, conjuring up, as it does, images of complexity that certainly don't fit with the reality of Domino. I use the word puzzle because a puzzle is a number of pieces of something that seemingly don't fit together but that, when arranged properly, form a complete picture. And Domino is just that; a complete picture formed from a number of pieces that don't necessarily seem to fit together.

The pieces of the Domino puzzle are the Internet, the World Wide Web, and Lotus Notes. In this chapter I discuss all three pieces separately, and then I explain how Domino combines all those pieces into a single, powerful communication tool.

The Net Net of the Net

Most of us have heard about the Internet only recently, yet it has been around since the 1960s. The Internet just didn't become a household term until its commercial use emerged in the mid-1990s. It is already radically changing how we do business and how we communicate with each other, but it has only just begun to exert its influence. Inventions and innovations such as the assembly line and telephone have had an immense impact on how we view the world and how we live our lives. So, too, will the Internet.

What exactly is it?

To understand the Internet, you must first know what a network is. An individual *network* is nothing more than two or more computers linked together, usually with a cable or telephone line (although there are also non-physical links between computers, such as cellular links). Linking computers allows the people sitting in front of them to communicate electronically with each other, just as two telephones connected with a telephone line allow people to communicate with each other.

The Internet is a network among networks, so to speak. To use an example: You have a computer network in your company and you have a friend who has a computer network in his company. Wouldn't it be great if a public network connected your company's internal network with his company's internal network? Then you could communicate with him electronically to let him know that you are bringing the beer to this Sunday's tailgate party and that he should bring steaks.

Well, such a network exists, and it's called the *Internet*. It can connect your network not only with your friend's network, but also with networks all over the world. If you are not connected to the Internet, you and your friend may very well show up to the tailgate party each with a cooler full of beer and nothing to eat — and that has trouble written all over it!

In the beginning

The Internet was born in the 1960s when a branch of the Department of Defense, Advanced Research Projects Administration (ARPA), started a computer network intended to enable the government to communicate in the aftermath of a nuclear war. One of the specifications for the network was that it be decentralized to provide a high level of fault tolerance. If nuclear war, an act of nature, or some other mishap were to destroy part of the network, traffic would dynamically reroute to another part of the network.

The result of ARPA's work was *ARPAnet* — an ancestor of the Internet. ARPAnet started out small, connecting only a few central computers in California with one in Utah. As military personnel, researchers, and educators discovered the usefulness of this network, which allowed them to communicate with others in different geographic locations, ARPAnet eventually grew to span the country.

As users pushed the limits of ARPAnet, they wanted better performance. (I guess some things never change; even today, we complain about the speed of the Internet, despite its being exponentially faster than the original ARPAnet.) The computer industry's successful transition from a mainframe paradigm to a server/client paradigm in the early 1980s only exacerbated that problem. At that time, rather than just a relatively small number of large multi-user computers attaching to ARPAnet, a larger number of smaller workstations were attaching, increasing traffic and really pushing the limits of ARPAnet.

In the early 1980s, the National Science Foundation (NSF), which incidentally is still involved in improving the Internet's performance (more on that later in this chapter in the gray-shaded sidebar called "The National Science Foundation's at it again!"), tried to use ARPAnet to connect a research system that the foundation had developed. ARPAnet, however, simply couldn't satisfy the foundation's needs. So the NSF built its own network, called *NSFnet*, which was a network backbone that connected regional networks. Researchers and educators, who were the only people permitted to use NSFnet, connected to a regional network that was connected to other regional networks by NSFnet. Because of the success of this new and faster network, ARPAnet, after more than 20 years of existence, drew its last breath in the early 1990s. NAFnet became the hardware and communications model upon which the Internet grew.

It's not just for professors anymore

By 1994, several independent commercial Internet networks had emerged, opening up the Internet for commercial use and making it a tool that was no longer confined to researchers and educators.

The Internet enables businesses and people to communicate in many new ways. Companies sell and market their products directly to consumers via the Internet. Employees can share information and stay in touch. Hobbyists can research genealogy, numismatics, bee keeping, or fly tying. Consumers can buy groceries, software, and cars, as well as sample a music CD before buying it. Outdoor enthusiasts can get the latest ski conditions, tee times, and even strange things like up-to-the-minute pictures of Pike's Peak — that's right, a new picture for each of the 525,600 minutes of the year (527,040 during leap year).

The Internet is open to anyone who has a computer; actually, you already can view Internet content with a television — and it probably won't be long before all you need is a wristwatch with a suitable display. Computer users normally connect to a commercial entity that connects them to a regional network, commonly called an *Internet Service Provider* (ISP).

The National Science Foundation's at it again!

Just as in the 1980s, when it improved the performance of the Internet by developing the NSFnet, the National Science Foundation is active in improving the performance of today's Internet. The NSF, in the last two years, has introduced vBNS (Very High Speed Backbone Network Service) and has been active in a project called *Internet II*, which will supplement the Internet by providing high-speed links for transmitting just graphics and video.

(Those media require a larger *bandwidth,* or capacity to move data, for timely transmission than most other Internet content, such as e-mail.)

Internet II, which will be available only to researchers and educators, will connect regional networks, called *gigapops* (gigabit capacity point of presence). Internet II will provide transmission speeds hundreds of times faster than what the Internet currently provides.

What Is the World Wide Web?

The Internet provides many services, including e-mail, file transfer, bulletin boards (also called newsgroups or discussion groups), Gopher, and the World Wide Web (more commonly known simply as *the Web*). The Web was added to the Internet in 1989 in an attempt to make the Internet easier to use.

The two basic components to the Web are *Web servers*, which are machines connected to the Web that store information, and *Web clients*, or machines connected to the Web that can access the information stored on Web servers using software called a *Web browser*.

You should be familiar with two terms in any discussion about the Web:

   ✔ **HTML (Hypertext Markup Language):** The language used to create the documents that are exchanged between Web servers and Web browsers.

   ✔ **HTTP (Hypertext Transfer Protocol):** The protocol used to exchange HTML documents between Web servers and Web browsers.

HTML and HTTP are the most basic tools of the Web. All computers that interact with the Web, whether they are servers or clients, must be able to understand HTML, and all Web clients must be able to take advantage of HTTP to retrieve information from a Web server. Though many other languages and protocols are used on the Web, these two are the common denominator among all Web interactions.

What Is Lotus Notes?

Lotus Notes is a software program that enables people to communicate with each other, and to share information in the confines of a corporate intranet or local access network (LAN). If I told you that Notes is *e-mail,* or an electronic way to send messages from one computer to another, you would have a good picture of what Notes is — but not a complete picture. Notes stores information on a *server,* which is a high-end computer with lots of storage space, in databases that can be shared by groups of users. The databases can be enhanced with a comprehensive security system, transferred to a laptop so you can work effectively while disconnected from the server, developed to process information, and enabled to automatically execute workflow processes.

The two basic hardware components to Lotus Notes are *Notes servers,* or computers that store and process information, and *Notes clients,* or computers that can access the information on the Notes servers.

To better describe the software components that make Notes so useful as a way to communicate, I have broken the discussion into a few different topics.

Get your objects here

A *Notes database* is an *object,* which in this case means a series of documents, that's stored on a Lotus Notes server and that can store many different types of information, including:

- **Text:** You can create documents that can be shared with other users in a Notes database.

- **File Attachments:** You can store files of any format in a Notes database. You may, for example, want to attach a spreadsheet or word processing file in a Notes database to make it available for review by a group of people.

- **Graphics:** You may want to create a Human Resources database that stores scanned résumés so that hiring managers can share them. You may even want to create a database that receives and then automatically redistributes faxes to the correct recipient's mail file, thereby eliminating the problem most offices have of receiving faxes that then sit unnoticed for hours at the fax machine.

- **Video:** You can store video files in a Notes database.

✔ **Voice:** You may want to create a Notes telephony application that enables your sales reps to call the Notes server from the road, listen to their mail messages (text messages converted to an electronic voice by text-to-speech recognition software), and respond to them by speaking into the phone. The server can embed their voice responses as an *object,* which in this case means a single digital file, in a mail message.

✔ **Relational data:** You can periodically transfer information in your Oracle, Sybase, Informix, or other relational database software into a Notes database, making it available to a laptop, a Web site, or another office.

Layman's application development

I have heard people call Lotus Notes a *development platform,* which means a series of software blocks that can be pieced together into a customized program, as opposed to a *software program* that performs only within its designed parameters. I don't know if I agree with the development people, but I see their intended point. You can develop your Notes application to be as different from my Notes application as a spreadsheet program is from a word processing program.

This very concept — Lotus Notes' design flexibility — is a key reason why the program is so popular to businesses. Notes can be made to do so many things just by someone tweaking it with a few simple programming tools. You can use two programming languages to develop your own specific Notes applications:

✔ @Functions and @Commands

✔ LotusScript

LotusScript is an advanced language that I do not cover in any detail in this book. The @Functions and @Commands language, although still powerful, is more of a layman's programming language; it is intuitive to use. You can create an exceptional Notes database, and therefore a Web site, using it, and you do not have to be a programming guru to understand it. (I touch on @Function and @Commands where necessary throughout this book.)

If you're interested in LotusScript, pick up a copy of *LotusScript For Dummies,* by Jim Meade. IDG Books Worldwide, Inc., publishes that book as well as the one you're reading right now.

Stronger than Fort Knox

Lotus Notes offers a comprehensive security system with which you can specify security for the server, databases, documents, sections, and fields.

- ✔ **Server:** You can grant or deny individuals or groups access to the server, and you can control what the people to whom you grant access may do on the server.

- ✔ **Databases:** You can grant or deny individuals or groups access to a database, and you can control what the people to whom you grant access can do in the database. For example, you may grant some people the ability to both create *and* read documents in the database but grant other people the ability to only read documents in the database.

- ✔ **Documents:** You can grant or deny individuals or groups the ability to read only certain documents in a database.

  The term *document* is synonymous with *record* if you are from the relational database world. Databases are made up of one or more documents.

- ✔ **Sections:** You can grant or deny individuals or groups the ability to edit or read sections of a document.

- ✔ **Fields:** You can grant or deny individuals or groups the ability to read fields within a document.

Replication is fun

In Lotus Notes, *replication* is the process by which a server *intelligently* copies (or replicates) a database from itself either to another server or to a workstation. What do I mean by intelligently copying? I mean that, instead of just dumping information from one machine to the other, the server determines what information should be replicated, and replicates just that information.

Suppose you want to make a 100-page corporate policy and procedures manual available to employees in both a New York office and a Tokyo office. You convert the manual into a Notes database so that each page of the manual is an individual document in the database. If you add a page to the database on the New York server, do you want to have to replicate all 101 pages when you call the Tokyo server, or would you rather save time and money by having to replicate only the one new document? I'll take a wild guess and assume the latter. Well, Notes replicates only the one page that was created. Lotus Notes is smart enough to replicate only those documents in a database that have been created, modified, or deleted since the database's last successful replication.

Replication in Notes also follows a security scheme that you can specify. For example, you may want to allow documents to replicate from the New York office to Tokyo, but not vice-versa.

The types of Lotus Notes replication are as follows:

- **Server-to-server replication:** The predominant reason for replicating from one server to another is to make sure that geographically dispersed offices share the same information.

- **Server-to-workstation:** The predominant reason for replicating from a server to a workstation (or even a laptop) is to enable yourself to work with the information in a database away from the office network; in an airplane, for instance.

E-mail

E-mail is the most popular use of Lotus Notes. The Notes server has a powerful mail-routing engine that's easy to administer, and the Notes client has an easy-to-use and understandable interface. You can replicate your mail database onto your laptop, which allows you to read, delete, and create mail messages while you are disconnected from the network, such as when you're on the beach. (Just don't get sand in that keyboard; what a mess!) When you connect with your company's server via the LAN, WAN, telephone line, or any other means, Notes automatically sends your new messages, retrieves the ones that came in while you were gone, and deletes from the mail database on the server all the files you marked for deletion while you were on the beach.

Calendaring and Scheduling

Calendaring and scheduling is another popular Lotus Notes feature. You can store your calendar in a Notes database (well, actually, in the same database where you store your mail). The easy-to-use calendaring and scheduling interface allows you to create a meeting notice, invite people to the meeting, and then do a free-time search into the invitees' calendars to see whether they are free to attend. Depending on the level of access you have, you may or may not be able to see their calendars, only whether their time is booked. Notes also offers an easy-to-use interface for accepting, declining, or delegating invitations when others send them to you. Once again, replication allows you to work with your calendar at the beach, just like it does with e-mail.

Work flows with workflow

Lotus Notes can improve workflow. Well, what exactly is *workflow*? Consider a simple project approval process: You have to write a proposal and bring it to your manager for approval. Contingent upon his approval, the proposal must go to a vice president, after which, contingent upon her approval, the proposal must go to the company's president. The process requires your proposal to change hands several times. It probably will also spend a fair amount of time just being invisible or lost as a less-than-top-priority addition to several people's rather cluttered desks. In one form or another, delayed action on your proposal is a fairly strong likelihood. Also, after that proposal leaves your hands, it's pretty hard to track who has it and what sort of reactions it's getting without you feeling pushy or looking foolishly over-eager to the bosses.

Notes can automate this example of inefficient workflow. You write the proposal in Notes and submit it for your manager's approval by clicking a button on the form. The Notes server automatically sends a mail message with a link to the proposal to your manager, requesting his approval. He adds his comments and submits it for vice presidential approval by clicking a button on the form. The Notes server automatically sends a mail message with a link to the proposal to the vice president, requesting her approval. She adds her comments and submits it for presidential approval by clicking a button on the form. The Notes server automatically sends a mail message with a link to the proposal to the president, requesting his approval.

The document stays in the database where you created it, so you can easily check on its status. If anyone along the line rejects the proposal, the workflow process ends. If you want, too, the process can have security implemented in such a way that only the manager can submit a proposal to the vice president, and only the vice president can submit it to the president.

Agents and your piece of mind

Agents, also referred to as *macros,* are programs that automate processes on the Notes server. You can create agents that execute when they're ordered to (manually), or after a certain amount of time passes, or when a document is created, modified, pasted, or mailed into a database.

You can create useful agents that perform such actions as sending a document to an archive after it has been in a database for six months. In a sales force automation database, you could have an agent that notifies any sales reps who haven't acted on a sales lead in five days that they must take action. The same agent can also notify a rep's manager if the rep hasn't taken action after a set number of days.

Workflow within Notes is all based on the agent technology. You can make an agent that, once the vice president signs off on a document, forwards the document to the appropriate person. Or, if the vice president doesn't sign off on the document, an agent may also be designed to notify the person who initiated the workflow process that the proposal was not approved, and to move the proposal from pending status to declined status. You may have a discussion database within which an agent executes after 30 days to automatically change the documents from active status to a closed-for-discussion status.

What Is Domino?

If you read this chapter straight through, you now know what the Internet is, and what the Web is, *and* what Lotus Notes is. So where does Domino fit in? "Lotus Notes meets the Internet" is a pretty good way to describe Domino. Lotus Domino is a technology that transforms Lotus Notes into an Internet applications server, enabling people who have Web browsers to view the content of and interact with Notes databases.

Domino allows you to leverage the open networking environment of the Internet at the same time as you leverage Notes' powerful features (such as the object store, ease of application development, security, replication, e-mail, calendaring and scheduling, workflow, agents, ease of server management, and search engine).

From an architect's viewpoint

So what parts go together to make up Lotus Domino? Well, before I introduce the pieces of Domino, I need to briefly introduce *URLs* (Uniform Resource Locators). A *URL* is the address of a Web site — for example, www.monks.com — that you type into your Web browser if you want to access a Web site. If you want to access a Domino Web site, you can type in one of the following two kinds of URLs from *any* standard Web browser, like Netscape Navigator or Microsoft Internet Explorer:

 ✔ **A traditional URL:** These are the common URLs used on the World Wide Web. For example, the URL

```
http://www.monks.com/htm/orders.html
```

opens the orders.html file in the htm directory on the www.monks.com Domino Web server.

 ✔ **Domino-specific URL:** These URLs only apply to Web pages built on a Domino Web server. For example, the URL

```
http://www.monks.com/sales.nsf/clients?OpenView
```

opens the `clients` view in the `sales.nsf` database on the `www.monks.com` Domino Web server.

I go into more detail about URLs in Chapter 5. For the following discussion on the parts of a Domino server, however, you need only this brief introduction to URLs.

A Domino server consists of two fundamental parts (see Figure 1-1):

✔ **HTTP Server:** Determines whether the requested URL is a traditional URL or a Domino-specific URL. If the URL is a traditional URL, it returns the requested HTML file, and if the URL is a Domino-specific URL, it gets help from the Domino engine before filling the request.

✔ **Domino Engine:** Allows Web browsers to access Notes databases, by automatically translating Notes elements (views, forms, documents, navigators, and the About Database Document) into HTML (Hypertext Markup Language).

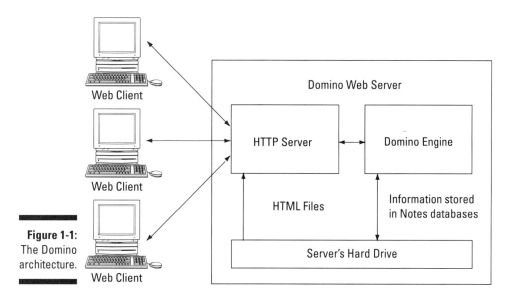

Figure 1-1:
The Domino architecture.

From a homeowner's viewpoint

If you manage or create Web sites yourself, your definition of Domino may be "a technology that eliminates pressure in the cranial cavity." That is, it eliminates headaches.

Domino allows you to build a Web site easily, using Notes design elements such as views, forms, navigators, actions, and agents. Any design changes that you make immediately become available to people visiting your Web site. Notes' replication technology allows you to make design changes while you are working on a computer that's disconnected from the network. Imagine flying the clear blue skies — or better yet, lying on a beach — as you make changes to your Web site! You can also distribute some of the design and content creation tasks to people located in different geographic areas. The Lotus Development Web site (which you can find at `www.lotus.com`) is a good example of one made up of over 100 Notes databases. Because you are building the site with Notes design elements, you can create the entire site without knowing a single bit of HTML. If, however, you are an HTML, Java, or CGI script guru, you can certainly implement those skills with Domino, as Domino supports those and other technologies.

Managing a Domino Web site is quite easy, too. The Public Address Book is a Notes database that stores the server's configuration information. Once again, the replication functionality of Notes allows you to do much of the server management while disconnected from the server.

It's All in a Name

I want to clear up some confusing terminology that you're likely to encounter. In this chapter, I said that the traditional Lotus Notes server requires a Lotus Notes client to access it. I also said that a Domino Web server is a Lotus Notes server running the HTTP server task. When you enable a Lotus Notes server as a Domino Web server, Web browsers as well as Lotus Notes clients can access the server.

Lotus has done something with the name of the traditional Lotus Notes server that can potentially confuse many people, including myself. Lotus has renamed the Lotus Notes server to the Lotus Domino Server. I believe Lotus has made this name change because market research showed that people responded more positively to *Domino* than to *Notes*. Thanks to Lotus' competitors, some people unjustifiably viewed Notes as an expensive and *closed* (too proprietary) technology.

This book deals with the Domino Web server, which is a Lotus Notes (or, as I just said, Lotus Domino) server that people can access with their Web browsers.

The only reason I make this clarification is that the installation chapter could confuse you if you don't realize that the Lotus Domino Server is synonymous with the Lotus Notes server and is different from the Domino Web server.

Chapter 2

Why Use Domino?

*I*n this technological age, we are constantly developing more effective and efficient forms of communication, one of which is the Internet. As we move closer to the 21st century, commerce and communication are radically changing due to the Internet. Distribution channels are being compressed (if not eliminated), services and products are improving, and business paradigms are changing. Domino can be your bridge to the 21st century.

A Bridge to the 21st Century

The next few sections present several examples of how the Internet is changing communication and commerce as we know it. Imagine that you are trying to buy a rare book. You have to call or visit countless specialty rare book shops and see if they have it — a process that could take months. That is, it could . . . if you didn't have access to the Internet. With the Internet you can search for the book just by clicking a button in your Web browser. You may end up getting the book from a person who is a part-time dealer working out of his basement — obviously someone you wouldn't find if you were roaming around the city and thumbing through the yellow pages looking for bookstores. The amazing thing about commerce over the Internet is that part-time business owners have no less commercial power there than do large metropolitan bookstores that spend millions of dollars a year in upkeep.

Eliminating distribution channels

If you want to buy a music CD, you don't buy it from the recording company, but from a middleman, usually a record store that tacks on a profit margin of more than 100 percent. Using the Internet, you can buy the CD directly from the recording company. Just visit the company's Web site, where you can listen to a sample of the music, pay for the CD, *and* arrange for shipping. The Internet will compress, if not eliminate, the distribution channel in most imaginable product and service situations. If a manufacturer can communicate with its customers easily and effectively, why would it need any other players in its distribution chain?

Software companies can go even further in improving their services than recording companies can. Many software companies already deliver the software via the Internet, thus eliminating not only the distribution channel but also the added cost and time of standard shipping.

Better products and services

When I was young, I was lucky in that my family had an encyclopedia collection. The problem was that, by the time I was using them to help me write papers in junior high school, the encyclopedias were about 15 years old. That didn't matter for most papers; after all, George Washington will always be the first President and the Louisiana Purchase will always be a pretty good real estate deal. But for some papers these encyclopedias were no help; the information I needed simply wasn't in them or was too outdated to be useful. Now I can use the Internet to find out the most up-to-date information in minutes.

You'd think that the people who make encyclopedias don't like that, but they've adapted to the Internet, too. Using the Internet, encyclopedia companies can improve their products by always offering up-to-date information and offering video and sound in addition to text and graphics, and by charging a fair price for just the information I use.

A better way to buy a car

If you've ever bought a car, you may well have dreaded going to a bunch of dealer lots and looking around. Using the Internet, you can go to an automobile search site and specify the type of car you want. The dealers come to you and tell you what cars they have that match your needs. You and they can then bargain for your price.

Domino is a bridge to the 21st century. (Did I say that already? Well, it's true!) It's not pie in the sky; it's a bridge that is here and now, and one that is travel-worthy.

A Capitalist's Tool

In Chapter 1, I talk about how Lotus Domino creates a powerful connection to the Internet. Businesses wishing to take advantage of the direct-market capabilities of the Internet can use Domino to link their services to the Internet's teeming consumer masses. Domino enables you to sell your products and services to your customers and to market to future customers. About 50 million computer users with Internet browsers are out there right now, and Domino quickly gives you access to them. Domino offers several features if you want to use the program to open up a commerce site:

- **Registration:** You can require users to register before they can gain access to your site (or even just a part of your site, like a discussion page). Domino comes with a template application that allows you to quickly and easily set up a registration process. All the names of people who register are stored in a Notes database so that you can easily refer to the list and generate reports or mailing lists based on it.

- **Authentication:** Authentication goes one step beyond registration. Through authentication you can determine not only who can access your Web site, but what they can do at the site. For example, you may allow only authenticated users to create documents or delete documents.

- **File distribution:** In your Lotus Domino Web site, you can attach to documents on the site files that people can download. Once again, you can also require people to register and provide a valid password before they can download a file.

- **Searching:** You can allow visitors to easily search your site. If you have all your products listed in a database, visitors can search for the product without having to open and read each document.

- **Collect payments:** You can use Domino.Merchant (see Chapter 19) to create a payment mechanism that requires users to submit a credit card number before allowing them to download a file or visit some area of your site.

- **Agent execution:** If people visit your site and find that you are out of a particular product, they can submit a request to contact them the next time information about the product appears in the site. The agent that you create automatically executes without your having to do anything.

Surf, Don't Scrap, Your Relational Data

Many companies have transactional systems built on a high-end RDBMS (Relational Database Management System) that allows them to enter and process thousands of transactions in minutes. A catalog company, for example, enters your order into a relational database when you call, and a bank's ATM machine processes your transaction with a relational database whenever you withdraw money from it.

A Domino database is not intended to replace these high-end relational databases. You can, however, enhance your transactional system with Domino. You can use Domino as the front end to your transactional database, which means that after people intuitively enter information with their Web browsers, Domino handles the process of integrating the information with the relational database. You can set up an exchange process so that as users enter information with their Web browsers, that information is either immediately or periodically transferred into the relational database for processing. The information can then be transferred back to the Domino system to give people easy access to that information.

Inputting made easier

A problem with large-scale relational databases is that they run on one centrally located machine, which can make entering information into the system complex for remote sites. Domino can simplify the process of entering information into the system by transferring to the centrally located relational database any information that users in satellite offices have entered into their Web browsers and sent to the database over the Internet.

Domino can also support the relational databases security model, so that if people cannot enter information directly into the relational database, they cannot enter it through their Web browsers, either.

Outputting made easier, too

Outputting information is much easier with Lotus Domino because Domino enables you to make any information stored in a relational database available to standard Web browsers. This means that you can easily make data stored in high-end relational databases available to satellite offices and customers.

Creating reports in a relational database takes a decent amount of programming knowledge. With Domino, you can create a report structure and pull in the relational data to easily create reports.

"Intranet" Isn't a Typo

The *Internet* is a public network that allows you to communicate and share information with people outside your organization. An *intranet* is a network within your organization that uses the same pieces as the Internet — Web servers, Web browsers, and the TCP/IP communication protocol — to allow employees to communicate and share information (confidential or otherwise) with each other.

Consider an example of a clinic where you want to enable doctors to use their Web browsers to look at patient information that is stored on a Web server. You certainly don't want this information available to people outside the clinic. With Lotus Domino, you can create a way for doctors to access the patient database even when the doctors are away from the office, while making that sensitive patient information safe from unauthorized outside users.

You can create an effective and secure intranet with Lotus Domino. The program offers you an extensive security system with which you can deny certain users access to an entire intranet site, deny them access to only certain documents on a site, or deny them access to only a certain part of a document on a site. For example, you may have an order processing system where a customer's name, shipping address, desired product items, and credit card information is available. You may want the employees in the order department, marketing department, shipping department, and accounts receivable department to see the customer's name, address, and items ordered, but only the people in the accounts department need to see the customer's credit card number.

Domino enables you to build Internet and intranet sites on the same computer. You can design the security model to make only certain information available for public use.

Super Mail

Lotus Domino allows you to take advantage of Lotus Notes' robust messaging features. Using Domino, you can allow people to read their e-mail on the Domino Web server with a Web browser but let the powerful Lotus Notes mail engine process and route the mail.

The mail program can send and receive mail messages and faxes. You can also enable people to check their mail with a telephone or send voice responses to other people's mail files when you take advantage of the Lotus Notes mail features.

Tight Security

Lotus Domino offers a dynamic and comprehensive security system. You can set a variety of security levels and methods by using Domino's easy-to-understand security tools. And once you set up your security system, you can modify it without any hair-pulling programming challenges.

What you can secure

Domino enables you to secure lots of information at various levels on your Web site. Each level can be modified to suit your needs and the needs of those who use your data.

  ✔ **Server:** You can grant or deny access to the Web server for individuals or groups, and you can control what the people to whom you grant access may do on the server.

  ✔ **Databases:** You can grant or deny access to a database for individuals or groups, also, and you can control what the people to whom you grant access may do in the database. For example, you could allow some people to create and read documents but others only to read documents.

  ✔ **Documents:** You can grant or deny individuals or groups the ability to read certain documents in a database.

  ✔ **Sections:** You can grant or deny individuals or groups the ability to edit or read sections or a document.

  ✔ **Fields:** You can grant or deny individuals or groups the ability to read fields within a document.

Dynamically changing

Being able to dynamically change the security is important. If you have an employee who is promoted to a management position, you now want her to have the ability to read and write documents, even though just yesterday, when she was not part of the management team, she could only read documents. Domino allows you to quickly change her security clearance throughout the entire site simply by adding her name to a *group,* which is a list that Domino uses to define who has access to what information on the server.

You may also want to take access away at the snap of your fingers — if, for example, you have someone in the company removed from a top-secret project and you want to immediately, not tomorrow or in ten minutes, make sure that he can no longer get access to confidential information about that project on the company's intranet. You can instantly change his level of access, even if you still want him to have access to other not-so-confidential information.

The ability to change the security dynamically and at the drop of a hat is crucial when developing an effective Internet or intranet site.

Ease of Site Management

The Domino Web server is relatively easy to manage, as are the content on the server and the design of the site. Domino makes difficult processes, such as changing one element in every Web page on your site, simple to accomplish.

Changing all the files

Suppose you have a non-Domino Web site consisting of hundreds of files that were created using a standard company form that included the company's logo. Today the company officially changed its logo. Since it's not a Domino Web site, you have to edit each and every one of the hundreds of files.

Now, if you have a Domino Web site and face that situation, all you need to do is make a single change to the logo in the form within which the documents were created. Suddenly every one of the hundreds of documents reflect the logo change whenever they're opened by a Web browser.

One place

If you have a standard Web server and a site composed of 100 Web pages, you have 100 files sitting on the computer's hard drive. You have a situation that could easily turn into a management nightmare (if it isn't one already).

All of the documents (Web pages) in a Domino Web site can be stored in a single database. If you have a site composed of 100 pages, how many files are on the hard drive? *One!* A single database file contains all 100 Web pages.

Development language is easy

Programming languages are hard to learn, and HTML (the common language of the Web) is no exception. All those <tags> and stuff — just too confusing! When creating a site with Domino, you work with standard Lotus Notes design elements:

- ✔ Views
- ✔ Forms

✔ Navigators

✔ About Database Document

✔ Actions

✔ Agents

You don't have to know a single thing about HTML to create a Domino Web site. You can build all of the elements using Notes' easy-to-use @Function and @Command language. You can also enhance agents by using LotusScript.

But you're not limited to just Lotus products and programs when developing your Domino Web site. If you do have HTML, Java, JavaScript, ActiveX, or CGI Scripting expertise, for example, you certainly can use those technologies to enhance your Domino Web site.

Automating Business Processes

Domino allows you to automate business processes. For example, say you have an application with which you want to archive certain documents after they have been inactive for 60 days. Domino eliminates the need to search for the documents and execute an export. All you need to do is set up an agent once, and periodically (you determine the interval) your agent archives documents that are inactive for 60 days. The agent you made runs without any further involvement on your part from now to the end of time.

Your organization may have some process that requires certain people at different levels of the organization to sign off on important documents, like invoices. Rather than some person having to walk around the office with the invoice and collect the required input and signatures, you can simply create a document on your Domino Web site and have Domino handle the task of forwarding the invoice.

Another example is if you have a commerce site where people order goods or services. Instead of determining what you need to send to accounts receivable, what you need to send to shipping, what you need to send to credit, and what you need to send to marketing, you can have Domino automate the process of disseminating the necessary information.

Well, that about sums up the information in this chapter. If you read Chapter 1 before this chapter, you now know what Domino is and what it can do for you. "So," you say, "when do I find out about how Domino works?" Well, I suggest you start with Chapter 3 for an overview of all the parts that make up a Domino server.

Chapter 3

A Look under the Hood

In This Chapter

▶ Installing the Domino Web server

▶ Configuring the Domino Web server

▶ Managing the Domino Web server

*T*his chapter covers installing the Domino Web server. Before I discuss that, however, I want to revisit a confusing issue that I mention in Chapter 1.

Lotus has renamed the traditional *Lotus Notes* server (the one that allows only a Lotus Notes client to view its contents and interact with it) to *Lotus Domino Server.* You may wonder why I mention this confusing use of terminology at the beginning of a chapter that covers installation. Well, what may be called the Lotus Domino Server isn't the same thing as a Domino Web server, which allows both Web browsers and Lotus Notes clients to view and interact with the server's content.

If you want a Domino Web server, you actually have to install and configure the Lotus Notes/Domino Server and then run the HTTP server task on the server. In this chapter I explain how to install and configure the Lotus Domino (Notes) Server, and then how to run the HTTP server task that enables the server to function as a Web server.

Enough of the name games already. In this chapter I cover a lot of ground. I cover all the basic steps of installing and configuring the Domino Web server, including system requirements and the intricate mysteries of *TCP/IP* (Transmission Control Protocol/Internet Protocol). Even if you work on a previously installed Domino Web server, you can benefit from my explanations of how Domino is set up — especially if what you want to do with your Domino Web server isn't working and you don't know why. So read on!

Installing the Domino Web Server

The steps required to install a Domino Web server are the same steps necessary to install the Lotus Notes Server, also known as the Lotus Domino Server. The Domino Web server pieces install automatically when you install Lotus Domino (Notes) Server. You just have to configure the server and then activate the Web part of it to make it a real Domino Web server. I explain in this section about how to start that process.

Network requirements

Your network requirements for your Domino Web server depend on whether you want to use it as an *Internet* site or an *intranet* site.

Set up your Domino Web server as an Internet site if you want people external to your network to have access to it. Most car manufacturers, for example, have Internet sites that communicate information to their customers, who, of course, are not part of their internal corporate computer network. Set up your Domino Web server as an intranet site if you want only people who are part of your internal network to have access to it. For example, some companies have intranet sites where their sales department employees share sales leads and account information.

The list below gives you an idea of what network procedures are required to set up Domino as an intranet site or as an Internet site.

- **Intranet site:** Connect the Domino Web server to an internal company network and configure TCP/IP as the protocol. Internal employees who have Web browsers can access the Domino Web server only via TCP/IP.

- **Internet site:** Connect the Domino Web server to the Internet and configure TCP/IP as the protocol. You can connect to the Internet via an Internet Service Provider (ISP). To enhance customer satisfaction, you should have a *constant connection,* meaning that users should be able to access your Domino Web server around the clock.

Operating system requirements

You can install your Domino Web server on a number of operating systems:

- Windows NT
- Windows 95
- OS/2

    ✔ Solaris/SPARC

    ✔ Solaris/IntelEdition

    ✔ AIX

Although *technically* you can install and run the Domino Web server under Windows 95, doing so isn't practical. Windows 95 simply is not powerful enough to work effectively as a server platform — so in a word (actually a contraction and two words), don't do it!

Hardware requirements

Your hardware requirements vary according to which operating system you install the Domino Web server on. To avoid performance problems, you should follow the recommended RAM and disk space requirements in Table 3-1 rather than the minimum ones Lotus offers in the Domino literature.

Table 3-1	Domino Web Server Hardware Requirements for Different Operating Systems			
Operating System	*Minimum RAM*	*Recommended RAM*	*Minimum Disk Space*	*Recommended Disk Space*
Windows NT	32MB	48MB	300MB	1GB
Windows 95	16MB	24MB	150MB	300MB
OS/2	32MB	48MB	300MB	1GB
Solaris	64MB	128MB	300MB	1GB
AIX	64MB	128MB	300MB	1GB

The recommended disk space of 1GB may seem high, but it ensures that the Domino Web server has plenty of disk space available for caching image files and file attachments, which improves its performance.

I do *not* recommend loading the Domino Web server on a computer using the Windows 95 operating system. That version of Windows isn't powerful enough to function as a server platform, and running Domino on a Windows 95 server will strain system resources. Use one of the other operating systems instead.

Stepping through the installation

I don't have enough pages in this book to cover the installation steps for every operating system, so I'm going to step you through installing Lotus Domino Server 4.5a on Windows NT 4.0. Other operating systems go through similar steps; check your system's documentation and the Lotus Domino/Notes manual for more specific information.

Be sure to close all open applications in Windows before you begin to install Domino. Open applications can disrupt the installation process. If you have any open applications, press Alt+Tab to switch to them; then close the applications.

The steps required to install a Domino Web server are the same steps necessary to install the Lotus Notes Server, also known as the Lotus Domino Server. The Domino Web server pieces install automatically when you install Lotus Domino (Notes) Server.

To install Lotus Domino Server 4.5a on your Windows NT server, follow these steps:

1. Choose Start⇨Run from the Windows NT taskbar.

The Run dialog box appears (see Figure 3-1).

Figure 3-1:
Type the
path to
Install.exe.

2. Type the path to the `Install.exe` **file and click OK.**

In this example, drive D is the CD-ROM drive that contains the Lotus Domino Server 4.5a disc. After you click OK, the installation program launches and the Lotus Domino/Notes Software Agreement appears (see Figure 3-2).

3. Read the agreement and, if you agree with it, click the I _Agree_ button at the bottom of the dialog box, below the Lotus Domino/Notes Software Agreement message.

The software registration dialog box appears (see Figure 3-3).

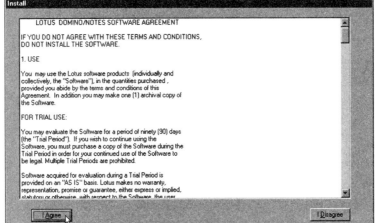

Figure 3-2:
The Lotus
Domino/
Notes
Software
Agreement
message.

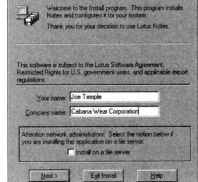

Figure 3-3:
The Lotus
Notes
software
registration
dialog box.

4. **Type your name in the Your name field and your company name in the Company name field, and then click the Next button.**

The Confirm Names dialog box appears (see Figure 3-4).

Figure 3-4:
The Confirm
Names
dialog box.

5. **Click Yes in the Confirm Names dialog box.**

   The Install Options dialog box appears (see Figure 3-5).

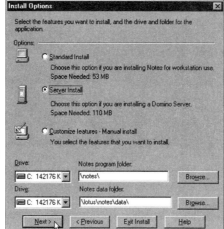

Figure 3-5:
The Install
Options
dialog box.

6. **Click the Server Install radio button in the Install Options dialog box.**

   The dialog box offers two other radio buttons:

   • **Standard Install:** Click this radio button if you are installing a
   Lotus Notes client on your workstation. Most of your users
   probably will use Web browsers to access the Domino Web server,
   so you probably won't need to install many Lotus Notes clients.
   You do need to install Notes clients on workstations where users
   will make design changes to the Domino Web site. (See Chapter 1
   for more about the differences between Lotus Notes clients and
   Web browsers.)

   Throughout the book I use the words *Domino Web site* to describe
   the content of your site and the place where users go to view the
   content. I use *Domino Web server* to describe the computer on
   which the site is hosted.

   • **Customize features — Manual install:** Click this radio button if
   you want to manually specify what features the Installation
   Program is to install. Figure 3-6 shows the features that you can
   decide whether to install.

7. **In the Notes program folder text box of the Install Options dialog
   box, type the path where you want the Install program to put the**

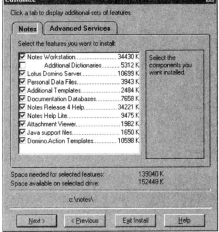

Figure 3-6:
You can
manually
specify
which
features to
install.

Notes program files; and in the Notes data folder text box, type
where you want the program to put the Notes data files.

The dialog box displays the drives on your system and their available
disk space. You can click the Browse buttons to look at your directory
structure and determine where you want to install the program and
data files. *Note:* Clicking the Browse buttons also lets you specify the
locations without having to type them in the text boxes.

8. **Click Next.**

The Select Program Folder dialog box appears (see Figure 3-7).

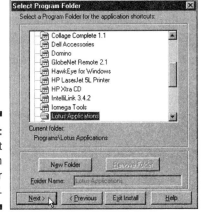

Figure 3-7:
The Select
Program
Folder
dialog box.

9. **Select the folder in which you want the Install program to place the application shortcuts (icons in the Windows interface that start the Domino Web server when you click them), or click the New Folder button to create a new folder for the application shortcuts.**

10. **Click the Next button.**

    The Begin Copying Files dialog box appears (see Figure 3-8).

Figure 3-8:
The Begin
Copying
Files
dialog box.

11. **Click Yes to begin copying files.**

    If you don't have enough disk space to install the selected program, the dreaded Not Enough Disk Space dialog box appears (see Figure 3-9). If that happens, you have the following options:

    • Select a different drive in which to copy the files.

    • Select the Customize features radio button in the Install Options dialog box, and deselect some features you had hoped to install (refer to Figure 3-6).

    • Press Ctrl+Esc to switch to the Windows Explorer, and then delete files from your hard drive to free disk space.

12. **Click Done in the Install Complete dialog box.**

    This box appears once all the files have been copied (see Figure 3-10).

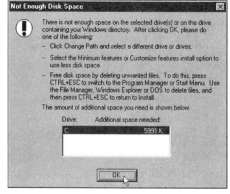

Figure 3-9:
You see this
message
box if you
don't have
enough disk
space to
copy files.

Figure 3-10:
Congratula-
tions!
You're
through
with the
install.

Setting Up the Domino Web Server

Copying the Domino Web server files to the server is only part one of getting the server up and running. Before you can run your Domino Web server, you must go through the setup process — part two. If you try to run the server before completing Setup, you just get an error message. (The third part of preparing your server is covered in "Starting the Domino Web Server" section later in this chapter — just in case you were wondering.)

To complete this second part of the Domino installation and setup, you must first get all the software configured properly, and then you must enable the TCP/IP port.

Doing the software shuffle

Before you follow the steps for setting up your Domino Web Server, you must be at a server workstation and your server must already have Lotus Domino Server (also called the Lotus Notes Server) installed. Now you're ready to set up your Domino Web server, as follows:

1. **Start the Lotus Notes software on the server by clicking the Start button in the Windows NT taskbar and following the path to the program folder that you specified in Step 8 of the installation process.**

   The installation procedures are detailed in this chapter under the heading "Installing the Domino Web Server." Once you start Notes, a blank workspace appears, along with the Notes Server Setup dialog box (see Figure 3-11).

2. **Click the appropriate radio button regarding whether this is the first Lotus Notes server in your organization, and then click OK.**

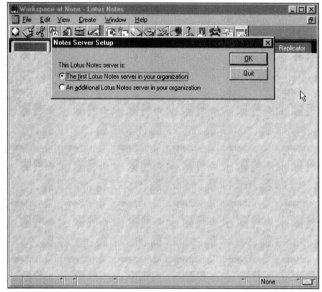

Figure 3-11:
The Notes
Server
Setup
dialog box.

The Notes Server Setup dialog box gives you two radio buttons to choose from:

- **An additional Lotus Notes server in your organization:** Click this radio button if your organization has an existing Certifier ID and Public Address Book. Notice that the Additional Server Setup dialog box (see Figure 3-12), which appears when you select this radio button, asks you to specify a server (in the Get Domain Address Book from area). The server that you specify is the one from which your new server obtains its server ID and the organization's existing Public Address Book.

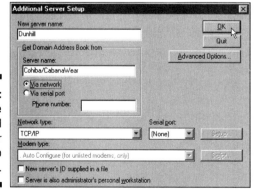

Figure 3-12:
The
Additional
Server
Setup
dialog box.

- **The first Lotus Notes server in your organization:** Click this radio button if this is the first Lotus Notes server in your organization. When you choose this option, the Setup program creates a *Certifier ID*, which is used to certify new servers and new Lotus Notes client users in your organization. The certification is necessary for the servers and clients to communicate. Choosing this option also causes the Setup program to create a *Public Address Book*, which stores information about the Domino Web servers in your organization and about the users and groups of users who access these servers.

You probably are installing the first Domino Web server in your organization, so I assume for the remainder of these steps that you selected the option titled The first Lotus Notes server in your organization. The First Server Setup dialog box appears (see Figure 3-13).

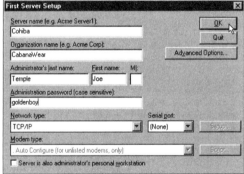

Figure 3-13: The First Server Setup dialog box.

3. **In the First Server Setup dialog box, type the name of your new Domino Web server, the name of your organization, and the name of your Domino Web server's administrator in the appropriate spaces.**

4. **Type the administrator's password in the Administration password box.**

   By default, this password must be a minimum of eight characters. (Step 8 tells you how to change this minimum password length, if you so desire.)

5. **Choose TCP/IP from the Network type drop-down list box.**

   TCP/IP is the required protocol for communicating with a Web server.

6. **Specify a Serial port and, if necessary, a Modem type from the appropriate drop-down list box.**

   The default Serial port selection is *(None)*. If the server uses a modem, you need to specify a serial port and a modem type. Talk to the network administrator to get this information.

7. *Don't* check the Server is also administrator's personal <u>w</u>orkstation check box.

This step is just my recommendation — but it's a pretty good one. The Domino Web server's workload is heavy enough just servicing all the users accessing it via Web browsers, without your adding to it. Why contribute to a possible server crash (and using it as a personal workstation certainly would) if you don't have to?

If you *can* conveniently use the server as a personal workstation, it's probably sitting on your desk, in which case you need to bolster its security. You should lock the server away in a room to which only you have a key; anything less compromises server security. People have told me that as long as they lock the keyboard nobody can access the server to cause problems, which is true. But somebody certainly can still cause severe problems simply by unplugging the server — users can't access an unplugged server, and unplugging a server can damage important files.

8. **Click Ad<u>v</u>anced Options to make other changes.**

The Advanced Server Setup Options dialog box appears (see Figure 3-14). The following list explains what each option means:

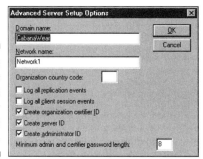

Figure 3-14:
Specify advanced server setup options.

- <u>**Domain name:**</u> For Domino, a *domain* is defined as all the servers and users in a Public Address Book. Setup uses the name of the organization as a domain name by default, and I see little reason to change it.

- <u>**Network name:**</u> A *network* to Domino is a group of continuously connected servers that share the same protocol. Setup defaults to Network1 as a network name. You may want to enter something more descriptive here. The network name affects the routing of Notes mail; unless your Domino Web site users will be taking advantage of Notes mail via their Web browsers, the network name has no significance.

- **Log all replication events, Log all client session events:** By default, these two check boxes aren't enabled. Check them if you want to record replication and user access to the Notes Log. Because checking these check boxes returns more information to the Notes Log, doing so may make future troubleshooting easier. The tradeoff, of course, is that you may find such heavy record-keeping to be information overload.

- **Create organization certifier ID, Create server ID, Create administrator ID:** By default, these three check boxes are enabled. You would disable any of these options only if you would rather use certain existing IDs than create new ones.

- **Minimum admin and certifier password length:** The default is eight. You can change this option if you want to change the required minimum password length.

9. **Click OK.**

   Setup displays a message box to tell you that it's creating files. Eventually the Time Zone Setup dialog box appears (see Figure 3-15).

Figure 3-15:
Select the
server's
time zone.

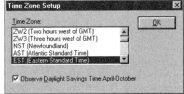

10. **Select the Domino Web server's time zone and indicate whether the region observes Daylight Savings Time.**

11. **Click OK.**

    A message box tells you that Setup is creating more files, and eventually another message box tells you that you have completed the setup process (see Figure 3-16).

Don't let Figure 3-16 fool you; you're two-thirds of the way through the process of getting your Domino Web server ready. If you feel confused by the word Notes on the screen in that figure, I certainly understand! Go to the first page of this chapter and read the first few paragraphs. That should clear things up.

Figure 3-16:
Notes
setup is
complete!

Enabling the TCP/IP port

Before you start up the Domino Web server, you must specify the TCP/IP port in the Server Document of the Public Address Book.

1. Launch the Lotus Notes client.

The Lotus Notes Workspace, which displays the Domino Web server's databases as rectangular icons, appears.

2. Click on the icon for the Public Address Book.

3. Choose View⟶Server⟶Other.

The View Other dialog box appears.

4. Double-click Server\Servers.

The server documents in your Public Address Book appear in the view pane.

5. Double-click on the name of the server for which you need to enable the TCP/IP port.

The server document opens.

6. Expand the Network Configuration section by clicking on the twisty (the triangular icon) next to the section name.

You see something like Figure 3-17. I've already specified my TCP/IP settings in this example.

7. Type TCPIP **in the Port field.**

8. In the Notes Network field, type the same name you used as the network name in Step 8 under "Doing the software shuffle" earlier in this section.

9. In the Net Address field, specify the Domino Web server's IP address.

10. Click the Enabled radio button.

11. Choose File⟶Save to save the server document.

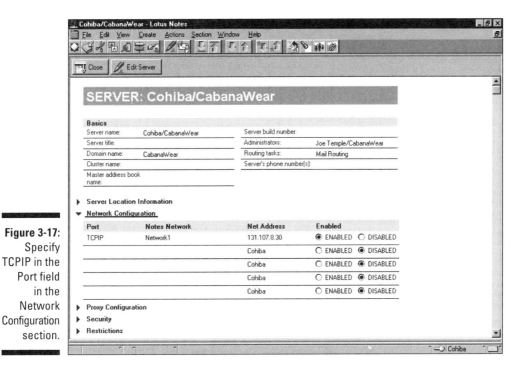

Figure 3-17:
Specify
TCPIP in the
Port field
in the
Network
Configuration
section.

Starting the Domino Web Server

This is the final step in getting the Domino Web server up and running on your Domino (Notes) Server. I assume in this section that you've loaded the Domino server software onto your server and have configured it according to the steps earlier in this chapter. If you haven't, or if someone has done it for you, you may want to briefly go through the previous sections of this chapter — just to be sure everything's kosher.

You can start the Domino Web server in a couple different ways: by typing a command at the main server workstation (or *console*) or by changing the Notes.ini file.

Type command at server console

You can type the **load http** command at the server console to start the Domino Web server. You must enable this command every time the server restarts. To do this, follow these steps:

1. **Start the Lotus Domino Server.**

2. **At the server console prompt, type** load http.

   See Figure 3-18. The prompt returns the date and time that the HTTP Web server (also known as the Domino Web server) started.

Load http command   Server console prompt

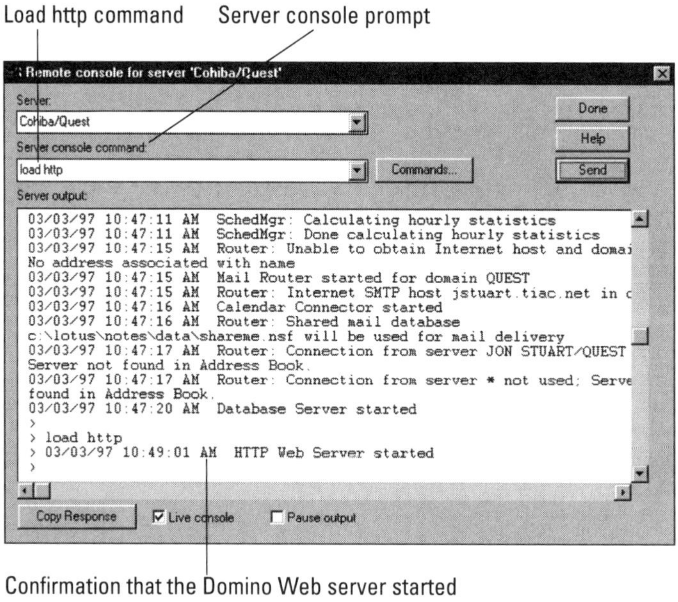

Figure 3-18:
The server
console.

Confirmation that the Domino Web server started

Start through Notes.ini

If you do not want to have to type **load http** every time the Domino Web server restarts, you can start the server via the Notes.ini file. Do the following:

1. **Open the** Notes.ini **file in a text editor.**

2. **Locate the ServerTasks= line.**

   The server tasks specified on this line start every time the server restarts. By default, this line specifies various tasks, such as Replica, Router, Update, and so on.

3. **Type** Http **at the end of this line.**

   See Figure 3-19. Now, every time you restart the server, it becomes Web-ready right away!

Figure 3-19:
The
Notes.ini
file.

```
notes - Notepad
File  Edit  Search  Help
EDITIMP22=PCX Image,0,_IPCX,,.PCX,
EDITIMP28=Binary with Text,0,_ISTRNGS,,.*,
EDITIMP29=WordPerfect 6.0/6.1,0,_IW4W,W4W48F/V0,.WPD,.WPT,.DOC,
EDITIMP30=Excel 4.0/5.0,0,_IW4W,W4W21F/V4C,.XLS,
EDITIMP31=Word for Windows 6.0,0,_IW4W,W4W49F/V0,.DOC,
EDITIMP32=GIF Image,0,_IGIF,,.GIF,
EDITIMP33=JPEG Image,0,_IJPEG,,.JPG,
EDITTEXP1=ASCII Text,2,_XTEXT,,.TXT,.PRN,.C,.H,.RIP,
EDITEXP2=MicrosoftWord RTF,2,_XRTF,,.DOC,.RTF,
EDITEXP3=CGM Image,2,_XCGM,,.CGM,.GMF,
EDITEXP4=TIFF 5.0 Image,2,_XTIFF,,.TIF,
EDITEXP5=Ami Pro,2,_XW4W,W4W33T/V0,.SAM,
EDITEXP21=WordPerfect 6.0,2,_XW4W,W4W48T/V0,.DOC,
EDITEXP22=WordPerfect 6.1,2,_XW4W,W4W48T/V1,.WPD,.WPT,.DOC,
EDITEXP23=Word for Windows 6.0,2,_XW4W,W4W49T/V0,.DOC,
DDETimeout=10
NAMEDSTYLE0=0200426173696300000000000000000000000000000000000000000000000000000101010000
NAMEDSTYLE1=0200427256C6C657400000000000000000000000000000000000000000000000000101010000
NAMEDSTYLE2=020048656164C696E65000000000000000000000000000000000000000000000000010101010
$$$NotesNIC=CN=Home/OU=Notes/O=NET, welcome.nsf, Notes NIC Welcome, Notes Network Information Cen
ServerTasks=Replica,Router,Update,Stats,AMgr,Adminp,Sched,CalConn, Http
ServerTasksAt1=Catalog,Design
ServerTasksAt2=UpdAll,Object Collect mailobj.nsf
ServerTasksAt5=Statlog
TCPIP=TCP, 0, 15, 0
Ports=TCPIP
LAN0=NETBIOS,0,15,0,,12288,
SPX=NWSPX, 0, 15, 0
COM2=XPC,2,15,0,,12294,19200,32,usrsp28.mdm
COM1=XPC,1,15,0,
COM3=XPC,3,15,0,
COM4=XPC,4,15,0,
COM5=XPC,5,15,0,
DisabledPorts=COM2,LAN0,SPX,COM1,COM3,COM4,COM5
LOG_REPLICATION=1
LOG_SESSIONS=1
```

ServerTasks= line

Chapter 4

Using Domino

● ●

In This Chapter

▶ Making things happen at the site

▶ Working with documents

▶ Searching

▶ Using Mail

▶ Creating your calendar

● ●

*U*sing the Domino Web server to build your Web site enables you to offer the functionality not only of being able to read documents on a Domino Web server, but also to edit, create, and delete them. There are a number of different user-friendly and intuitive ways to navigate through a Domino Web site and execute actions.

You can search a single view (which is the Domino-speak equivalent of a group of *Web pages*) of the Domino Web site for words or phrases, or you can search a single database, a group of databases, or all the databases on the Domino Web server. The search language is powerful enough that you can do compound searches with Boolean logical operators such as AND. For example, you can search for documents that contain the words blue AND red.

The Domino Web server opens the powerful Notes mail and calendar features to a standard Web browser. You can use a Web browser to read your mail and create mail messages. You can also view your calendar, and create and send invitations for meetings. And if you receive an invitation from someone, the Domino Web server allows you to use your Web browser to either accept or decline the invitation.

In this chapter I discuss how users can work with Domino to access information on a Domino server. I also tell how you can create and manipulate documents stored on the server, use Domino's powerful Boolean search engine, and do some mail and calendaring functions.

Even if you're a developer and already know a lot about the subjects covered in this chapter, I suggest you read it anyway. I include some tips every now and again throughout the chapter that you may find useful when building your Domino Web site.

The Interface

The following few sections cover how users access the Domino Web server and how they go about opening databases.

Accessing the Domino Web site

To open a Domino Web site, you type its *URL* or Uniform Resource Locator, which is a Web address like `www.idgbooks.com`, into your Web browser. As a server administrator, you decide what users see when they type the Domino Web server's URL into their Web browsers. The default displays for the user a list of links to the databases on the server (see Figure 4-1). By simply changing an option in the server document, you can display a home page, a listing of links to all the documents on the site, or a specific document.

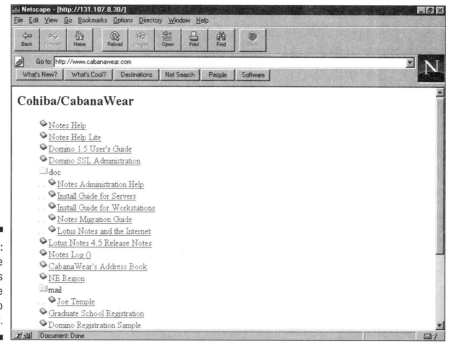

Figure 4-1:
Links to the
databases
on the
Domino
Web server.

Opening databases

After you type the site's URL into your browser and a page appears on your browser screen with the listing of links to databases on the Domino Web server, you open the database by clicking any of the links. The home page appears (see Figure 4-2). You can also, rather than clicking the database's link, type in the URL that specifies the name of the database and then type the `?OpenDatabase` action, which tells Domino to open the database.

Web browser view versus Notes view

If you view information on the server, be aware that there are a few differences between what you will see on a Notes client interface and what you will see on a Web browser interface. Figure 4-3 shows a typical view as seen on a Notes client, and Figure 4-4 shows the same view as seen on a Web browser. Some of the differences:

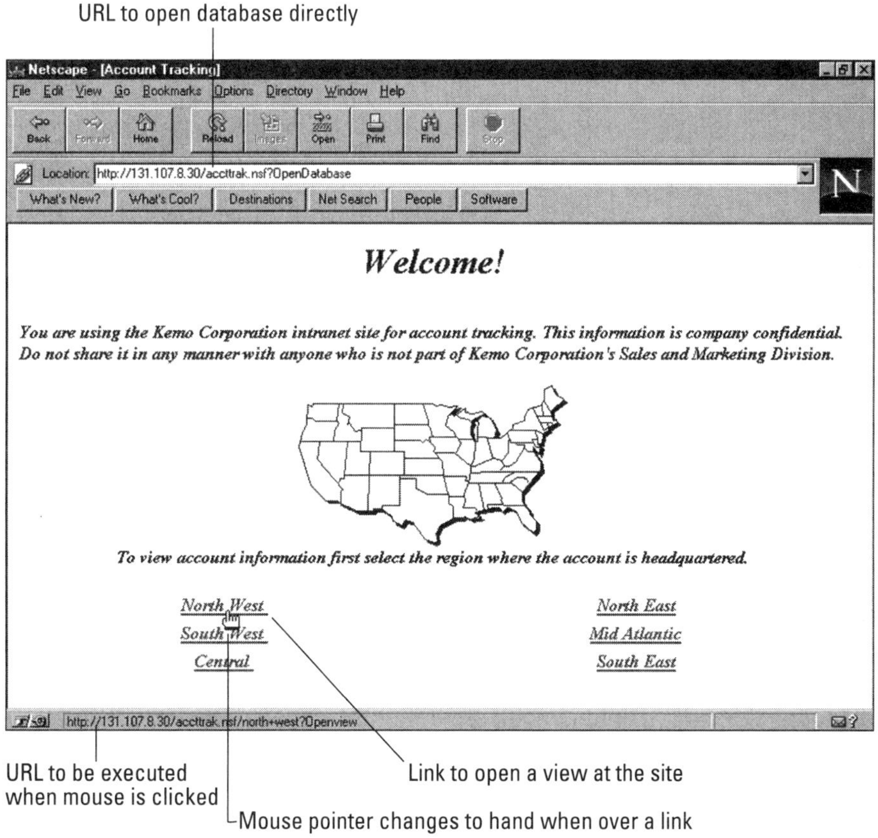

URL to open database directly

Figure 4-2:
The home
page of a
database.

URL to be executed
when mouse is clicked

Link to open a view at the site

Mouse pointer changes to hand when over a link

- ✔ **Number of documents displayed:** The Web browser displays fewer documents than does the Notes client. You can use the elevator bar in the right margin of the Web browser to scroll up and down so that you can view documents that fall off the screen.

- ✔ **Opening documents:** Notice that the documents in the Web browser seem to be underlined; this indicates that they are links. To open a document, simply click the link. To open a document on a Notes client, on the other hand, you must double-click the link.

- ✔ **Closing documents:** Using a Web browser, if you have a document open on-screen and you want to return to the view that displays all the documents, you click the Back icon or the Previous link. In Notes, you press Esc.

- ✔ **Navigating to views:** The Web browser does not provide a menu for maneuvering through a Web site; so to move around, you must rely on links and buttons that have been designed into the application. To open a view using the Notes client, you can click its name in the navigation pane.

- ✔ **Collapsing and expanding views:** If you want to expand or collapse a view in the Web browser, you click the links. If you want to do the same thing in Notes, you use a menu option.

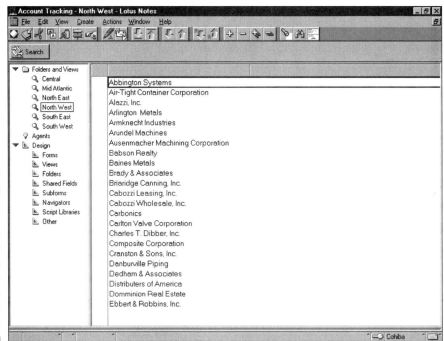

Figure 4-3:
View as seen with a Notes client. The navigation buttons are part of the client's program.

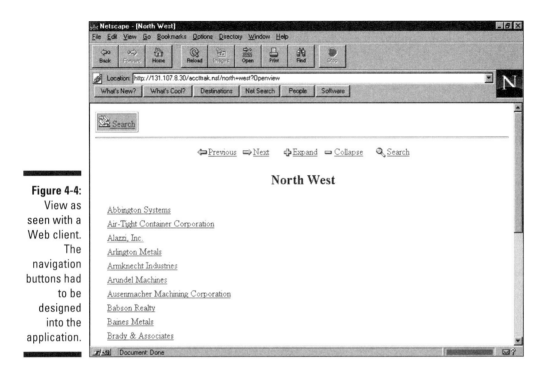

Figure 4-4:
View as
seen with a
Web client.
The
navigation
buttons had
to be
designed
into the
application.

Moving and Executing

Basically, users have four ways of maneuvering around and executing commands in a Domino Web site:

- ✔ Clicking links
- ✔ Clicking action buttons
- ✔ Clicking hotspots on navigators
- ✔ Typing URLs

Your Web browser or Notes client does most of the work for you if you use any of the "clicking" methods. Typing a URL, however, requires a tad more personal involvement in the process.

Clicking links

Clicking links (often called *hypertext links* or *hyperlinks*) is a standard way to navigate through most Web sites. Links are represented by underlined text or by graphics.

You can find links in views and documents, and in the About Database document (see Chapter 3 for more details about this document), which you also can use as a home page.

When you format ordinary text for your Domino Web site, avoid underlining the text if at all possible. In Web sites, underlined text generally indicates a link, so users may get confused if nothing happens when they click text that you have underlined.

Figure 4-4 shows good examples of links that move your browser to another part of the site and/or execute an action. The view alphabetically lists each company by name down the left-hand side. These names, which are set off by underlining, are links to documents. Clicking them moves you to other documents. The links at the top of the view (Previous, Next, Expand, Collapse, and Search) are examples of links that execute an action if you click them.

You also commonly find links in documents. Figure 4-5 shows a document containing an example of a link that executes a command and an example of a link that navigates the user to another part of the Domino Web site.

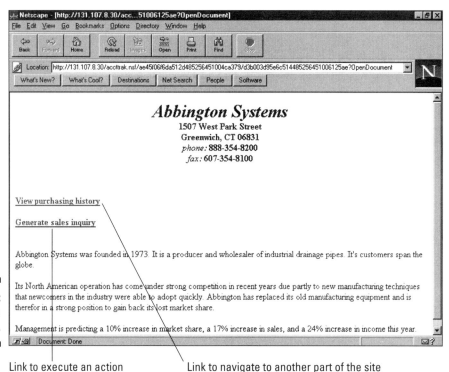

Figure 4-5:
Links in a
document.

Link to execute an action   Link to navigate to another part of the site

Clicking action buttons

Clicking graphic buttons is another way to maneuver through a Domino Web site and to execute preprogrammed actions. Figure 4-6 shows examples of action buttons that execute commands — the Search Web Server, Search Database, and Search View buttons. The figure also has examples of links (Previous, Next, and company) that maneuver you to other views in the Domino Web site.

Buttons that execute commands you can do from a view, such as the Search buttons in Figure 4-6, are the only buttons that appear in the view's action-button bar. For example, a button designed to execute a command that edits a document doesn't appear in the view's action-button bar because you cannot edit a document in a view. You must first open the document to edit it.

Action buttons can also appear in a document. Figure 4-7 shows action buttons in a document that can execute a search and edit a document, as well as maneuver you to another view. Just like in a view, only buttons issuing commands that can be performed in a document appear in the document's button bar.

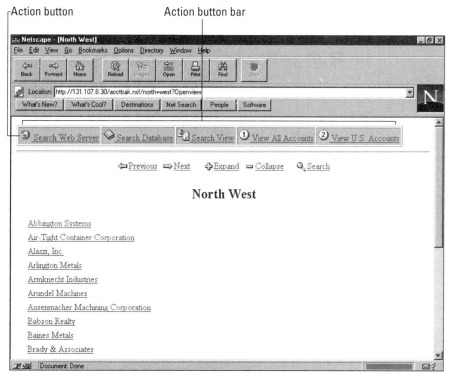

Figure 4-6:
Action buttons in a view.

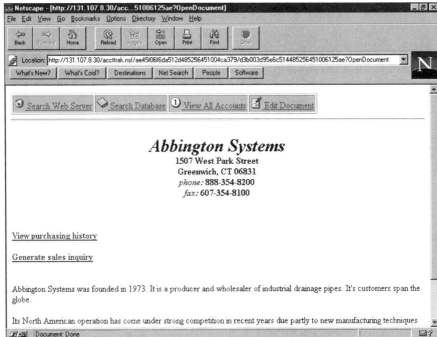

Figure 4-7:
Action
buttons in a
document.

Clicking hotspots on a navigator

Navigators are *image maps* (one large graphic or a series of interconnected small graphics) in which you enable areas of the images as *hotspots* to perform certain functions. Navigators are often used as Domino Web site home pages, but you can also use them throughout a site to help users move around it or execute actions. For example, a user can click the hotspots on your home page and be taken to a database file in another part of the site.

Figures 4-8 and 4-9 show the same navigator. If you click different areas of this image of Australia, you navigate to a different part of the Domino Web site or you execute an action.

In Figure 4-8, you know the mouse pointer is positioned over a hotspot because it looks like a hand with a pointing finger instead of a normal pointer-arrow. The status bar at the bottom of the screen displays the action that clicking this hotspot executes. Clicking the part of the image map represented by the Western Australia portion opens a view called Western Australia.

In Figure 4-9, the mouse pointer is positioned over a hotspot represented by the South Australia portion of the image map and the status bar tells you that clicking the hotspot executes a search of the All Documents view for any documents that contain the text string "South Australia."

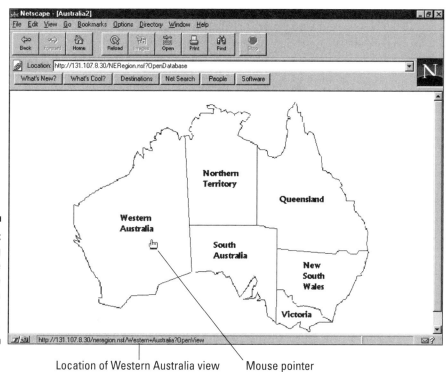

Figure 4-8:
Clicking
here
opens the
Western
Australia
view.

Location of Western Australia view   Mouse pointer

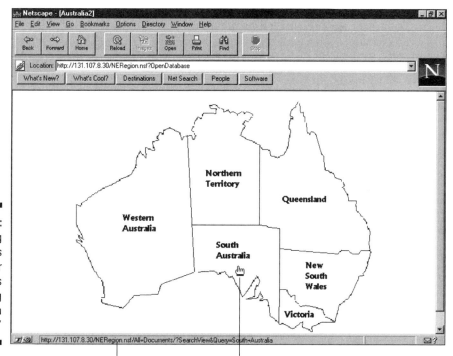

Figure 4-9:
Clicking
here starts
a search for
documents
containing
"South
Australia."

Search query enabled   Mouse pointer

Just as links and action buttons can both maneuver you to another part of the Web site or execute an action, so can hotspots in navigators.

Typing URLs

All of the coding that allows links, action buttons, and navigators to maneuver you through the Domino Web site or execute actions is in the form of URLs (see Chapter 5 for more on this topic). Domino uses special Domino-specific URLs that execute actions.

Just as you can click a button to execute a URL that a developer has programmed into the button, you can also type a URL directly into your Web browser. Such an approach isn't exactly user-friendly, though, because so many URLs are rather long, not to mention a bit cryptic.

In Figure 4-9, for example, the status bar shows the URL that executes when you click the South Australia hotspot. If you type the same URL into your Web browser, it executes the search action on the All Documents view in your Domino Web site (which means the search engine scans every document in the site). Typing in that URL executes the search action no matter where you are on the Internet.

The syntax that comprises the search URL requires a protocol, server name, database name, view name, and action name to perform the search. Considering the increased time and potential for error in typing URLs, you may want to stick with clicking buttons.

Working with Documents

Domino creates an easy-to-use environment for interacting with the site. When I say *interact*, I don't mean users can just read documents. I mean they can read, create, edit, delete, and execute processes that affect documents. That Domino makes these functions easy for you to do, whether you are the site administrator or a user, is reason enough to fall in love with it.

Opening documents

The most common way to open a document is to click the document's link on a view page. The values that appear in the first column of the page are underlined, indicating that they are links; clicking the underlined value opens a document.

You can also open documents by clicking action buttons or navigator hotspots programmed to open specific documents. Additionally, typing the same URL programmed into the action button or navigator hotspot opens the same documents. See "Moving and Executing" earlier in this chapter for more about how such buttons, hotspots, and URLs are used.

Creating documents

The Web browser doesn't inherently furnish a menu for creating documents, so you must find another way, the most common of which is to use an action button. Since you can't use a menu, you must create new documents by clicking action buttons that were programmed into the view by the developer. Figure 4-10 shows an action button that you can click if you want to compose a new document.

You can't create documents if the Domino Web site administrator doesn't give you the required authority. Of course, if you're the Web site administrator, you can do whatever you want.

Action button to compose documents

Figure 4-10: A view with an action button for composing documents.

Netscape - [North West]

File Edit View Go Bookmarks Options Directory Window Help

Back Forward Home Reload Images Open Print Find Stop

Location: http://131.107.8.30/accttrak.nsf/north+west?Openview

What's New? What's Cool? Destinations Net Search People Software

Search Web Server Search Database Search View View All Accounts Compose Document

⇐Previous ⇒Next ⊹Expand ⸻Collapse Search

North West

Abbington Systems
Air-Tight Container Corporation
Alazzi, Inc.
Armknecht Industries
Arundel Machines
Ausenmacher Machining Corporation
Babson Realty
Baines Metals
Brady & Associates
Briaridge Canning, Inc.

Document: Done

Editing documents

When you click a link to open a document, that document opens in read mode. When the document is open in read mode, you can execute an edit action that changes the document from read mode to edit mode. Since the Web doesn't furnish a menu for editing documents, you must find another way, the most common of which is to use an action button.

Figure 4-11 shows an action button that puts documents in edit mode, and a document after that button has been clicked. You can see that the fields appear with rectangles around them when they are in edit mode. Compare the way the document looks here to the way it appeared in read mode (refer to Figure 4-7).

You must receive the required authority from the Domino Web site administrator before you can edit a document.

Edit action button

Field in edit mode

Delete action button

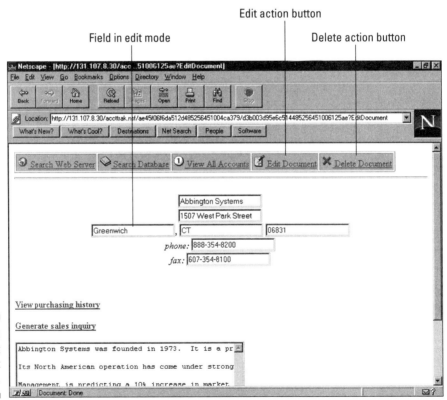

Figure 4-11:
A document
in edit
mode.

Deleting

You delete documents the same way as you edit them, except the button that you click has been programmed to delete the document instead of edit it. Figure 4-11 shows a delete action button in the button bar. If you click the delete button, it deletes the currently displayed document.

As with most editing functions, you can't delete the document if the Domino Web site administrator hasn't given you the required authority.

Clicking the button deletes the document, and then a screen confirming the delete action appears (see Figure 4-12).

Figure 4-12:
The Delete
confirmation
screen.

Filling in fields

Entering information in fields when you are creating or editing documents is a pretty straightforward process. Each of the fields is represented by a rectangle (see Figure 4-13).

You can press Tab to move from one field to the next as you enter information.

All you need to remember when you enter information in fields is that a field may require a certain data type, such as numbers, or may require some type of value, or that a value may not be in excess of a maximum number of characters. If you run into one such field requirement, don't worry; nothing is going to blow up on you. You just get a friendly and intuitive message when you try to save the document, telling you that you need to change one of your fields.

Field

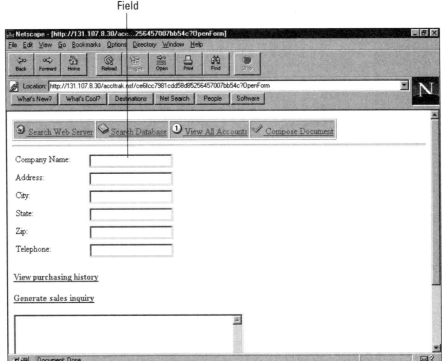

Figure 4-13:
Fields in
edit mode.

Keyword fields

Domino offers a special type of field called a *keyword field*. Instead of requiring site visitors who are creating documents to type information, the keyword field presents them with a predefined list to select from. As a user, you may see a keyword list if the document has an assigned status, and you have only three options: Open, Open pending approval, and Closed.

Keyword fields can be presented to users in three different ways:

- ✔ **Radio button:** Allows the user to select only one item.
- ✔ **Check box:** Allows the user to select more than one item.
- ✔ **Dialog box:** Allows the designer to determine whether the user can select one or more items. To select from the list, the user simply scrolls through the choices by clicking on the up or down arrows that are part of the box.

Figure 4-14 shows the three different options for keyword fields.

Check box   Radio button

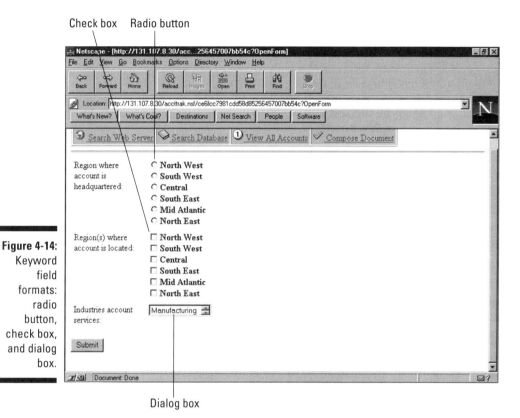

Figure 4-14:
Keyword
field
formats:
radio
button,
check box,
and dialog
box.

Dialog box

Submitting

When you finish editing or composing a document you can submit it. Submitting the document saves it in the Notes database. In edit mode, every document has a submit button (refer to Figure 4-14) that you click to save the document on the Domino Web server. Other people visiting the site can then view the edited document.

Searching

Domino allows you to search a single database or a group of databases on a server. To execute a search, you can click a link, an action button, or a navigator hotspot that the site designer has set up. You can also type in the URL syntax for searching (see Chapter 14).

A database must be Full Text Indexed to be searchable. On the Domino Web server, the administrator must enable a Full Text Index. (See Chapter 14 for more information on enabling full-text indexing on the Domino Web site.)

Search interface

Once you are presented with the Full Text Search screen (see Figure 4-15), you can build a search. Follow these steps:

1. **Type the text you are searching for in the Search for the following word(s) box.**

   You can specify individual words or phrases.

2. **Select a limit to the number of documents that the search returns.**

   Your options are All, which returns all documents that match the search criteria, and 10, 50, 100, and 250.

3. **Select how you want the results sorted.**

   You have the following sorting options:

   • **Relevance:** Sorts the documents based on how well they match the search string. Generally speaking, a document with multiple occurrences sorts before a document that has a single occurrence, but the length of the document also affects the sort order. For example, a short document with only one occurrence may sort before a longer document with more than one occurrence.

   • **Oldest first (by date):** Sorts documents in ascending order of their creation dates. For example, a document created in January sorts higher than a document created in February of the same year.

   • **Newest first (by date):** Sorts documents in descending order of their creation dates. For example, a document created in December sorts higher than a document created in November of the same year.

4. **Decide whether you want to enable the Find exact word matches only option.**

   This option makes the Domino search engine return only documents that contain the exact word specified. If you do not select this radio button and you search for the word *find,* documents with the words *find, finding*, and *finds* are returned. If you do select this radio button, only documents with the word *find* are returned.

5. **Decide whether you want to enable the Find word variations as defined by thesaurus option.**

   This option makes the Domino search engine return documents that contain the word specified, as well as documents that contain synonyms of that word. If you select this radio button and you search for the word *find*, documents with both *find* and *locate* are returned. If you do not select this radio button, only documents with the word *find* are returned.

6. **Click the Search button when you finish.**

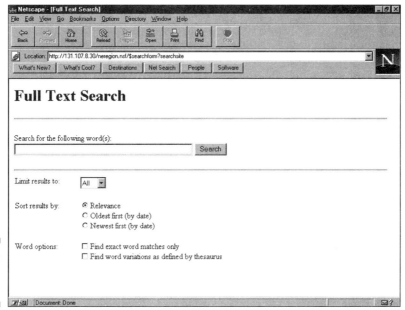

Figure 4-15:
The Search
form.

Searching with Boolean logic

The Domino Web server allows you to use Boolean logic operators such as AND and OR in the Search for the following word(s) field. You can also set conditions apart with parentheses. Some examples of Boolean search criteria:

- ✔ **Dog** AND **Cat:** Documents must contain both of the words Dog and Cat to match the criteria.

- ✔ **Dog** OR **Cat:** Documents must contain at least one of the words Dog or Cat to match the criteria.

- ✔ **(Dog** OR **Cat)** AND **Goat:** Documents must contain the word Goat, and must contain at least one of the words Dog or Cat.

- ✔ **(Dog** AND **Cat)** OR **Goat:** Documents must contain the word Goat, or both of the words Dog and Cat.

Using Mail

If you are a Notes mail user, Domino enables you to view your mail with a Web browser. Additionally, you can view your mail from any machine with a Web browser, even if you don't have your Notes.ID. To use a Web browser to view your mail, you must authenticate yourself by specifying your name and a password, so that people without your password cannot read your mail.

Reading your mail

You access your mail file the same way you access any other Domino Web server database:

1. **Type the Domino Web server's URL in your Web browser.**

   A list of the databases on the Domino Web server appears.

2. **In the list of databases on the server, click the link that represents your mail database.**

   An authentication dialog box appears.

3. **Type your name and password in the authentication dialog box, and click OK.**

   Your mail database appears, with links to the different views (see Figure 4-16).

4. **Click whichever view link you want.** The view appears (see Figure 4-17). You can use a number of different views: all the documents in the mail files, calendar items, to-do items, meetings, deleted documents, and so on.

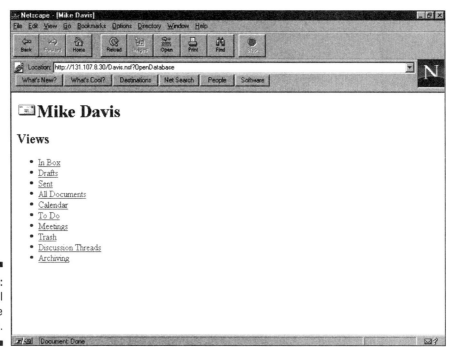

Figure 4-16:
Mail database views.

Link to create a meeting invitation   Link to create a to-do item

Link to create a mail message   Link to view a mail message

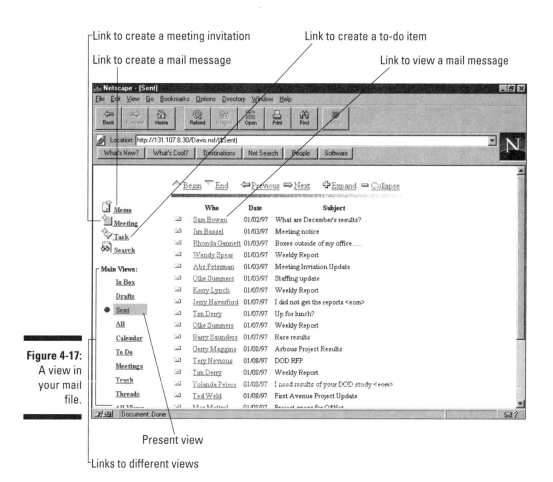

Figure 4-17:
A view in
your mail
file.

Present view

Links to different views

Sending mail

You can create mail messages with your Web browser and have the powerful mail router on the Domino Web server handle the delivery. To create a mail message:

1. Click the Memo link.

The memo form appears (see Figure 4-18).

2. In the *To* field, *cc:* field, or *bcc:* field, type the names of the people to whom you want to send the memo.

Names that you specify in the bcc (blind carbon copy) field are not visible to other recipients of the message.

Submit button   Action buttons

To field

Carbon copy field

Blind carbon copy field

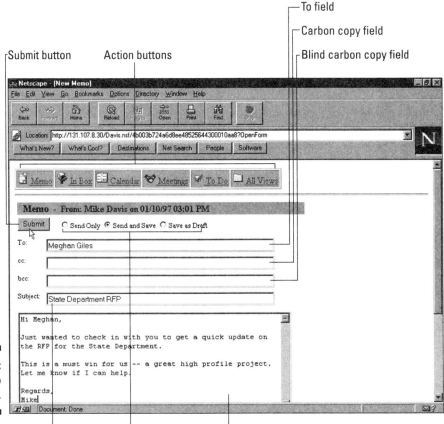

Figure 4-18:
The memo
form.

Subject field   Send / save options   Body field

3. **In the Subject field, type a title for the document that will appear in the recipients' views.**

4. **Type your message into the Body field.**

5. **Choose one of these send/save option radio buttons:**

   • **Send Only:** Sends the message but does not save it.

   • **Send and Save:** Sends the message and saves it in the database.

   • **Save as Draft:** Saves the message but does not send it. You can open the message at a later date and send it.

6. **Click the Submit button.**

You can easily move to another view when the memo form is open, simply by clicking one of the action buttons that appear in the button bar above the form.

Calendaring

The mail database has a calendar function, so you can keep a schedule of events, appointments, and that sort of thing, on the Domino Web server.

Viewing your calendar

To view your calendar, click the Calendar action button or the calendar link in your mail database. Figure 4-19 shows the Two Day calendar view.

You can view your calendar two days, one week, two weeks, or one month at a time. You can click the links at the top of the view to switch the view. The Today link brings you to the present day's items. The Year link shows you a yearly calendar but does not display your appointments. The Previous and Next links allow you to cycle through days, weeks, or months.

Link to compose a calendar item   Link to switch to today   Link to scroll to previous days, weeks, or months   Links to show yearly calendar without links

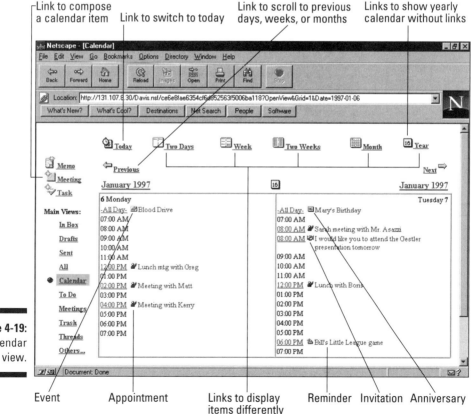

Figure 4-19: Calendar view.

Event   Appointment   Links to display items differently   Reminder   Invitation   Anniversary

Five types of times appear in the calendar: appointments, events, anniversaries, invitations, and reminders, each of which has its own icon.

Creating calendar items

Creating calendar items is easy. Just follow these steps:

1. **Click the Meeting link.**

   The Invitation form appears (see Figure 4-20).

2. **If you are creating an entry other than an invitation, click the Appointment, Event, Reminder, or Anniversary link, whichever is appropriate to your entry.**

3. **Type a description of the meeting in the Brief Description field.**

4. **Type the date of the meeting in the Date field.**

5. **Type the time in the Time field.**

6. **Leave the Not for public viewing check box unchecked unless your mail file is public domain and you do not want other people to see this particular entry.**

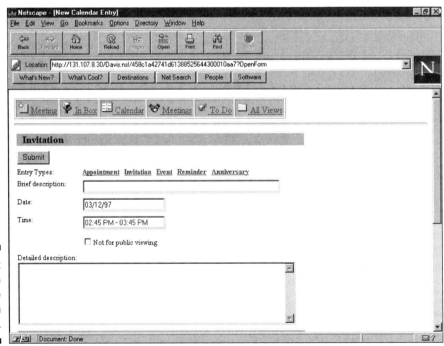

Figure 4-20:
The top
of the
invitation
form.

7. **Type a detailed description of the meeting in the Detailed description field.**

8. **Type the names of the people you want to invite to the meeting in the Send invitations to field (see Figure 4-21).**

9. **Choose any file attachments in the File Attachments field.**

10. **Choose any Mail Options:**

   - **Importance:** Determines how the invitation is flagged in the recipients' mail file.

   - **Delivery Priority:** Determines how quickly the invitation is mailed.

   - **Delivery Report:** Specifies how you want the delivery report returned to you.

11. **Click the Submit button.**

That sums up this chapter. Using Domino is very intuitive, and the added flexibility of working with your favorite Web browser is why everyone's excited about Domino.

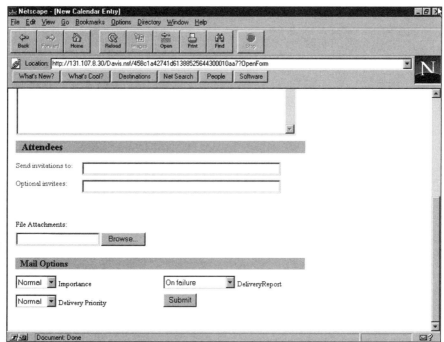

Figure 4-21:
The bottom of the invitation form.

Chapter 5

U-R-Cing URLs Everywhere!

*Y*ou see *Uniform Resource Locators* (URLs), such as www.idgbooks.com, everywhere you look nowadays. Many television advertisements, for example, whether they be for cars, magazines, mutual funds, or kids' toys, show the company's URL at the bottom of the screen. Just what are these mysterious things called URLs?

Think of URLs as a really good street address. If you and I want to meet at my office, I just have to give you the street address, right? Unfortunately, nope. I have to give you the street address. I have to give you the city, because there is more than one Main Street in the world. I not only have to *tell* you the directions, but we have to converse back and forth to make sure you were clear on the directions. I also have to give you parking directions. And even after all that, one of the first questions I ask you when you arrived at my office is, "Did you have any trouble finding the place?"

With URLs you don't have the same problem. If you were planning to visit my virtual office — my Web site — I would just have to give you the URL, right? Right! All you need to do is type my URL into your trusty Web browser and, just like that, you are visiting my virtual office — no directions, no wrong turns, no parking, and no getting cut off by obnoxious drivers and watching *them* making obscene gestures.

People visiting your Domino Web site not only will be using URLs to find the site, but also will be utilizing them to maneuver through and interact with the site; Domino's use of URLs goes beyond your average Web server's use of them. Before you can understand how Domino uses URLs, you need to understand the components of a typical URL.

The Bits and Pieces of Internet URLs

Here is an example of a typical URL:

```
http://www.marinebiology.com/whales/titleist.htm
```

Using the above URL as an example, you can see that a URL consists of the following four components:

- ✔ **Protocol:** A protocol of `http` indicates a URL that points to a World Wide Web server (also called a Web server). Another protocol you might see is *ftp*, which indicates a URL that points to a *File Transfer Protocol* (FTP) server.

- ✔ **Network location:** A unique name, such as `www.marinebiology.com`, that identifies an Internet server. You can substitute the server's TCP/IP address (for example, `131.107.8.30`) for the network location name.

- ✔ **Path or directory:** Part of the directory structure on the Internet server. The server's hard drive might have a number of directories that categorize HTML files logically. For example, `whales` may be one directory, `sharks` another, and `squid` another, each of which would contain related files.

- ✔ **File name:** A single HTML file located on the Internet server — in our example, `titleist.htm`.

The example here shows that the `titleist.htm` HTML file is located in the `whales` directory of the `www.marinebiology.com` World Wide Web server. If users want to display the home page (usually named *index.htm*) of this particular Web server, they just type **http://www.marinebiology.com** into their Web browsers.

URLs can be *absolute* or *relative*.

- ✔ An *absolute URL* is one in which the entire Internet address, including protocol, network location, optional path, and file name, is specified; for example:

  ```
  http://www.marinebiology.com/whales/titleist.htm
  ```

- ✔ A *relative URL* is one in which one or more of the components are missing; for example:

  ```
  www.marinebiology.com
  ```

If a user specifies a relative URL, the browser fills in the blanks based on the current Web page. For example, if the user types **www.marinebiology.com** into the browser while viewing another World Wide Web document, the browser will fill in the missing protocol to produce `http://www.marinebiology.com`.

The Bits and Pieces of Domino URLs

Domino URLs are the same as other Internet URLs, with a few exceptions. First, because a Domino Web server displays documents that are neatly stored in a Notes database rather than files stored willy-nilly on the server's hard drive, the path and file name components in a Domino URL refer to databases and documents. Also, Domino URLs include additional components that allow users to interact with the Domino Web site. In the next few paragraphs I describe the pieces of a URL and give you developers a few tips on how to include some of those pieces (such as Notes object IDs) in your server's URL.

Dissecting Domino URLs

Domino URLs don't look too dissimilar from regular, everyday URLs. Sometimes they just have more question marks. Here is an example of a Domino URL:

```
http://www.marinebiology.com/whales.nsf/
              titleist?OpenView&ExpandView
```

A Domino URL consists of the following five main components:

- ✔ **Protocol:** A protocol of `http` (standard for Domino URLs), as explained in the previous section, indicates a URL that points to a World Wide Web server. Since Domino lets you attach and detach files without using FTP, you don't need the `ftp` protocol specification if you use Domino. In addition to `http`, you'll also see the `https` protocol specification, which indicates that you can do secure transactions with the Domino Web site.

- ✔ **Host or Network location:** This unique name (`www.marinebiology.com`) identifies an Internet server. You can substitute the server's TCP/IP address (for example, `131.107.8.30`) for the network location name.

Do not confuse the name of the Internet server with the name of your Notes server. Even though they are on the same machine, the name you give the Notes server when you install it has no bearing on the domain name that users will specify from their browsers.

✔ **Notes Object:** This particular Notes object refers to the `whales.nsf` database and the `titleist` view. When you specify a database as the Notes object, you can use the name of the database, or you can use its ReplicaID. When you specify other objects as the Notes object, you can specify the name of the object, its UniversalID (also called *unique ID* or *UNID*), or its NoteID. See the section "Calling all IDs" following this list for definitions of these IDs and to find out about including the database objects' IDs in the URL.

I recommend using the names of databases and objects instead of their IDs; this convention makes any necessary troubleshooting much easier.

Examples of Notes objects are

- Databases
- Views
- Navigators
- Forms
- Documents

✔ **Action:** The action specifies what you want to do with the Notes object. In the example, the action specifies to open the titleist view. If you do not specify an action in the URL, Domino defaults to the ?Open action. Actions can

- Open databases, views, and forms
- Open, edit, and delete documents
- Execute *agents* (also known as *macros* and *procedures*)
- Navigate to other Web sites

✔ **Argument:** You can control how the action executes by specifying arguments. In the example, the &ExpandView argument displays the `titleist` view in expanded format.

Calling all IDs

As I explain in the previous section, when you specify a database as the Notes object, you can use the name of the database, or you can use its ReplicaID. When you specify other objects (such as views and forms) as the Notes object, you can specify the name of the object, its UniversalID, or its NoteID. (For information on how to specify the name of an object in a URL, see "Actions that open things" later in this chapter.)

Inserting ReplicaIDs

Though I recommend using the names of databases and objects in URLs instead of their IDs, I'd be remiss if I didn't explain how to put ReplicaIDs in a URL. You can use the Clipboard to include the database's ReplicaID in the URL:

1. Select File➪Database➪Design Synopsis.

The Design Synopsis dialog box appears (see Figure 5-1).

2. Check the Replication check box.

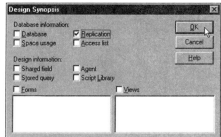

Figure 5-1:
The Design
Synopsis
dialog box.

3. Select OK.

The design synopsis appears (see Figure 5-2).

4. Highlight the ReplicaID.

5. Select Edit➪Copy.

The ReplicaID is now in the Windows Clipboard (or its UNIX equivalent) and can be pasted when creating the URL.

6. Move the cursor to where you want to create the URL (whether it be in an action button, navigator hotspot, text link, or such) and start to create the link.

7. Paste the ReplicaID into the URL.

After you paste the ReplicaID into the URL, be sure to remove the colon (:). Otherwise your users get an error when they use the URL.

Inserting UniversalIDs

The NoteID is an eight-character combination of letters and numbers that uniquely identifies an object within a single replica copy of a database. The UniversalID (also called _unique ID_ or _UNID_) is a 32-character combination of hexadecimal digits that uniquely identifies an object across all replica copies of a database. An object's NoteID changes between replica copies; the UniversalID doesn't.

ReplicaID

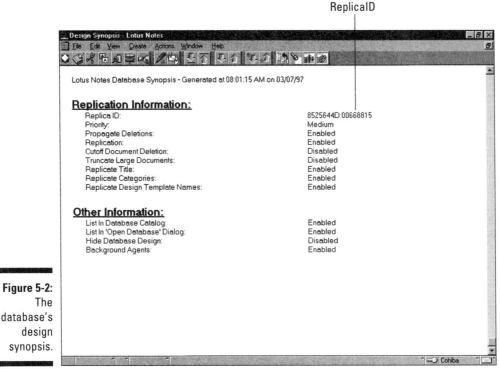

File Edit View Create Actions Window Help

Lotus Notes Database Synopsis - Generated at 08:01:15 AM on 03/07/97

Replication Information:
Replica ID:	8525644D:00668815
Priority:	Medium
Propagate Deletions:	Enabled
Replication:	Enabled
Cutoff Document Deletion:	Disabled
Truncate Large Documents:	Disabled
Replicate Title:	Enabled
Replicate Categories:	Enabled
Replicate Design Template Names:	Enabled

Other Information:
List In Database Catalog:	Enabled
List In 'Open Database' Dialog:	Enabled
Hide Database Design:	Disabled
Background Agents:	Enabled

Cohiba

Figure 5-2:
The
database's
design
synopsis.

I can't recommend strongly enough that you use the UniversalID instead of the NoteID to identify an object. Actually, I recommend using the name of the object to identify it, but if you definitely want to use an ID, go with the UniversalID rather than the NoteID.

Two different sets of steps apply for obtaining UniversalIDs. One set applies to getting the IDs for documents, and the other set works for views. Follow these steps to obtain a document's UniversalID:

1. Launch the Lotus Notes client.

The Lotus Notes Workspace, which displays the Domino Web server's databases as rectangular icons, appears.

2. Click the icon for the database that contains the document.

3. Choose View➪Go To.

The Go To dialog box appears.

4. Click the name of the view that contains the document and click OK.

The database opens.

5. Click the document in a view to select it.

6. Select File⇨Document Properties, or click the right mouse button and select Document Properties.

The Properties for Document InfoBox appears (see Figure 5-3).

A three-line ID appears at the bottom of the InfoBox. The first line is 39 characters long. If you remove "*OF,*" "*ON,*" colons, and minus sign (–) from the line, the remaining 32 characters comprise the UniversalID. If you don't omit the colons and minus sign when you type the UniversalID into the URL, your users get an error when they use the URL. In the ID shown in Figure 5-3, for example, you would remove the bold elements of the following line to get the 32-character UniversalID:

ID: OFACFAF2A5**:**D95A9B3B**–ON**85256450**:**005379B9

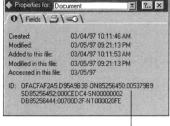

Figure 5-3:
The
Properties
for
Document
InfoBox.

First line of ID
contains the
UniversalID

Unfortunately, you can't highlight the UniversalID so you can't utilize the Clipboard like you did with the database's ReplicaID. You must pull out your trusty pencil and a piece of paper and start copying down the 32-character ID — but remember to leave out those items so noted in the last paragraph.

7. Move the cursor to where you want to create the URL (whether it be in an action button, navigator hotspot, text link, or such) and start to create it by typing the UniversalID that you wrote down.

These steps get you started when you want to put the UniversalID for a document in a URL. To continue creating the link (action button, hotspot, and so forth), see the appropriate chapter in this book.

I should tell you about another way to get the UniversalID for documents. You can type **@Text(@DocumentUniqueID** into either a completed field or a column formula. Doing so gets you the 32-character UniversalID, with the colons and minus sign omitted. You can then copy it to the Clipboard and paste it into your URL.

To get the UniversalID for a design element, such as a view:

1. **Select <u>V</u>iew⇨<u>D</u>esign to expand the Design folder in the navigation pane.**

   If `Design` does not appear at the bottom of the View menu, select <u>V</u>iew⇨<u>S</u>how⇨<u>D</u>esign, to expand the Design folder.

2. **Select the Views folder.**

   All the views in the databases appear listed in the view pane.

3. **Click on the name of the view from which you want to get the UniversalID.**

4. **Select <u>D</u>esign⇨Design <u>P</u>roperties.**

   The Properties for Design Document InfoBox appears (see Figure 5-4).

5. **Go to Step 6 for getting the UniversalIDs for documents (immediately preceding this series), read the instructions about deleting OF, ON, colons, and minus signs, and then follow Step 7 of that same list.**

A Closeup of Actions

Including actions in URLs enables your Domino Web site visitors to open certain elements, interact with documents, and search your site. As a developer, you also can use an action to force all site visitors to log in before they enter the site.

Actions that open things

This section introduces the commands that enable you to open design elements in the database. Actions like ?OpenServer, ?OpenDatabase, and ?OpenNavigator perform specific functions that every Lotus developer uses when designing his or her Domino Web server.

?OpenServer

Use the *?OpenServer* action to open a server. The only components necessary are the protocol and network location (see "The Bits and Pieces of Internet URLs" earlier in this chapter for explanations of these terms). The following example opens the `www.architecture.com` Domino Web server.

```
http://www.architecture.com/?OpenServer
```

?OpenDatabase

Using the *?OpenDatabase* action opens a particular database on a server. You can use the database's name or its ReplicaID to specify the database you want to open; if you use the ReplicaID, be sure to omit the default colon. These URLs open the `tribeca` database:

```
http://www.architecture.com/tribeca.nsf/?OpenDatabase
http://www.architecture.com/8525644600521DD4/?OpenDatabase
```

?OpenView

You use the *?OpenView* action to open a particular view in a database. You can use the view's name or its UniversalID to specify the view you want to open. These URLs, for example, open the `Residential Buildings` view in the `tribeca` database:

```
http://www.architecture.com/tribeca.nsf/
          Residential+Buildings/?OpenView
```

```
http://www.architecture.com/tribeca.nsf/
          EE4D221F60A9E82F8525644600564750/?OpenView
```

You also can use the view's NoteID in ?OpenView to specify the view, but because the NoteID can change between replica copies of the database, I strongly advise against using it.

In the place of the view name or UniversalID, you can use `$defaultview` to open the default view in the database. The following URL, for example, opens the default view in the `tribeca` database.

```
http://www.architecture.com/tribeca.nsf/$defaultview/
          ?OpenView
```

Follow these steps to specify a default view in your database:

1. **Choose View⇨Design to expand the Design folder in the navigation pane.**

   Select View⇨Show⇨Design if `Design` does not appear at the bottom of the View menu.

2. **Click the Views folder.**

   The views in your database appear in the view pane (see Chapter 6 for more about the various Domino panes).

3. **Double-click the view you want to set as the default.**

   The view appears in Design mode.

4. **Choose Design➪View Properties, or click the right mouse button and select View Properties.**

   The Properties for View InfoBox appears (see Figure 5-5).

Figure 5-5:
The
Properties
for View
InfoBox.

5. **Select the Options tab.**

6. **Check the Default when database is first opened box.**

7. **Save the view.**

The ?OpenView action offers optional arguments that you can use to control how the view displays:

- ✔ **Count=*n*,** where *n* is the number of rows to display

- ✔ **Start=*n*,** where *n* is the number of the row that should display first

- ✔ **Collapse=*n*,** where *n* is the number of the row to display in collapsed format

- ✔ **Expand=*n*,** where *n* is the number of the row to display in expanded format

- ✔ **CollapseView,** to display the entire view in collapsed format

- ✔ **ExpandView,** to display the entire view in expanded format

The following examples demonstrate how to structure the syntax for these additional arguments:

```
http://www.architecture.com/tribeca.nsf/
          Residential+Buildings/?OpenView&Start=5&Count=15
```

```
http://www.architecture.com/tribeca.nsf/
          Residential+Buildings/?OpenView&ExpandView
```

?OpenForm

Use the *?OpenForm* action to open a particular form in a database, allowing users to create documents in your Domino Web site. You can use the form's name or its UniversalID to specify the form you want to open. These URLs open the Buildings form in the tribeca database:

```
http://www.architecture.com/tribeca.nsf/Buildings/?OpenForm
```

```
http://www.architecture.com/tribeca.nsf/
          7006D60F12ADB9CB852564460056038F/?OpenForm
```

You can use the form's NoteID in ?OpenForm to specify it, but because the NoteID can change between replica copies of the database, I strongly advise against using it.

In the place of the form name or UniversalID, you can use $defaultform to open the default form in the database. The following URL, for example, opens the default form in the tribeca database:

```
http://www.architecture.com/tribeca.nsf/$defaultform/
          ?OpenForm
```

To specify a default form in your database, follow these steps:

1. **Choose View➪Design to expand the Design folder in the navigation pane.**

   If Design does not appear at the bottom of the View menu, choose View➪Show➪Design.

2. **Click the Forms folder.**

   The forms in your database appear in the view pane.

3. **Double-click the form that you want to set as the default.**

   The form opens in Design mode.

4. **Choose Design➪Form Properties, or click the right mouse button and select Form Properties.**

   The Properties for Form InfoBox appears (see Figure 5-6).

5. **Click the Defaults tab.**

6. **Click the Default database form check box.**

7. **Save the form.**

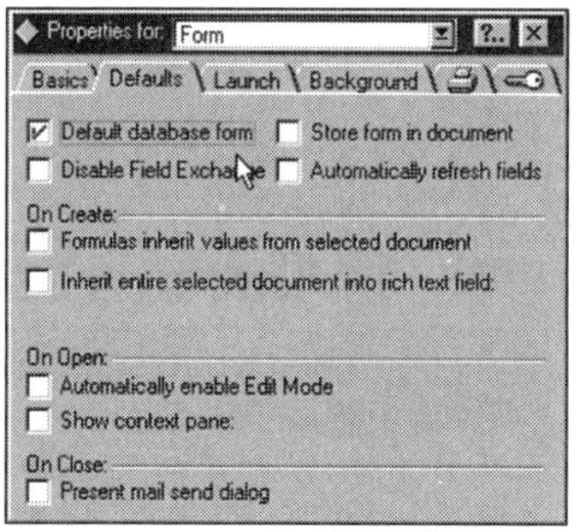

Figure 5-6:
The
Properties
for Form
InfoBox.

?OpenNavigator

The *?OpenNavigator* action opens a particular navigator in a database. You can use the navigator's name or its UniversalID to specify the navigator you want to open. These URLs, for example, open the `Real Estate` navigator in the `tribeca` database:

```
http://www.architecture.com/tribeca.nsf/Real+Estate/
              ?OpenNavigator
```

```
http://www.architecture.com/tribeca.nsf/
              9458902791182DB98525644E00725592/?OpenNavigator
```

As with the other ?Open actions, you can use the navigator's NoteID to specify it. The NoteID, however, can change between replica copies of the database, so I strongly advise against using it.

In the place of the navigator name or UniversalID, you can use `$defaultNav` to open the databases' folders navigator, which lists all the views in the database. The following URL, for example, opens the folders navigator in the `tribeca` database.

```
http://www.architecture.com/tribeca.nsf/$defaultNav/
              ?OpenNavigator
```

?OpenAgent

Use the *?OpenAgent* action to open a particular agent in a database. You can use the agent's name or its UniversalID to specify the agent you want to open. (After all the Remember paragraphs in this chapter, you don't even want to *think* about using the agent's NoteID to specify it, do you?) These URLs, for example, open the `Process Inspections` agent in the `tribeca` database:

```
http://www.architecture.com/tribeca.nsf/
            Process+Inspections/?OpenAgent
```

```
http://www.architecture.com/tribeca.nsf/
            453E8E23CB10C5AB8525644E007393CF/?OpenAgent
```

?OpenAbout and ?OpenHelp

You use the *?OpenAbout* action to open the "About Database" Document in a database. This URL, for example, opens the "About Database" Document in the `tribeca` database:

```
http://www.architecture.com/tribeca.nsf/$about?OpenAbout
```

The *?OpenHelp* action opens the "Using Database" Document in a database. This URL, for example, opens the "Using Database" Document in the `tribeca` database:

```
http://www.architecture.com/tribeca.nsf/$help?OpenHelp
```

Actions that work with documents

This section introduces the actions that you use to work with documents in the database. Actions like ?OpenDocument, ?EditDocument, and ?DeleteDocument perform specific functions that every Lotus developer uses when designing his or her Domino Web server.

Use the *?OpenDocument* action to open a particular document in a database. You can use the document's DocumentKey or its UniversalID to specify the document you want to open.

You can use the document's NoteID in document actions to identify documents in a database. The NoteID, however, can change between replica copies of the database, so I do not recommend using it in this manner.

The DocumentKey is a value in the first sorted column of a view. For example, in the Residential Buildings view, which contains listings of apartment houses (see Figure 5-7), the first sorted column in the view lists the name of each document in the view. The values in this column are the DocumentKeys. (When you use a DocumentKey to open a document, remember that the value is not case sensitive.) If more than one document matches the requested DocumentKey, the first matching document in the view is opened.

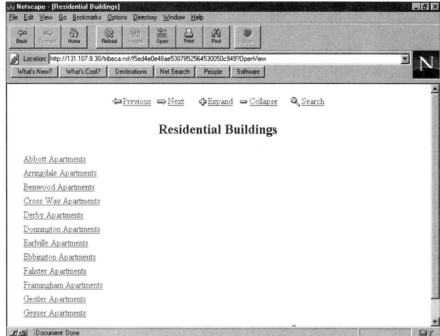

Figure 5-7:
The
Residential
Buildings
view.

The following URLs open the Donnington Apartments document in the Residential Buildings view:

```
http://www.architecture.com/tribeca.nsf/
          Residential+Buildings/
          Donnington+Apartments?OpenDocument
```

```
http://www.architecture.com/tribeca.nsf/
          Residential+Buildings/
          FE5AF631812B82F0852564530050F5FC?OpenDocument
```

Use the *?EditDocument* action to edit a particular document in a database. You can use the document's DocumentKey or its UniversalID to specify the document you want to edit.

The following URLs edit the Donnington Apartments document in the Residential Buildings view:

```
http://www.architecture.com/tribeca.nsf/
          Residential+Buildings/
          Donnington+Apartments?EditDocument
```

```
http://www.architecture.com/tribeca.nsf/
         Residential+Buildings/
         FE5AF631812B82F0852564530050F5FC?EditDocument
```

Use the *?DeleteDocument* action to delete a particular document in a database. You can use the document's DocumentKey or its UniversalID to specify the document you want to delete.

These URLs delete the `Donnington Apartments` document in the `Residential Buildings` view:

```
http://www.architecture.com/tribeca.nsf/
         Residential+Buildings/
         Donnington+Apartments?DeleteDocument
```

```
http://www.architecture.com/tribeca.nsf/
         Residential+Buildings/
         FE5AF631812B82F0852564530050F5FC?DeleteDocument
```

Actions for searching

One of the most useful functions you can offer your site visitors is the ability to search your Domino Web site. Giving your users the ability to search your site saves them time and often ultimately determines whether they locate the information they came to your site to find in the first place. You must have a grasp of the following URLs to be capable of designing search functionality into your site. Refer to Chapter 14 for more information on how to make your Domino Web site searchable.

Use the *?SearchView* action to search a view in a database. The syntax looks like this:

```
http://Host/Database/View/
         [$SearchForm]?SearchView[ArgumentList]
```

The *$SearchForm* optional parameter tells the server to display the Full Text Search window so that the users can create a search. *ArgumentList* is an optional parameter that the server ignores if you specify a $SearchForm. If you specify an ArgumentList and not a $SearchForm, the server doesn't display the Full Text Search window; instead, it displays the Search Results window with the documents that match the search criteria you specified in the ArgumentList parameter.

The syntax of the ArgumentList is as follows:

```
&Query=SearchString;SearchOrder;SearchThesaurus;
         SearchMax;SearchWordVariants
```

✔ **SearchString:** Specify the word or phrase you are searching for.

✔ **SearchOrder:** Specify the value 1, 2, or 3, where 1 is for a "Relevance" sort, 2 is for an "Oldest first" sort, and 3 is for a "Newest first" sort. The default is 1.

✔ **SearchThesaurus:** Specify TRUE or FALSE, where TRUE finds word variations as defined by the Thesaurus and FALSE finds only exact matches. The default is FALSE.

✔ **SearchMax:** Specify the maximum number of matching documents to display. The default is 0, which means to display all matching documents.

✔ **SearchWordVariants:** Specify TRUE or FALSE, where TRUE finds variants of the word you are searching for and FALSE doesn't. TRUE is the default.

The following URL, for example, presents you with a search form so that you could create a search criteria to search the Residential Buildings view:

```
http://www.architecture.com/tribeca.nsf/
         Residential+Buildings/$SearchForm?SearchView
```

And this URL tells the server to search the Residential Buildings view for the word Donnington:

```
http://www.architecture.com/tribeca.nsf/
         Residential+Buildings/
         ?SearchView&Query=Donnington
```

Use the *?SearchSite* action to search a group of databases or all databases on the Domino Web server. It works in conjunction with the Search Site database, which lists all the databases that are part of the search group (see Chapter 14 for more information). Its syntax looks like this:

```
http://Host/Database/[$SearchForm]?SearchSite[ArgumentList]
```

The only two syntax differences between the ?SearchSite and ?SearchView actions are that the ?SearchSite action doesn't have a view component and that ?SearchSite tells the Domino Web server to search a group of databases rather than a view. The ?SearchSite action uses the same arguments as the ?SearchView action.

This URL, for example, presents you with a search form with which you could create a search criteria to search a group of databases on the Domino Web server, as specified in the Search Site database:

```
http://www.architecture.com/srchsite.nsf/
         $SearchForm?SearchSite
```

An action that forces a login

If you want to force a user to specify a name and password before allowing him or her access to your Domino Web site, you can append the &login parameter to the URL. When a user executes the following URL, she is presented with a dialog box that asks for a name and password. If the user does not specify a name and correct password, the Domino Web server doesn't grant access to the site.

```
http://www.architecture.com/tribeca.nsf/?OpenDatabase&login
```

For more about security measures such as this, see Chapter 15.

Part II
Start Your Engines

The 5th Wave   By Rich Tennant

"Ronnie made the body from what he learned in Metal Shop,
Sissy and Darlene's Home Ec. class helped them in fixing up
the inside, and then all that anti-gravity stuff we picked
up off the Web."

In this part . . .

Building an engine and building a Web site have a couple of things in common. You need lots of parts to make something that runs well and is useful. Leave any one component on the garage floor, such as a wrist pin or a ?Open field value, and you've got a lot of expensive machinery that doesn't do what you want.

With Domino, however, you don't need to see a mechanic. Just pick up this book and start poring over this part. I cover a host of design tools in these chapters — forms, fields, views, actions, and navigators. These are the basic tools by which you make your Domino Web server. (Sorry; I don't do carburetors. That's another book.)

Chapter 6

Working with Lotus Notes Design Elements

* *

In This Chapter

▶ Creating a database

▶ Investigating the design elements

▶ Understanding the design interface

▶ Creating design elements

▶ Getting help

▶ Finding a hidden Design mode

* *

I suspect that one of the reasons you're interested in Domino is that you can use Domino to give people who have Web browsers, whether they are internal or external to your company, the ability to read, create, delete, and modify documents in your Notes databases. In Chapter 1 I cover the basic differences between using a Notes client to access a Domino Web server and using a Web browser to access it. Understand that, even though users will interact with your Domino Web site with Web browsers, you use a Notes client for doing all your design and maintenance work. This chapter introduces the Lotus Notes database design interface. Through this interface, you create your Domino Web site.

In the next few pages you find some of the basic information you must have in order to create a Domino Web site. If you are familiar with Lotus Notes application development, don't expect to find much new information here. Very little is different between developing a Notes database that is viewed in the traditional Notes way (using a Notes client), and developing one that is viewed at a Domino Web site with an ordinary Web browser.

License to Design

Lotus Notes has three types of licenses (or programs); some licenses can do everything you want to do, and others aren't appropriate for Web server design. Before you can start designing a Web site with Domino, you must make sure that you've got the right Notes license for the job.

 ✔ **Lotus Notes:** This license type is sort of the granddaddy of them all. The Lotus Notes license is the only one that lets you design a database. To create your Domino Web site, you must have this full-function license.

 ✔ **Lotus Notes Desktop:** For a lower price, the Lotus Notes Desktop license type offers a subset of the Lotus Notes license type's functionality. No way can you design a database with this license! As a matter of fact, if you have a Lotus Notes Desktop license, *Design* isn't in any menu, nor is a Design folder found in the Navigation pane.

 ✔ **Lotus Notes Mail:** This is another lower-priced license that offers even less functionality than the Lotus Notes Desktop license.

You can easily make sure that you have a Lotus Notes license type. Just follow these steps:

1. **Launch the Lotus Notes client.**

   The Lotus Notes Workspace, which displays the Domino Web server's databases as rectangular icons, appears.

2. **Choose File⇨Tools⇨User ID.**

   Up pops a dialog box asking for your password.

3. **Type in your password and click OK.**

   The main Lotus Notes screen appears and the Basics tab is highlighted.

4. **Click the Basics tab or press Enter.**

   You can press Enter because the Basics tab is already selected by default. You see one of the three license types listed next to License.

If your license type is Lotus Notes Desktop or Lotus Notes Mail and you want to upgrade it, you need to talk to your system administrator.

Creating a Database

After you install the Domino Web server software and set up the connections (see Chapters 3 and 4 for details), the next and most elemental process of designing a database is creating a database. Basically, you can create a database by copying an existing database or creating a new one.

Copying an existing database

Copying a Lotus Note database is easier than photocopying a piece of paper. Well, maybe not quite as easy as walking up to a photocopier, inserting a coin, and pressing a button — but close.

Suppose you have an existing discussion database where your sales reps share ideas with each other, and this database concept has worked out so well that you want your marketing people to do the same thing. Never mind paying a consultant $125 an hour to build an exact copy of the database, and never mind going back and forth copying and pasting forms and views from the sales database to the new marketing database. You simply create a copy by following these steps:

1. **Make sure that the database you want to copy is added to the Workspace.**

   To add a database to the Workspace, choose File⇨Database⇨Open and select the name of the database you want added.

2. **Click the database you want to copy.**

3. **Choose File⇨Database⇨New Copy.**

   If the New Copy option is grayed out, you didn't select a database in the previous step; go back to Step 2 and try again. The Copy Database dialog box appears (see Figure 6-1).

4. **Type the server name in the Server field.**

   Keep Local, the default, as the server name if you want to store the database on the machine you are working on; otherwise, specify the name of the server you want to store the database on.

5. **Type the database title in the Title field.**

   The database title is the name users see when they view the list of databases on your Domino Web server. So if you want your users to see Big Kahuna Surf and Bike Emporium, type that name in the Title field.

6. **Type the filename and directory under which the database is to be stored in the File Name field.**

7. **Check any optional settings by clicking the appropriate box under Copy.**

   You use these settings to set a size limit for your database, alter its encryption scheme, set up database security, and so on. See the bulleted list following these steps for an explanation of the options.

8. **Click OK.**

Figure 6-1:
You use the
Copy
Database
dialog box
to set up
your new
database's
parameters.

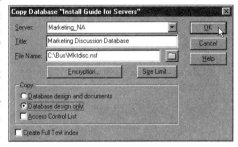

If you are creating a copy of the database for the purpose of replication between Notes servers, be sure to choose File⇨Replication⇨New Replica instead of File⇨Database⇨New Copy. Databases must have matching Replica IDs to replicate with each other. When you make a replica copy of a database (by using File⇨Replication⇨New Replica), you ensure that the ReplicaID for the new database is the same as that of the original.

"What on earth is replication?" you may ask. Replication is the process of synchronizing databases. For example, you may have a corporate-wide sales account database that is stored on the servers in all your regional sales offices. When a document is added to the database on the Dallas server, the replication process updates the databases on the servers in all the other regional sales offices so that they all include the Dallas document and are thereby synchronized. You can also replicate between a server and a laptop, so if you are in a hotel room and you make a design change to a database, you can replicate the change via your modem to the server in your office.

When you want to copy an existing database and you follow the Steps 1–4 in "Copying an existing database" defined earlier in this chapter, you see the Copy Database dialog box shown in Figure 6-1. This box has several elements for you to set so that your database functions the way you want it to. Here's a brief description of each element.

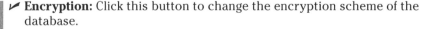

✔ **Encryption:** Click this button to change the encryption scheme of the database.

Do not change the default setting of Do not locally encrypt this database. If you change the setting, users will be unable to open the database with their Web browsers.

✔ **Size Limit:** Clicking this button brings up a dialog box where you can set the size limit for your database. You can specify a size limit for the database of 1GB, 2GB, 3GB, or 4GB. The default is 1GB. After the specified size limit has been reached, no more documents can be added to the database. (But you can cheat a little and replicate the database to increase its size. I tell you how in the section called "Replicating a Database" later in this chapter.)

✔ **Copy Database design and documents:** Click this radio button if you want to copy the design and documents from the original database. Select this option if you want an exact copy of the database. And I mean *exact* — every design element, document, paragraph, word, letter, and punctuation mark.

✔ **Copy Database design only:** Click this radio button if you want to copy just the design from the original database. Select this option if you don't want to copy any of the database's documents, but just its design elements, such as views, forms, navigators, and fields (see "Understanding the Design Elements" later in this chapter for more information on design elements).

✔ **Access Control List:** Clicking in this box puts a check mark in it. You check the box if you want to copy the Access Control List (ACL), which controls security, from the original database. If you want to select this option, make sure that you're listed in the ACL; otherwise, you may not be able to make design changes. See Chapter 15 for more about the ACL.

✔ **Create Full Text Index:** Check this box if you want to create a Full Text Index, which allows users to search your site. Keep in mind that this option requires additional disk space to hold the index that's created. If you do not presently have a lot of disk space on the server, don't worry about it; you can always decide to create a Full Text Index in the future. However, people using Web browsers can't search the database until a Full Text Index is created (see Chapter 14 for more information on Full Text Indexes).

Creating a database from scratch

More often than not, you'll find that you are creating brand-new databases rather than copying existing ones. Creating a new database from scratch is unquestionably — especially if you lack kitchen skills, as I do — easier than baking a cake from scratch. (Okay, so maybe I lied about copying a database being easier than photocopying, but I am telling the truth here.)

To create a database, follow these steps:

1. **Choose File➪Database➪New, or press Ctrl+N.**

   The New Database dialog box appears (see Figure 6-2).

2. **Specify the server name in the Server text box.**

   Click the down arrow and scroll until you find the server name that you want.

   The default for the Server text box is Local; keep that as the server name if you want to store the database on the machine you work on. Otherwise, type in the name of the server where you want to store the database.

3. **In the Title text box, type in your database title.**

   The database title is the name users see when they view the list of databases on your Domino Web server.

4. **In the File Name text box, type in the filename and directory under which you want to store the database.**

5. **Set as appropriate the optional settings for Encryption, Size Limit, and Create full text index for searching.**

   Details about these settings are in the bulleted list of the section "Copying an existing database" earlier in this chapter.

6. **Click the Template Server button and, from the scroll box, select a template name on which to base the design of your new database.**

   The template server defaults to Local, which indicates the hard drive of the machine on which you are working. If you select the Show advanced templates check box, both the default templates and the templates that are specified as advanced appear in the scroll box. This option is confusing because none of the templates that ship with the software is marked as *advanced.* So if you select this check box, you don't notice a change in the scroll box.

7. **When you're finished, click OK.**

Figure 6-2:
Use the
New
Database
dialog box
to create
your Notes
database
from
scratch.

Replicating a Database

Replicating a database is different from *copying* a database. As I noted in the section on "Copying an existing database," when you make a new copy of a database, the copy's ReplicaID differs from the original database's. You want to make a replica copy of a database, however, when the ReplicaID for the new database must be the same as the ID for the original database.

You want the ReplicaID's to match in certain situations. For example, what if you exceed the capacity limit of your database and you still need room? You can change the preset size limit of a database by replicating it. Replicating a database to increase the size limit is actually quite simple. Follow these steps:

1. **Select the database on the Workspace.**

2. **Choose File⇨Replication⇨New Replica.**

   The New Replica dialog box appears (see Figure 6-3).

3. **Specify the server name in the Server text box.**

   Click the down arrow and scroll until you find the name that you want.

4. **In the File Name box, type the database's directory and file name.**

   You must choose either the name of the original database or the directory.

5. **Click the Size Limit box and set the server's reserved storage capacity for your database.**

   See the section "Copying an existing database" earlier in this chapter for information on specifying a size limit (capacity) for your database.

6. **Click the Create: Immediately radio button.**

   Setting the Immediately button ensures that your database is made right now. You want instant gratification, don't you?

7. **Click in the Copy Access Control List check box.**

   Checking this box ensures that the ACL for your database is copied. Make sure that you are listed in the ACL; otherwise, you may not be able to make design changes. (For a definition of ACL, see the bulleted list in "Copying an existing database," earlier in this chapter.)

8. **Choose OK.**

   You just created a replica copy of the database.

Figure 6-3:
Using the
New
Replica
dialog box
is the only
way to
increase
the size
limit of your
existing
database.

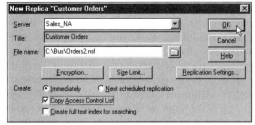

After you create the new replica copy, delete the old database by clicking its icon and choosing File➪Database➪Delete.

Understanding the Design Elements

After you create the database, you can begin customizing it by creating and/or editing design elements. You can create and customize a number of design elements to make your Domino Web site look great while at the same time satisfying all the expectations your demanding users will have of a high-quality interactive site. One of the nice things about building a Web site with Domino is that you don't have to be a programming guru to build a great site, because working with these design elements is fairly intuitive.

You can't get by without these elements

I once heard a story of a great football coach who would always begin practice by holding up a football and saying to his team, "Gentlemen, this is a football." The idea was that before he could get his team to think about all the technical and mechanical aspects of the game and all the strategical nuances, the coach needed to start his team off at square one.

Excuse my ignorance on exactly who the coach was. He may have been a football coach; I'm a baseball (Red Sox) fan. For all I know, the coach was Pat Riley holding up a basketball. Anyhow, I'm saying something similar: "Ladies and gentlemen, these are fields, forms, and views." Before you can build a championship Domino Web site, you must first understand these basic building blocks of a Domino design.

✔ **Fields:** Fields are the most basic building block in Notes. They store text, numbers, time, file attachments, and other information. The information users see when they are at views or read documents, whether it be something that somebody typed, pasted, or attached, or the result of a formula or an agent, can be stored in fields.

A few fields in Domino have special names, such as $$Return, $$ViewBody, and $$NavigatorBody, among others (see Chapters 16 and 18 for more information on these fields). These specialized fields enable you to customize the site's appearance.

✔ **Forms:** To provide a structure for people to create and read documents on your Domino Web site, you need to use *forms*. A form in Domino is like any other form, such as a tax form. Every year you create a tax document by entering information into a blank tax form. Just as the tax form has a structure (little boxes going down the right-hand side) for you to enter your salary information, the amount of interest you have earned, and the amount of your deductible, a form at your Domino Web site provides the structure for users to enter information. When users enter the information into the form and then save it, they create a document on the Domino Web site.

✔ **Views:** Listings of the documents at your site are called *views*. Think of a view as a table of contents for your site. Views are better than a simple table of contents, however, because you can customize Views to do many different things. For example, you may want to enable only certain people, such as upper management, to see certain views, or you may want to set up a number of views at your site so that your customers in the Northeast are in one view and your customers in the Southeast in another. You can do these types of things by manipulating views.

You'll love what these elements do

If you want to really impress your friends and family, get to know these design elements. (Once again, you need not be a programming guru to work with them.) These design elements allow you — whatever your programming skills — to make a Domino Web site that knocks everybody's socks off.

✔ **Navigators:** Images that provide a graphical way for users to maneuver through your Domino Web site are called *navigators*. Navigators can take users to documents, views, other navigators, or other Web sites. You can also design navigators to perform special functions, such as creating a document or executing a search.

✔ **Actions:** Buttons at the top of either a form or a view that allow users to maneuver through your Domino Web site or perform special functions are called *actions*. They work much the same way as navigators do, but actions are presented to the user as a button at the top of a form or view instead of as a full-page image map.

✔ **Agents:** Background processes that run on the server and automate applications are called *agents*. You can create agents that perform certain functions automatically. For example, one of your agents can archive any documents that have not been modified in 90 days. Another agent can send a notification to a sales rep and his manager if a particular sales lead has not been acted upon in 30 days. And yet another can generate notifications automatically when an account becomes past due.

✔ **About Database Document:** You can use the *About Database Document* as your site manager home page. You can add text, file attachments, and links that allow users to maneuver through your Domino Web site.

✔ **Subforms:** *Subforms* are a grouping of fields and/or images that you can add to a form. If you find that you are adding the same fields and images to a number of forms, you can group all the forms into a subform, make the overarching design changes to the subform, and then add the subform to the forms.

Using subforms for grouping images and fields has several advantages. If you decide after you create your database that you want to change an image that is displayed in a form, you don't have to go to every single form where you added the image. Instead, you only need to go to the one subform to make the change, and that change then reflects in all the forms that include the subform.

The Design Interface

After you create a database, you're ready to move on to creating design elements. In this section, I show you the interface you use to create and modify design elements.

Main database window

Soon after you create the database, you see a window with two panes: the Navigation pane and the View pane (see Figure 6-4). These panes enable you to work with design elements in specific ways.

Navigation pane

The Navigation pane lets you select and open views and folders. Because you use the Notes client only for doing design work, you need concern yourself only with the Design and Agents folders in the Navigation pane. The other views and folders are specific to the Notes client.

You can resize the panes by pointing at vertical border that separates the panes. When your mouse pointer touches the border, the pointer turns into a vertical bar with horizontal arrows (see Figure 6-4). Drag it to the left or right to resize the pane.

View pane

The other pane you see when you first create your database is the *View pane.* In Figure 6-5, the View pane is active. This pane enables you to select and open documents and design elements. If you open the database and can see only the Navigator pane, choose View➪Design to display the Navigator and View panes. Figure 6-5 shows what the view pane looks like when the database has a number of views.

Menu SmartIcons Cursor to resize pane

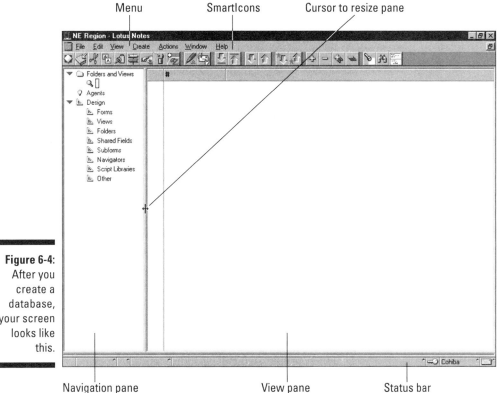

Figure 6-4: After you create a database, your screen looks like this.

Navigation pane   View pane   Status bar

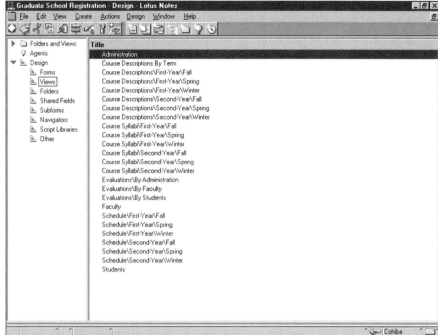

Figure 6-5:
The View
pane
enables you
to open
documents
and design
elements.

Design window

You should be familiar with another window with a different set of panes. When a design element is in Design mode, the Action pane and Design pane appear.

You must have the full version of Lotus Notes before you can make design changes to your database. You can't make design changes using a Lotus Notes Desktop or Lotus Notes Mail license.

To put an element in Design mode, do the following:

1. Choose View⟶Design.

This action displays the Design pane.

2. Click the Design folder.

This action will expand the Design folder in Navigation pane to display design elements.

3. Click the design element you want to include in your database.

The View and Action panes appear, each showing a different perspective of the design element you selected.

4. Double-click the design element in the View pane to view the properties of the element.

Figure 6-6 shows a design element as viewed in Design mode.

Design pane

The Design pane appears automatically as soon as the design element is in Edit mode. You specify in the Design pane a formula for a given design element. For example, if you want a field that automatically calculates today's date, you specify the formula @Today in the design pane.

Action pane

The Action pane displays the action buttons associated with a form, subform, or view. For example, if you have an action button that allows users to create documents when they click it, the name of that action button appears in the Action pane. (See Chapter 11 for information on creating action buttons.) If you don't see the Action pane in the Navigator pane, choose View⇨Action Pane to display it.

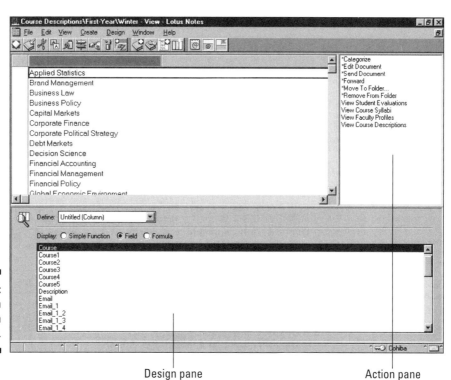

Figure 6-6:
A view in
Design
mode.

Design pane   Action pane

What a savior

After you put the design element in Design mode, you can make modifications. You must save your modifications after you make them. You can choose from a few different ways to save the form:

- ✔ Press Esc and then select Yes in the dialog box.
- ✔ Press Ctrl+S.
- ✔ Choose <u>F</u>ile➪<u>S</u>ave.

If you're working on a form in Design mode and you want to test your modifications without having to save the form, test it, and then get the form back into Design mode, do the following:

1. **Choose <u>D</u>esign➪<u>T</u>est Form.**

   A dialog box appears and asks you if you're sure you want to test the form.

2. **Click <u>Y</u>es in the dialog box.**

   If your form is a new one that hasn't yet been named, simply enter the name of the form and click OK. Your form reappears.

3. **Test your modifications.**

   The form reacts just as if you had saved all the modifications you made to it.

4. **When you finish, press Esc to return to Design mode.**

   Save your form either before or after you test it using these steps.

The important InfoBox

The *InfoBox*, also commonly referred to as (and shown in figures as) the *Properties box,* allows you to easily change things such as formatting, security, and default values of a design element, and to set or change many other design-element-specific properties.

You can bring up an InfoBox a couple different ways. First, put the view into Edit mode by double-clicking the view. Next, do one of the following:

- ✔ Choose Design➪View Properties.
- ✔ Click the right mouse button and choose View Properties.

Figure 6-7 shows the Properties for Form InfoBox, which allows you to specify some of these properties:

- ✔ Form name
- ✔ Form type
- ✔ Background color

Note that Figure 6-7 just shows the property options under the Basics tab of the InfoBox. Click the Background tab to see the background color option.

Figure 6-7:
The InfoBox
for a form
contains
lots of
settings you
can change
for your
forms.

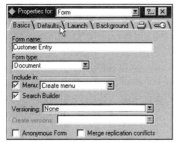

Figure 6-8 shows an InfoBox for views, which (surprise!) allows you to specify some of these properties for the view.

- ✔ **Name:** You can put in this field the name for a view. The view name you specify here is the one that appears when users view through their Web browsers the list of views on the Domino Web site.

- ✔ **Alias:** This is the name of the view you should use when referring to the view in formulas. For example, you may have a view called North West Account Profiles with an alias of NWAcctProfiles. You use NWAcctProfiles anytime you refer to the view in a formula. Using an alias, you can change the name of the view without having to update every formula in your entire Domino Web site that refers to the view — a task that could take days.

- ✔ **Comment:** A comment is more or less a note to you, the view designer, regarding something about the view.

- ✔ **Style:** You can specify whether the view is the standard style or a calendar style (see Chapter 4, Figure 4-19, for an example of a calendar-style view).

Figure 6-8:
Use the
View
InfoBox to
change the
view's
name, alias,
or style, and
to add a
comment
about the
view.

Getting Good Help

You can activate context-sensitive help in any InfoBox (or anywhere else in Design mode) simply by pressing F1. Doing so brings up a dialog box with links to the desired information.

Figure 6-9 shows the result of pressing F1 while in the active window shown in Figure 6-7. Notice that three of the first few links in the dialog box specifically refer to the properties in the active InfoBox:

- ✔ Name this form and add it to the Create menu?
- ✔ Make this form the default?
- ✔ Change the background of this form?

Figure 6-9:
Context-
sensitive
help
boxes are
available
throughout
the Notes
program.

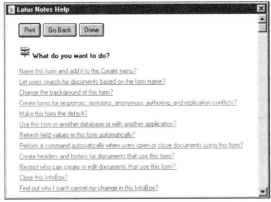

The other links refer to more general help topics. You either click these links to view the information or you print out the information in the links by clicking the Print button. Click Go Back to see a more general help box. Clicking Done when you're finished returns you to the active program window (in this case, the View InfoBox).

If You Can't Find Design Mode

Throughout this book, I present numbered steps for creating and modifying design elements. The steps do not make sense under three conditions. This section addresses those conditions and explains the steps you must follow to remedy the condition so that the steps make sense under all scenarios.

In this book, I begin all the steps for creating or modifying design elements with a variation of the following three steps to get the Design option in the View menu:

1. **Launch the Lotus Notes client.**

   The Lotus Notes Workspace, which displays the Domino Web server's databases as rectangular icons, appears.

2. **Click a database icon.**

3. **Choose View➪Design.**

One of three conditions exists when Design won't appear in the View menu (Step 3). One condition must be remedied by your server administrator, one can't be remedied unless you have a backup of the database, and the other is easily remedied.

 ✔ **Lotus Notes License type:** As I mentioned at the beginning of this chapter, you must have a full Lotus Notes license type for the Design menu option to appear. Follow the steps in the "License to Design" section at the beginning of this chapter to make sure you have a full Lotus Notes license. If you do not have a full Lotus Notes license, you must talk to your system administrator to get it upgraded. If you have a full Lotus Notes license type, refer to the next condition.

 ✔ **Hidden database design:** It is possible to hide the design of a database so that people can't make future changes. Database designers might also hide the design of a database to prevent people from "borrowing" (also called *stealing*) the design that they worked so hard to create. If the design of a database is hidden, the Design menu option doesn't appear. To verify whether or not the design of a database is hidden:

1. Click the database's icon.

2. Choose File➪Database➪Properties.

The Properties for Database InfoBox appears.

3. Click the Design tab.

The first line under the tab says either Design is not hidden or No Design Information Available. The database's design is hidden if the line says No Design Information Available. You cannot unhide the design of a database. Your only option to make design changes is to find a backup copy of the database in which the design is not hidden.

If the first line under the tab says Design is not hidden, refer to the next condition.

✔ **Show Design disabled:** This condition is the most common reason for Design to not appear in the menu. To enable Show Design:

1. Click the database's icon.

2. Choose View➪Go To.

The Go To dialog box appears.

3. Click a view or folder name and click OK.

It doesn't matter which view or folder you click, because all you want to do is open the database to access a particular menu option.

4. Choose View➪Show➪Design.

Notice that there was not a check mark next to the Design option in the menu. If you repeat this step, you'll notice a check mark next to Design. Be careful if you repeat the step, however, because each time you do so you toggle the check mark on and off. The end result you want is to have Domino put a check mark next to Design.

After you finish these steps, the Design menu option appears within the View menu.

Chapter 7

Welcome to Our Home

*Y*ou only get one chance to make a first impression. It is probably second nature to you that if you want to make a good first impression when meeting someone, you look him in the eye, give a warm "Hello," a firm handshake, and begin to converse intelligently. Or if you want to make a good impression when someone is walking into your office for the first time, you make sure the reception area is presentable and the receptionist welcomes her, offers to take her coat, and offers her something to drink (no scotch please — unless, of course, it is after 10:00 a.m.).

You haven't been creating Web sites as long as you've been meeting people, and you don't actually see people visiting your Web site face to face. But you still are making a first impression to people when they visit your site for the first time.

Just as it is when you meet people, you only get one chance to make a first impression with your Domino Web site. When people visit your site for the first time, you want them to receive a friendly greeting and to have a favorable visual impression of the site.

Still, the home page needs much more than just a good appearance. You may have a good first impression of someone if he is dressed nicely, is well groomed, has shined shoes, and gives a good handshake; but if he opens his mouth and exposes you to a monologue that is punctuated with expletives, he's ruined your first impression of him. Similarly, you don't want your site to merely offer a nice initial impression but then insult or disappoint its visitors with aggressive Web "profanity," in the form of an inept, unintuitive interface or plain, sterile, meaningless drivel.

A successful home page not only must affect an impressive appearance, but also must offer useful information and an intuitive interface for easy maneuvering. Some of the things you should include in the home page:

✔ A link to a brief description of your company and services

✔ Information for first-time visitors, especially if you require site registration

✔ Directions and links for maneuvering through the site's content

✔ Directions on searching for information

What Users First See

When users want to visit your Domino Web site, they simply type your site's URL into their Web browsers. Your job is to determine what you want the Web server to return to their browsers at that point. You may, for example, have the Web server

✔ Display a list of all the databases on your server, with the titles of the databases set as hypertext links

✔ Display a specific database's home page

✔ Display a specific view within a database

✔ Display an HTML file on your server's hard drive

To configure what users will see, you can use the Web server's *server document,* located in the Public Address Book.

Configuring the server document

Every Domino Web server has a server document. The server document should be customized to fit your needs. You probably want to change certain settings anyway, just because the changes make sense. To customize the server document:

1. **Launch the Lotus Notes client.**

   The Lotus Notes Workspace, which displays the Domino Web server's databases as rectangular icons, appears (see Figure 7-1).

Public Address Book

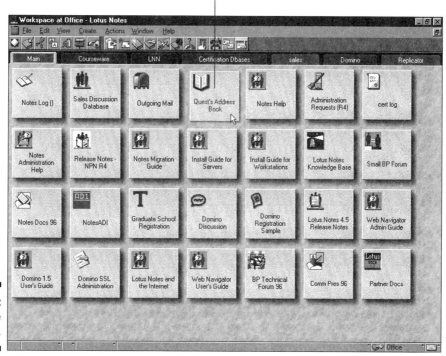

Figure 7-1:
The
Workspace.

2. Click the Public Address Book icon.

3. Choose View➪Server➪Other and then double-click Server\Servers.

The server documents appear in the view pane.

4. Double-click the name of the server that you want to customize.

5. Expand the HTTP Server section.

The Mapping section (see Figure 7-2) of the server document contains the Home URL field. The value in this field determines what users see when they type your URL in their browsers. The default field value is /?Open, which displays the list of databases on the server (see Figure 7-3) to Web browsers.

6. Make whatever changes you deem appropriate and choose File➪Save to save the document.

Be sure that Yes is specified in the Allow HTTP clients to browse databases option in the Security settings section of the server document (see Figure 7-4). Yes is the default, and if you change it, site visitors can't browse through the list of databases on your server.

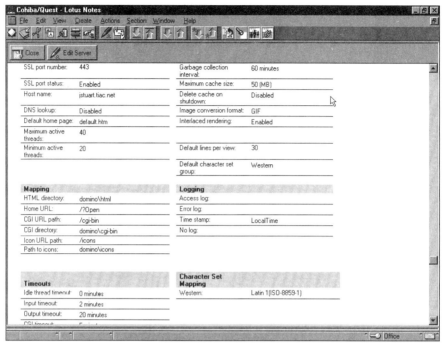

Figure 7-2:
The
Mapping
section of
the server
document.

Figure 7-3:
What a
Web
browser
sees if
you have
/?Open in
the Home
URL field.

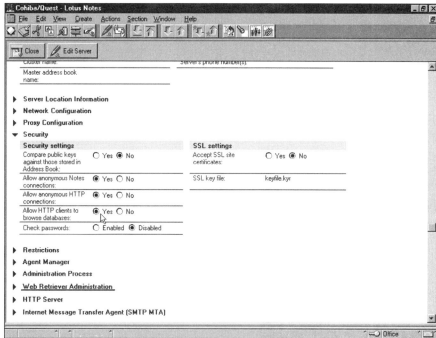

Figure 7-4:
The
Security
section of
the server
document.

The value in the Home URL determines what is displayed when users type your Domino Web site's URL into their Web browsers. Table 7-1 shows the result of what is displayed to users' Web browsers based on the field value specified in the Home URL field.

Table 7-1	**Examples of Values in the Home URL Field**
Field Value	**Result**
/?Open	Displays the list of databases on the server
/prodref.nsf/Main+Navigator	Displays the Main Navigator pane in the Product Reference database
/prodref.nsf/Customer	Displays the Customer view in the Product Reference database

When you specify a navigator or view name in a URL or in the Home URL field, be sure to enter the plus sign (+) wherever you want a space to appear. For example, to specify *Main Navigator* in a URL, you enter Main+Navigator.

The Basics section (see Figure 7-5) of the server document contains the Default home page field. If you want an HTML file on your server's hard drive to display when users specify your server's URL in their Web browsers, enter the name of the HTML file in this field. In this event, you must also make sure that you leave the Home URL field in the Mappings section blank. If you do not specify a directory for the HTML file, Domino looks for the file in the directory specified in the HTML directory field, which is in the Mapping section of the server document.

Save the server document after making your changes by pressing Ctrl+S.

Creating an About Document

One of the easiest ways to create a home page is to use the About Document. Every database has an About Document. Your About Database Document can include:

- ✔ Text, which you can format
- ✔ Graphics

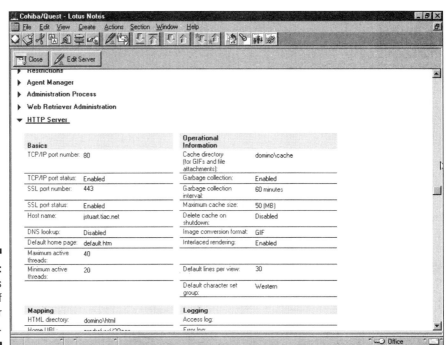

Figure 7-5: The Basics section of the server document.

✔ File attachments

✔ Links to databases, views, and documents

 A standard feature among Web applications is that users can click underlined text to execute a link or action, so you want to avoid underlining any text you add to the About Document. Underlining text that doesn't link to something else could confuse users.

Making changes to the About Database Document

To make changes to the About Document:

1. **Launch the Lotus Notes client.**

   The Lotus Notes Workspace, which displays the Domino Web server's databases as rectangular icons, appears.

2. **Click the icon for the database that contains the About Database Document you want to edit.**

3. **Choose View➪Design.**

   The database opens. If Design does not appear in the menu, select View➪Show➪Design.

4. **Select the Other folder in the navigation pane.**

5. **Double-click the "About Database" Document design element in the view pane.**

6. **Do one of the following to save design changes:**

   • Press Ctrl+S.

   • Click the Save SmartIcon.

   • Press Esc and select Yes in the dialog box.

   • Choose File➪Save.

Creating links

After you put the About Document in Design mode, you can start typing. Remember that you're typing the information that is the first thing users see when they first open your site. Be sure to make it informative and to the point.

When you're comfortable with the information you have entered, you're ready to create links. *Links (also called hypertext links or hyperlinks)* are words and phrases that users can click on to maneuver to different parts of your Domino Web site. Links appear on your users' screens as underlined text.

You can turn more than just text into a link. You can copy images to the Clipboard and then paste them into the About Database Document to use as links. To enable an image as a link, follow the same steps you would use to make a word or phrase a link.

To create a link:

1. **Highlight the word or phrase that you want to act as the link.**

2. **Choose <u>C</u>reate➪<u>H</u>otspot➪<u>U</u>RL Link.**

   The Properties for URL Link Object InfoBox appears (see Figure 7-6). If you have text that begins with `http://` in the Clipboard, the Properties for URL Link Object InfoBox doesn't appear. Domino is smart enough to know that you intend to use the information in the Clipboard as the URL that you want the users' browsers to open when they click on the hotspot. If you want the InfoBox to appear, simply copy some text that does not begin `http://` to the Clipboard.

Figure 7-6:
The
Properties
for URL Link
Object
InfoBox.

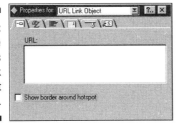

3. **Type in the formula box the URL that you want users' browsers to open when they click on the hotspot.**

   An example would be `http://www.manssiere.com`. If you want to use the Windows Clipboard to paste a URL into the formula box, be sure to paste the URL to the Clipboard before you perform Step 2.

4. **Click the other tabs in the Properties for URL Link Object InfoBox if you want to make formatting changes to the hotspot.**

Creating Notes links

You can easily create links in the About Document to documents, views, and databases. Document links, view links, and database links will appear to your users as small icons. You should add text beside the icons to inform your users about the links.

To create a link to a document, view, or database, follow these steps:

1. **Select the document, view, or database to which you want to link.**

2. **Choose Edit⇨Copy As Link.**

   Depending on whether you want to create a link to a document, view, or database, choose Document Link, View Link, or Database Link. See Figure 7-7.

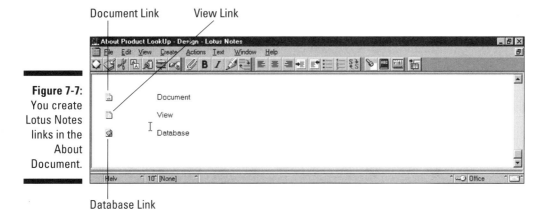

Document Link   View Link

Database Link

Figure 7-7: You create Lotus Notes links in the About Document.

Using a Navigator as a Home Page

Another way to create a home page is to use a navigator. A *navigator* is an image map with hotspots. The hotspots can act as links to documents, views, other navigators, other databases, or other Web sites. You can even enable the hotspots so that your visitors can *interact* with the Domino Web site. For example, you can create hotspots that users can click to compose a document or execute a search.

The hotspots on the image should give users visual cues that suggest where selecting them will lead. For example, if you create a Domino Web site to furnish tourism information on Europe, setting the navigator as a picture of Europe makes sense. Each country could serve as a visual cue to the sort of information users receive if they click on it. Clicking on Spain would take users to information on touring Spain, and clicking on Italy would take them to information on touring Italy.

Creating Navigators

Creating a navigator, like creating the other design elements that compose your Domino Web site, is simple and straightforward:

1. **Copy an image to the Windows Clipboard.**

   Because navigators are image maps that enable visitors to maneuver through your site, you want to be sure to select an appropriate image. You can create a navigator out of an image in any format that you can copy to the Clipboard in Windows. If you're using a UNIX server, you need to use the X Windows equivalent of the Clipboard to perform this function.

2. **Choose Create⇨Design⇨Navigator.**

   A blank navigator design window appears (see Figure 7-8).

3. **Choose Edit⇨Paste to paste the image from the Clipboard.**

   The image appears (see Figure 7-9).

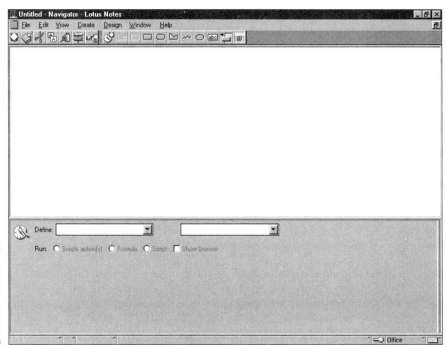

Figure 7-8: A blank navigator design window.

Figure 7-9:
An image of
Australia as
a navigator.

After you determine what parts of the image to use for creating
hotspots, you can define the area users click on as either a rectangle or
a polygon (see Figure 7-10). Do one of the following:

- Choose Create➪Hotspot Rectangle, or click the Hotspot Rectangle
  SmartIcon, to enable a rectangular area of the image as a hotspot.

- Choose Create➪Hotspot Polygon, or click the Hotspot Polygon
  SmartIcon, to enable a polygon-shaped area of the image as a
  hotspot. To use the polygon drawing tool, just click the mouse
  where you want to start drawing, move the mouse cursor to
  where you want to change direction in the drawing, click again to
  change direction, and finally, double-click to finish the drawing.

4. **In the Design pane, make sure that the hotspot's name is specified in
   the Define box.**

5. **Click the Simple action(s) radio button or the Formula radio button.**

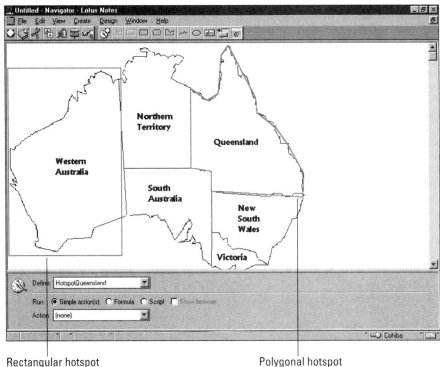

Figure 7-10:
Creating
hotspot
objects on
parts of the
image.

Rectangular hotspot   Polygonal hotspot

6. Depending on what you did in Step 5, choose a simple action from the Action drop-down list box or type a formula in the blank text window.

For more about these choices, see the section "Design options explained" following this list.

7. Press Ctrl+S to save the navigator.

After you save the navigator you are prompted to give it a name, unless you have already specified one in the navigator's InfoBox.

Design options explained

The options for navigators provided in the Design pane are Simple action(s), Formula, and Script; you can use Simple action(s) or Formula. The Script choice option is for using LotusScript in agents that run on your Domino Web server. You cannot use LotusScript in form events, database events, actions, or buttons.

✔ **Simple action(s):** Use the Simple action(s) option (see Figure 7-11) to enable your users to open a navigator, a view, a link, or a URL.

Figure 7-11:
The Simple
action(s)
options.

✔ **Formulas:** You can create formulas that enable your users to maneuver to another part of the site or to execute a command, such as the `@Command([Compose];"`*formname*`"` formula) used to create a document.

You can type your formula in the formula box in the Design pane (see Figure 7-12).

Figure 7-12:
The
Formula
box.

Auto Launching

After you have created a home page (using an About Document or navigator), you want to remove any confusion your users might experience if you require them to specify the About Document or navigator in the URL syntax they use to get to your site. To that end, you should set up your home page to launch automatically whenever your users look at the database:

1. **Choose File➪Database➪Properties.**

    The Properties for Database InfoBox appears (see Figure 7-13).

Figure 7-13:
Specify a
launch
option for
the home
page.

2. Click the Launch tab.

3. Click one of the following options:

- Open "About database" document.

- Open designated Navigator.

- Open designated Navigator in its own window.

4. If you are launching a navigator, designate which one in the InfoBox.

An HTML Home Page

If you already have a home page created in HTML, you can use it in your Domino Web site. To use an HTML file as a home page:

1. Copy the file into the HTML directory.

The HTML directory is specified in the HTML directory field (see Figure 7-14) in the Mapping section of the server document in the Public Address Book.

2. Specify the name of the HTML file in the Default home page field in the Basics section of the server document (see Figure 7-14).

3. Be sure to leave the Home URL field, in the Mapping section of the server document, blank.

If you have an entry in this field, the server ignores the HTML file you specify in the Default home page.

HTTP Server section expanded

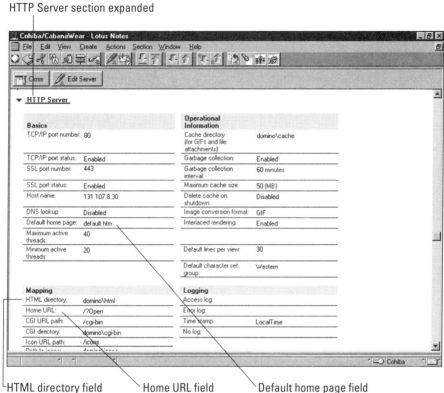

HTTP Server section expanded

Figure 7-14:
The HTTP
Server
section of
the server
document.

HTML directory field   Home URL field   Default home page field

Chapter 8

Creating Forms

. . . .

. . . .

*B*efore I discuss creating forms with you, I must answer the question, "What is a form?" The best way to answer is to introduce *documents* and differentiate them from forms. Documents are the content of a Domino Web site; as you navigate through a Domino Web site, you look at documents — and views and navigators, but I discuss those later in the book (see Chapter 10 for more information on views and Chapter 12 for more information on navigators). For now, just concentrate on documents and forms.

If you own an office furniture store and your Web site has information on each type of computer table you sell, and you set up your site so that customers can view individual pages featuring each type of computer table, these individual Web pages are documents in Domino parlance. The document for a particular type of computer table includes information on its price, its size, its weight, its color, what materials were used in its construction, and what some of its particular features are, such as a scratch-resistant top or foldable legs.

A form in Domino, like any other form you have ever filled out, serves to give the document structure. When you create a document, you actually type the information into a form. During tax time, you fill out a 1040 form, which asks you to specify such data as income, interest, number of dependents, and so on, and provides little boxes on the right-hand side in which you fill in your answers. After you fill in the form, you have a tax document that you submit to the IRS. Like a tax form, a Domino form provides structure for entering information into your Notes database.

Forms not only are used to enter information, but also to display information in a document. Consider the 1040 U.S. tax form; it's the form that determines the appearance of the information you enter. For example, your name appears at the top of the form and your answers appear in the right-hand column. The IRS could very easily change the form so that your answers appear on the left-hand side. The data stays the same, but the document looks different because the form changed. So you can think of a form that's displaying information as a sort of window through which people view the contents of a document.

You use forms to capture information and store it in a Notes database as well as to view information in the database. A Notes database may have a number of forms. For example, a discussion database has at least two forms: one for a main document that introduces a discussion topic and another for responses to the main document.

Creating Forms

You must create at least one form for your Domino Web site so that documents can be created. If you decide to make your Domino Web site interactive so that users can create documents with their Web browsers — which is, after all, one of the main reasons for creating a Domino Web site in the first place — you must create a form that they can use.

Creating a form from scratch

Your users access your Domino Web server with a Web browser, but you do all your design work in Notes.

 You use the Lotus Notes client for all your design work. Your version of Notes must be a full Lotus Notes client, not a Lotus Notes Desktop or Lotus Notes Mail client. You can use the Notes client on the server or a workstation.

 I recommend that you do design work for Domino Web sites on a workstation, because using the server jeopardizes its integrity or security. The workstation doesn't need to have a continuous connection to the server — that is, it doesn't have to be connected via a *local area network* (LAN) or *wide area network* (WAN). You can perform replication over phone lines, the Internet, LANs, WANs, cellular connections, and so on. You can even do your design work on a laptop in an airplane and then replicate your design changes when you're done.

To create a form, do the following:

1. Launch the Lotus Notes client.

The Lotus Notes Workspace, which displays the Domino Web server's databases as rectangular icons, appears.

2. **Click the icon for the database where you want to create the form.**

3. **Choose Create➪Design➪Form.**

   The design window for the form appears (see Figure 8-1).

4. **Add text, graphics, or fields to the form.**

5. **Name the form by choosing Design➪Form Properties and typing the name into the Form name box.**

6. **Save the form.**

   If you didn't name the form in Step 5, a dialog box appears on-screen and prompts you to do so now. You can save the form in one of these four ways:

   - Press Ctrl+S.
   - Press Esc, and then click Yes in the dialog box.
   - Choose File➪Save.
   - Click the File Save SmartIcon.

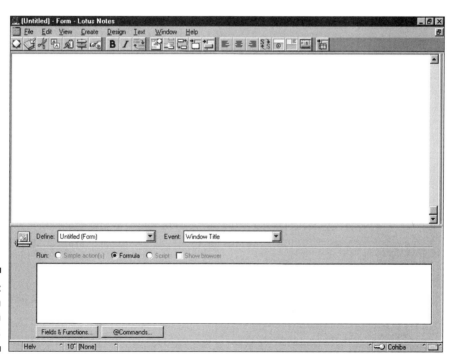

Figure 8-1:
The form design window.

To close the Properties for Form InfoBox (or for that matter, any of the InfoBoxes I discuss throughout the book) click the X in the upper-right corner of the box.

Editing an existing form

You may find it necessary to edit a form. If you create a database based on a template, you probably will have to make changes to the form quite often. Follow these steps:

1. **Launch the Lotus Notes client software.**

   The Notes Workspace appears.

2. **Double-click the icon for the database where you want to create the form.**

   The database opens.

3. **Choose <u>V</u>iew⇨<u>D</u>esign.**

   The Design folder in the Navigation pane expands. If Design does not appear in the View menu, choose <u>V</u>iew⇨<u>S</u>how⇨<u>D</u>esign.

4. **Click the Forms folder.**

   The forms in the database appear in the view pane.

5. **In the View pane, double-click the name of the form that you want to edit.**

   The form appears in Edit mode.

The form or database can inherit its design from a design template. *Inheritance* is simply the process by which the server updates the design of databases based on a parent (or master) template. Any modifications you make to a design element can be overwritten when the inheritance process (a server task called "Design") updates the design element based on the template. If the form or database inherits its design from a design template, you receive a warning when you try to edit the form (see Figure 8-2). It lets you know that any changes you make to the form will be overwritten when the Design server task runs (which it does by default at 1:00 every morning).

To prevent your design changes from being overwritten, disable the design inheritance for either the form or the database. To disable design inheritance for the form, follow these steps:

1. **Click the form name in the View pane.**

2. **Choose <u>D</u>esign⇨Design <u>P</u>roperties.**

   The Properties for Design Document InfoBox appears (see Figure 8-3).

Figure 8-2:
This box
warns you
about
design
changes
getting
overwritten.

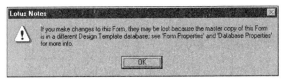

3. **Click the Design tab.**

You see various check boxes of options for the document's design. Right now you're only interested in the one about refresh/replace.

4. **Check the box next to Do not allow design refresh/replace to modify.**

Figure 8-3:
Disable
design
inheritance
for the form.

To disable design inheritance for the database, do the following:

1. **Choose Design⇨Design Properties.**

The Properties for Database InfoBox appears (see Figure 8-4).

2. **Click the Design tab.**

You see various check boxes of options for the database's design. Right now you're only interested in the one about inheriting the design.

3. **Uncheck the Inherit design from template check box.**

4. **Press Ctrl+S to save the form.**

Changing background color

You may decide to change the background color of a form. Maybe you want to make it stand out to the user, or perhaps you want it to match the background of your entire site. Regardless of why you want to change the background color, Domino makes it easy. Just follow these steps:

Figure 8-4:
Disable
design
inheritance
for the
database.

1. **Open the form in Design mode.**

   See Steps 1–5 in "Editing an existing form" at the beginning of this chapter.

2. **Open the form's InfoBox.**

   You can open the form in the following ways:

   - Choose <u>D</u>esign⇨Form <u>P</u>roperties.
   - Click the right mouse button, and then choose Form Properties.
   - Click the Design Form Properties SmartIcon.

   No matter which way you choose, the Properties for Form InfoBox appears.

3. **Click the Background tab.**

4. **Click the arrow next to the color box.**

   The color palette appears (see Figure 8-5).

5. **Click a color.**

   The form's background magically becomes the color you chose.

6. **Press Ctrl+S to save the form.**

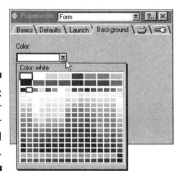

Figure 8-5:
The Color
palette for
background
color.

What You Can Add to a Form

The form is the basic structure of your Domino Web site. If your Web site is a house, the form is the frame of 2x4s and 2x8s. After the frame of a house is completed, the things that make the house enjoyable and interesting to live in, such as windows, doors, floors, lights, plumbing fixtures, and appliances, can be added. Similarly, with your Domino Web site, the features that you add to the form are what make it interesting and enjoyable to work in (or for those of you who tend to burn the candles at both ends at work — live in). All of the items that are added to a form are dynamically translated on-the-fly to HTML by the Domino Web server and are presented to a Web browser when requested. Some of the features that you can add to a form are:

- ✔ **Static Text:** You can specify words that appear in every document that was created with the form. You can use the static text you make to create links that execute actions or navigate users to other parts of the site. This chapter covers creating and using static text in your documents.

- ✔ **Fields:** In your forms, fields display the data. Fields are one of the features that make a Domino Web site truly interactive; when people with Web browsers create documents on your site, they're typing information into fields.

- ✔ **Special fields:** Domino supports a number of special fields, with *reserved names,* that execute certain actions. For example, on a form, you can create a field and give it the reserved name of HTML. Any form that contains a field called HTML displays just the contents of that field when viewed through a Web browser. Even if the form contains other fields, only the contents of the HTML field is displayed.

- ✔ **Action buttons:** Action buttons appear at the top of forms, and, when clicked, can execute actions or navigate users to other parts of the site (see Chapter 11 for more information).

- ✔ **File attachments:** Users can download files that you attach to the form, and can upload files to the Domino Web server (see Chapter 17 for more information).

- ✔ **HTML:** Domino allows you to use what is referred to as *passthru HTML,* which enables you to embed HTML into the form to add enhancements that you couldn't present to the user via standard Notes functionality (see Chapter 20 for more information).

- ✔ **Graphics:** You can paste graphics from the Windows Clipboard into the form, or you can use passthru HTML to display a graphic file located on the server's hard drive in the form.

- ✔ **Submit button:** By default, every form has a submit button at the bottom of the form. When users click this button, they submit, and therefore create, a document on the Domino Web server. You cannot remove this button, but you can change its location (see Chapter 18 for more information).

This chapter deals with adding static text to the form (but it doesn't address enabling it as a link — that's in Chapter 7); the other items also each require separate chapters.

Most of your users probably connect to your site via a telephone line, so keep their phone bills and frustration levels in mind as you design your Domino Web site. By all means, make the site interesting, but try to hold your use of graphics and other elements that take time to download and to draw on the user's screen to a minimum. Your users will appreciate the savings of money and time you offer.

Adding and Removing Static Text

Static text refers to the standard words and phrases that appear on all documents created using a particular form. For example, the 1040 form (sorry to start talking about taxes again!) has static text that asks something like "What is your income?" and "How many dependents do you have?" Every tax document turned in to the IRS has this same standard static text. The answers on each of the forms are different, but the static text is the same.

You can turn static text into links that your site visitors can click to execute an action or navigate to another part of the site (See the section "Creating links" in Chapter 7 for more information on creating links).

Adding static text to a form

Adding static text to a form is fairly straightforward. Follow these steps:

1. **Open the form in Design mode.**

   See Steps 1–5 in "Editing an existing form" earlier in this chapter.

2. **Start typing away.**

   You can also paste stuff from the Windows Clipboard, if applicable.

3. **Save the form.**

Removing static text

Removing static text is pretty straightforward, too. Follow these steps:

1. **Open the form in Design mode.**

   See Steps 1–5 in "Editing an existing form" earlier in this chapter.

2. **Highlight the text that you want to delete.**

3. **Delete the text.**

   You delete text by doing one of the following:

   - Press Del.

   - Press Backspace.

   - Choose Edit⇨Clear.

   - Choose Edit⇨Cut.

4. **Press Ctrl+S to save the form.**

Formatting Static Text

When you use the Domino Web server to create a form, you can only approximate what your form looks like when viewed by a Web browser, because the Domino Web server converts your text styles to HTML tags. So, as you create a form, you should periodically test out its appearance on a Web browser. Also, keep in mind that different Web browsers interpret formatting differently.

A number of options are available for formatting text. You do the formatting via the Properties for Text InfoBox. You can open this InfoBox in several ways. Just follow these steps:

1. **Open the form in Design mode.**

   See Steps 1–5 in "Editing an existing form" earlier in this chapter.

2. **Open the Properties for Text InfoBox.**

   You open the InfoBox in one of the following ways:

   - Choose Text⇨Text Properties.

   - Click the right mouse button, and then choose Text Properties.

   - Press Ctrl+K.

   - Click the Text Properties SmartIcon.

   The Properties for Text InfoBox appears (see Figure 8-6).

3. **After the Text InfoBox appears, highlight the text you want to format and select formatting options from the InfoBox.**

By using the options in the Properties for Text InfoBox, you can change the way the static text appears. For example, you can change the size of the text, make it bold or italic, center it, and so forth.

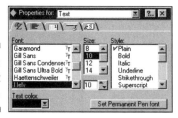

Figure 8-6:
The Text
InfoBox.

Specifying text size

You use the Size scroll box of the Font tab in the Properties for Text InfoBox to change the size of selected static text on your Domino site. When you specify the size of the text (or the text's *point size*) you want, refer to Table 8-1 to see how the Notes point sizes are mapped to HTML text size.

Table 8-1	How Notes Point Sizes Are Mapped to HTML
Notes Point Sizes	*Maps to HTML Text Size*
Less than 9	1 (smallest; used for footnotes and such)
9 – 10	2
11 – 12	3 (often used for regular type)
13 – 14	4
15 – 18	5
19 – 24	6
Greater than 24	7 (largest; used for main headings)

Features supported in the Format tab

Domino supports the HTML Bold, Italic, Underline, Strikethrough, Super-script, Subscript, and Text Color features through the Style scroll box of the Text InfoBox's Font tab. Figure 8-7 shows how the formatting appears in Notes and Figure 8-8 how it appears in a Web browser.

Web users expect underlined text to signify hyperlinks, so keep in mind that underlining words that aren't links may stir up some user confusion.

Domino supports point size, but perhaps not in the way you expect. Also, HTML does not have a corresponding formatting effect for typeface, shadow, emboss, and extrude (all of which are on the Format tab). Because of this deficiency in HTML, Web browsers don't support those type attributes at all.

✔ **Point size:** As Table 8-1 shows, point sizes do not translate exactly as you might expect them to. They are mapped to an HTML size.

✔ **Typeface:** When a Web browser accesses documents, Domino converts them to HTML on-the-fly. Because the concept of typefaces hasn't yet been built into HTML, typefaces don't translate exactly as you might expect. The typeface of text appears in the Web browser according to settings in the Web browser itself.

Features supported in the Alignment tab

The Properties for Text InfoBox includes a tab for positioning your text on the screen. The Alignment tab looks like several lines of text in a stack. Features supported in the Alignment tab are left, right, and center alignment, and bulleted and numbered lists.

HTML places limitations on Alignment features, too, just like it does with the other tabs of the Properties for Text InfoBox. Features not supported in the Alignment tab owing to an absence of a corresponding HTML effect are Full Justification, No Wrap Alignment, Indentation, and Interline Spacing. Figures 8-9 and 8-10 compare the appearances of alignment options between a Lotus Notes client and a Web browser. Figures 8-11 and 8-12 show how certain formatting options appear on a Lotus Notes client versus how they appear on a Web browser.

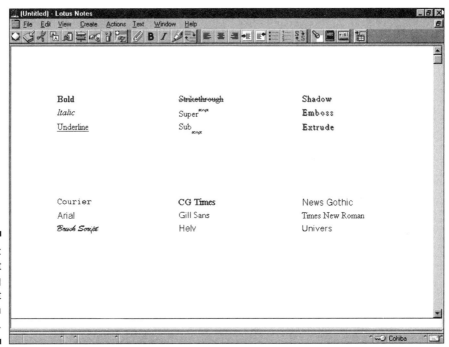

Figure 8-7: Text formatting as it appears in Notes.

These formatting features do not translate

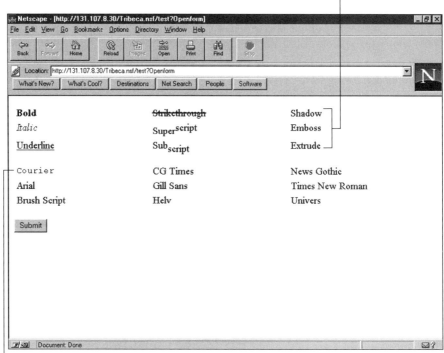

Figure 8-8:
Text
formatting
as it
appears in
a Web
browser.

Courier translates to Web browser's monospace font

Left alignment   Center alignment   Right alignment

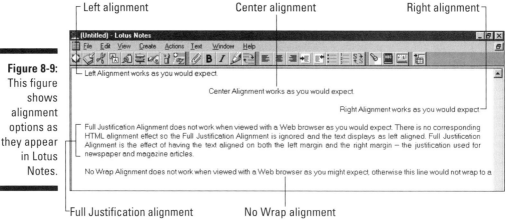

Figure 8-9:
This figure
shows
alignment
options as
they appear
in Lotus
Notes.

Full Justification alignment   No Wrap alignment

Left alignment translates

Center alignment translates

Right alignment translates

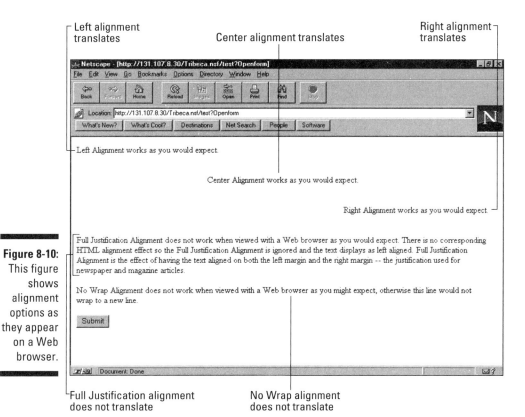

Figure 8-10: This figure shows alignment options as they appear on a Web browser.

Full Justification alignment does not translate

No Wrap alignment does not translate

Bulleted list   Numbered list

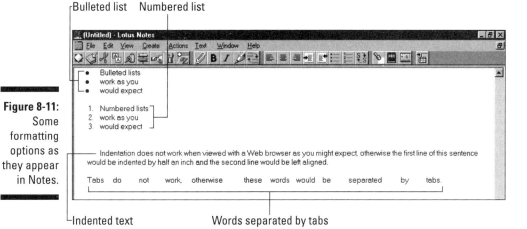

Figure 8-11: Some formatting options as they appear in Notes.

Indented text

Words separated by tabs

Bulleted lists translate   Numbered lists translate

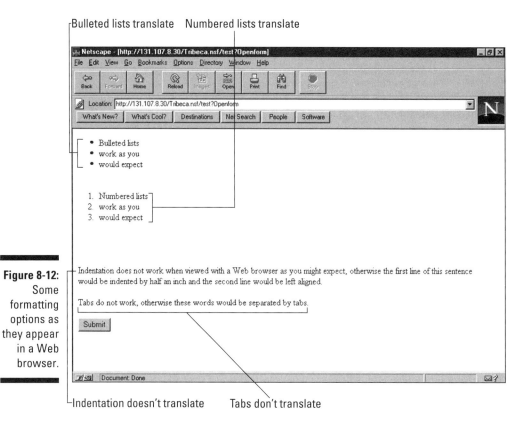

Figure 8-12:
Some
formatting
options as
they appear
in a Web
browser.

Indentation doesn't translate   Tabs don't translate

Some features not supported at all

Here are some more Lotus Notes/Domino features that you should know
aren't supported by Web browsers:

✔ Tabs

✔ Multiple spaces between words (unless using the monospaced font)

If you want to align numbers or preserve multiple spaces between words
when your Domino pages are viewed by a Web browser, format the text with
a *monospaced* (fixed-width) font, such as Courier in Windows. Figure 8-13
shows a sentence that has three spaces between each word formatted in the
Lotus Notes Helv typeface (which kind of looks like Helvetica) and the same
sentence formatted in the monospace Courier typeface. Notice that the
multiple spaces between the words are preserved with Courier but not with
Helv. Figure 8-13 also shows an aligned column of numbers formatted in Helv
and an aligned column of numbers formatted in Courier. Notice that the
spaces placed before the numbers to properly align them are ignored in
Helv, making the numbers appear aligned.

Spaces don't translate   Spaces translate when formatted with a monospace font

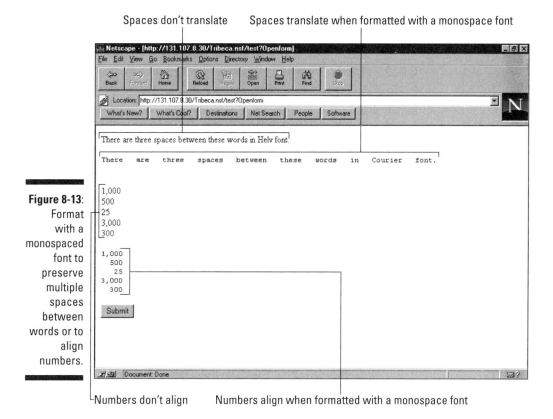

Figure 8-13:
Format
with a
monospaced
font to
preserve
multiple
spaces
between
words or to
align
numbers.

Numbers don't align   Numbers align when formatted with a monospace font

Aligning Text in Columns

Because tabs and multiple spaces between text do not correspond to any HTML formatting effects, they don't translate for viewing by a Web browser. If you want columns of information to appear in your form, put the information into a table and then hide the border of the table.

To create a table, follow these steps:

1. Launch the Lotus Notes client.

The Lotus Notes Workspace, which displays the Domino Web server's databases as rectangular icons, appears.

2. Click the icon for the database that contains the form to which you want to add a table.

3. Choose View⇨Design.

The database opens. See Chapter 6 if Design does not appear in the View menu.

4. **Click the Forms folder.**

   The names of the databases' forms appear in the view pane.

5. **Double-click the name of the form to which you want to add a table.**

   The form appears in edit mode.

6. **Place the cursor where you want to insert a table on the form.**

7. **Choose Create⇨Table.**

   The Create Table dialog box appears (see Figure 8-14).

Figure 8-14:
The Create
Table dialog
box.

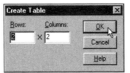

8. **Enter appropriate values for Rows and Columns.**

9. **Click OK.**

   The table appears on the form. You can key text or numbers into the table now.

10. **To hide the table's border, put the cursor in the upper-left cell of the table.**

    When the table is viewed by a Web browser, the entire table adopts the border format of the upper-left cell of the table. For example, if the upper-left cell has a border, the entire table has a border; if the upper-left cell has no border, the entire table doesn't have a border.

    Because the entire table adopts the border format of the upper-left cell of the table when viewed with a Web browser, I recommend that you remove the border from just that cell, so that when you do design work on the form with the Lotus Notes client, you can see where the table is located.

11. **Choose Table⇨Table Properties.**

    The Properties for Table InfoBox appears (see Figure 8-15).

12. **Click the Set All To 0 button.**

    The border disappears from the cell.

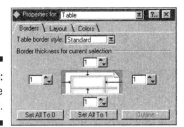

Figure 8-15:
The Table
InfoBox.

If you decide not to hide the table border, the table appears across the entire width of the screen. You can resize the columns by adding more of them, or by choosing View⇨ Ruler and manually resizing them by dragging the vertical bar to the left or right, or by changing the cell width under the Layout tab in the Properties for Table InfoBox.

Ease of Site Management

The most important concept to understand about forms is how they ease site management. Imagine that you have a site containing a document for each of 1,000 products. Further, imagine that each document was created using a form that has your company address typed at the top. On any other type of Web server, each of the 1,000 documents exists in a separate file on the server's hard drive. Also on any other type of Web server, if your corporate address changes, you must open and edit each of the 1,000 documents individually to change the address.

Now, on a Domino Web server, each of the 1,000 documents is stored in a single Notes database. All the documents contain different information, but they are displayed through the same form. If you make a change to the form, all the documents created from that form reflect that change. On a Domino Web server, therefore, you only change the company address in the form once, instead of opening, editing, and closing 1,000 separate documents — which would take . . . how long? Well, maybe not quite forever.

Chapter 9

Getting the Feel for Fields

● ●

In This Chapter

▶ Adding fields

▶ Understanding the Keywords data type

▶ Creating formulas for the Keywords data type

▶ Implementing security through fields

▶ Calculating fields

● ●

*I*f you read Chapter 8 before this chapter, you know that you and your site visitors use *forms* to create content (that is, documents) on the Domino Web site, and you know how to add static text to forms. Yet static text alone does not enable you or your site visitors to create content; the forms must have *fields* where people can input data.

A form without fields would be like a society in which we were all the same color and dimension, all had the same level of intelligence and wit, all wore loincloths, and all liked to eat peas. Life would be boring. There would be no uniqueness. So while the static text is the same between documents created with the same form, fields allow you and your users to enter information into those documents that differentiates them from other documents.

For example, if you are creating an account tracking intranet site, you want your sales reps to be able to create new documents for new accounts. The forms that your sales reps use to create those documents must have fields in which they can type names, addresses, e-mail addresses, and so on, for the new accounts.

A field contains a single type of information, such as text, numbers, date and time, computed values, attachments, or objects. In this chapter, I discuss the many uses of fields.

Adding Fields to a Form

As with static text, you add fields to a form when you have the form in Design mode. You add fields to forms by using a Lotus Notes client; you cannot add them using a Web browser (although you can use a Web browser to input information into a field). Adding a field to a form is easy:

1. **Choose View⇨Design.**

   If you don't see the Design option in the View menu, choose View⇨Show⇨Design. The Design folder in the Navigation pane expands.

2. **Click the Forms folder.**

   All the forms in the database appear in the View pane.

3. **Double-click the name of the form to which you want to add a field.**

   The form opens in Design mode.

4. **Put the cursor where you want to add the field.**

   If you are creating a field in which you want users to input information, be sure to add static text that informs users of the field's purpose.

5. **Choose Create⇨Field, or click the Create Field SmartIcon.**

   The field, named Untitled if no other field on the form has that name (or Untitled2 if a field on the form does have that name), is added at the cursor location. The Properties for Field InfoBox appears (see Figure 9-1).

6. **Type the field's name into the space for Name on the InfoBox.**

7. **Click the arrow on the Type drop-down list and specify the field's data type.**

   You can choose from eight data types:

   - **Text:** Contains letters, punctuation, and numbers not used mathematically.

   - **Number:** Contains numbers used mathematically. You can format numbers as currency, scientific, or percentage, and you can specify the number of decimal places (the default is 2 decimal places, but you can specify 0 through 15), as well as whether to enclose negatives in parentheses and whether to punctuate numbers in the thousands with commas.

Field added at cursor location and called Untitled   Field InfoBox

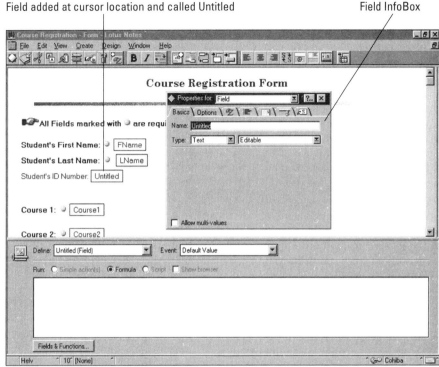

Figure 9-1:
The Field
InfoBox
appears
when you
add a field.

Speaking of numbers: When you create a zip code field, be sure to specify the Text data type, because if you specify the Number data type, you can't store zip codes that begin with a zero. You can see how that would make the folks on the East Coast less than delighted. Also, when you create a telephone number field, be sure to specify the Text data type as well, because if you specify the Number data type, you can't enter telephone numbers by using the dash format (800-555-5555).

- **Time:** Contains dates and/or times. You can format a Time field to display just date, just time, or both, and you can specify whether to display the year or month portion of the date or the seconds portion of the time. Also, you can use the values in Time fields for calculations. For example, you may want to automatically calculate a project due date for 60 days after a document is composed.

- **Rich Text:** Contains text, file attachments, graphics, and objects. You can format individual text items. For example, you could type "*Lotus Domino For Dummies* is the best book I have ever read" in a Rich Text field and format the book title in italics while leaving the rest of the words in regular type. You can format any type of field, but only Rich Text fields allow you to format individual items within the field. The content in Rich Text fields cannot be displayed in a view column, so you should make sure that any field you specify as a Rich Text field does not include information you plan on displaying in a view (see Chapter 10 for more information on creating views).

- **Keywords:** Allows users to choose values from a predefined list. The items can be displayed in a radio button, check box, or dialog list interface. If you use the dialog list interface, you can make it so users can select only the items that you have predefined, or you can allow them either to select one of the predefined values or to specify their own. You can either type the predefined values into the field, or you can create a formula that generates the values. (See "Keyword Fields Are Key" later in this chapter for more details.)

- **Authors:** A security field that allows people who have Author access in the database's Access Control List (ACL) to edit documents. If a user has Author access in the database's ACL, he must be listed in a document's Authors field before he may edit the document. (See Chapter 15 for more information on the Authors field and the ACL.)

- **Readers:** A security field that allows people to read documents. If a document has a Readers field and you aren't listed in it, you may not read the document, regardless of the level of access you have in the database's ACL. That's right, even if you have Manager access, you must be listed in the Readers field to read the document!

- **Names:** Displays the Notes user-naming convention in an easier-to-understand format. Forget that this one's even an option; you never use it. This option has no significance if your users are accessing the database with Web browsers.

8. **Click the drop-down list next to the Type box and specify whether the field is Editable or Computed.**

   An Editable field allows users to input values, whereas a Computed field generates the inputted value with a formula.

9. **If you selected the Number or Time data type, format how you want input to appear on-screen.**

   You set how your input looks by filling in the appropriate formatting options that appear automatically in the InfoBox as soon as you specify either the Number or Time data type.

10. **Check the Allow multi-values check box if you want users to enter multiple values in a field.**

    Allowing multiple values comes in handy for a Readers field. Suppose you want two people to be able to read a document, and you type their names into the Readers field and separate them with a comma — for example, "George Herbert, Walker Bush" — but you don't specify that the field is to allow multiple values. The Domino Web server, rather than interpreting these names as two different people, only allows a person named "George Herbert, Walker Bush" to read the document. (You can bet the Clinton White House enables the Allow multi-values check box!)

You can test to see how a newly added field looks on a form without having to leave Design mode. This feature enables you to quickly test fields on the fly as you add them. Follow these steps:

1. **With the form still in Design mode, choose <u>D</u>esign⇨<u>T</u>est form.**

    A dialog box appears asking you whether you want to save the form.

2. **Click <u>Y</u>es.**

    The form appears as it would on the Notes client in Edit mode. Keep in mind that fonts, spacing, and other formatting look different when viewed via a Web browser.

3. **Look at the field you created and note whether it looks okay.**

4. **Press Esc when you're finished.**

    This returns you to Design mode. If you didn't like the way your new field looks in Step 3, you can change it in Design mode and start all over again from Step 1.

Keywords Fields Are Key

By utilizing the Keywords data type, you can make your Domino Web site much easier to use. Instead of expecting users to type information into a form's fields, you can let them choose information from a list of options. Obviously, such an approach doesn't make much sense on most types of answers, but if you had a product orders database, you'd want people to choose from a list the product that they want to order.

Suppose you have a security application that specifies employee hair color. You don't want the application to let people categorize their hair as "Green," or "Gray, but really brown," or "Brown, black, or red, depending on the day of the week," or "Purple with a blue stripe" — that would be totally unruly. You want your employees to select from "Black," "Blonde," "Gray," "Brown," "Red," or "Bald"; if they're something in between, you still want them to make an approximation that allows you to categorize them. You can see how limiting options works well in this application, for if this were the security application for the Chicago Bulls and you did not utilize the Keywords data type, Dennis Rodman would fall into about 30 different categories.

Creating a Keywords field

1. Add the field to the form.

Follow Steps 1 – 6 under "Adding Fields to a Form" earlier in this chapter.

2. Choose Keywords from the Type drop-down list.

3. Choose Editable from the drop-down list next to the Type list.

You use the Keywords data type to give your users options when they input values into the field. Using a Computed field instead of choosing the default Editable defeats the purpose of using the Keywords data type, because the Computed option doesn't let users input values.

4. Choose one of the options from the Choices drop-down list.

See the list under "Keyword choices by formula" later in this chapter and also look at Figure 9-2.

Web browsers support only the first two of the five options in the Choices list. Keep that in mind if your Domino site will mainly be used from the Internet instead of your corporate intranet. Because this book is about Domino Web servers, I focus on the first two options.

- **Enter choices (one per line):** The designer types the users' choices into the InfoBox of the field he or she is creating.

- **Use formula for choices:** The designer creates a formula that generates the users' choices. See "Keywords choices by formula" later in this section for more about this option.

- **Use Address dialog for choices:** Not supported by Web browsers.

- **Use Access Control List for choices:** Not supported by Web browsers.

- **Use View dialog for choices:** Not supported by Web browsers.

5. Depending on your selection in Step 4, either type the choices or type a formula in the Field InfoBox's formula box.

Click the List Window button to enlarge the display of the formula box. If you selected Enter choices (one per line) in Step 4, you can click the Sort button to sort the choices.

Figure 9-2:
Different
ways to
generate
users'
choices.

6. **Enable the Allow values not in list check box if you want to let users enter values that you didn't predefine into the field.**

   I recommend against checking this box. When you enable this option, Web browsers display a rather unintuitive field (see Figure 9-3), defeating the purpose of using the Keyword data type in the first place. Experiment with it to see what I mean.

7. **Click the Allow multi-values check box if you want to let your users enter more than one value in the field.**

   For example, if you have a customer tracking application and you want a keywords field that specifies the states where the customer has offices, you want the field to allow anywhere from one to 50 separate values.

8. **Click the Interface tab.**

   I can think of no other way for me to describe which of the tabs is the Interface tab other than to say it is the one with the little picture that looks like a candle on its side in a box. (Okay, maybe I could also describe it as a firecracker on its side in a box.)

9. **Select an Interface option.**

   You can choose from check boxes, radio buttons, and a dialog list on this tab. See "Interface options" later in this section for more details.

10. **Do not check the refresh or helper options on the Interface tab.**

    The Don't display entry helper button, Refresh fields on keyword change, and Refresh choices on document refresh options all have no effect on Web browsers, so you don't need to check the boxes on the Interface tab.

11. **If you select Check box or Radio button in Step 9, specify the number of columns in which you want the boxes or buttons to appear.**

    By default, buttons or boxes appear one on top of the other in one column. Disregard the Frame drop-down list; Web browsers don't support this option.

Interface options

I mention in Step 9 of the "Creating a Keywords field" list earlier in this chapter that you can choose from one of three interfaces for your field. On the Interface tab of the Properties for Field InfoBox, you can choose to display keyword fields as a check box, radio button, or dialog list.

- ✔ **Check box:** Allows users to choose more than one value by clicking on each one.

- ✔ **Radio button:** Allows users to choose only one value by clicking on it. All other values are deselected when the user clicks one radio button.

- ✔ **Dialog list:** Allows users to choose values from a drop-down list. As the Web site developer, you can specify whether users can choose more than one value from the list. If you specify in the Properties for Field InfoBox that the field allows multi-values, users can choose more than one value by pressing Ctrl while they click their preferred values.

The section "Controlling how many rows display in a Keywords field" at the end of this chapter explains how you can specify the number of rows that display in the Dialog list.

Figure 9-3 shows the three different interfaces, and illustrates how the Dialog interface appears if you select the Allow values not in list option, the Allow multi-values option, or both. Notice that when you select Allow values not in list, the Keywords field looks and acts the same as does a Text field viewed on a Web browser.

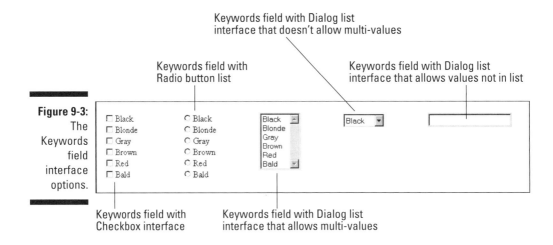

Keywords field with Dialog list
interface that doesn't allow multi-values

Keywords field with
Radio button list

Keywords field with Dialog list
interface that allows values not in list

Figure 9-3:
The
Keywords
field
interface
options.

Keywords field with
Checkbox interface

Keywords field with Dialog list
interface that allows multi-values

Keywords choices by formula

I mention in Step 4 of the "Creating a Keywords field" list earlier in this chapter that designers can choose Use formula for choices from the Choices drop-down list of the Properties for Field InfoBox to use a formula that generates field choices for the user. Using a formula to generate the choices is useful when the values users can select are constantly changing.

For example, say you have a Domino Web site that serves as a virtual bookstore, and you want your users to choose the books they want to order from a list of titles, rather than manually type the book titles into a field. You could create a formula that pulls the titles from your inventory database. Another benefit of that approach is that anytime you add or discontinue a book title, the change reflects immediately in the Keywords list; you don't get the lag time and mistakes that occur when you have to manually make the changes in your inventory databases and update your Keywords fields.

Two very useful ways to generate formulas are with the @DbColumn and @DbLookup formulas.

Taking choices from a column

You can use the @DbColumn formula to generate the values from a column, using the following syntax:

```
@DbColumn("[class]":"[cache]";"[server]":database;view;column)
```

Note that two of the separators in the formula are colons (:) and three are semicolons (;). I point this out because I don't want you to make the same mistake I often do of separating all the arguments with semicolons and then wondering why the formula doesn't work correctly.

Here's an example:

```
@DbColumn("":"";"":sales.nsf;Account Profiles;1)
```

The following list explains the components of the @Dbformula syntax:

- ✔ class: Indicates the type of database in which the column you are doing the lookup to is located. To specify a Notes database you use either "", or "Notes".

- ✔ cache: Indicates whether to cache the formula result for future lookups. Web browsers don't support caching of results, so you can simply specify "" for this parameter.

- ✔ server: Indicates the name of the Domino Web server in which to find the column you're using for the lookup. You can specify "" if it's the same Domino Web server you're using for the lookup.

✔ database: Indicates the name of the database in which to find the column to which you're doing the lookup. You can specify " " if it's the same database you're using for the lookup.

✔ view: Indicates the name of the view in which to find the column you're using for the lookup.

✔ column: Indicates the number of the column (starting with 1 and counting from left to right) that contains the values you want returned.

Include all columns when counting from left to right, including hidden columns. When you count columns, put the view in Design mode so you can see any hidden columns.

Figure 9-4 shows an @DbColumn formula that returns the first column in the All Course Descriptions view of the gradreg.nsf database. The server parameter is specified as " ", which means that the gradreg.nsf database is on the same Domino Web server as the database from which the formula is being executed.

Figure 9-4:
The
@DbColumn
at work.

Figure 9-5 shows the result of the @DbColumn formula that appears in Figure 9-4. The values that you see in the Keywords field are the values in the first column of the All Course Descriptions view in the gradreg.nsf database.

Figure 9-5:
The result
of the
@DbColumn
formula
shown in
Figure 9-4.

Finding specific choices in a view

You don't have to generate an entire column to obtain values from it.
Instead, you can use the @DbLookup formula to generate specific values
that match a criteria, using one of the following syntax:

```
@DbLookup("[class]":"[cache]";"[server]":database;view;key;column)
```

or

```
@DbLookup("[class]":"[cache]";"[server]":database;view;key;field)
```

 Note that two of the separators in the formula are colons (:) and four are
semicolons (;). I point this out because I don't want you to make the same
mistake I often do of separating all the arguments with semicolons and then
wondering why the formula doesn't work correctly.

Here are a couple of examples:

```
@DbLookup("":"";"":sales.nsf;Account Profiles;New;1)
```

or

```
@DbLookup("":"";"":sales.nsf;Account Profiles;New;Name)
```

The @DbLookup formula mainly has the same components as the
@DbColumn formula, except that it also has these components:

- ✔ key: Identifies the documents for which to search. The Domino Web
  server finds all the documents that have a value in the first sorted
  column of the specified view that match key.

- ✔ field: Identifies the name of the field that contains the value that the
  formula returns from the documents that match the key. As an alternative to specifying a field name, you can specify the number of the
  column that contains the value.

Figure 9-6 shows an @DbLookup formula that returns the value in the second
column in the Course Descriptions By Term view of the gradreg.nsf
database for all documents that have the value Winter in the first sorted
column of the Course Descriptions By Term view. Notice that the server
parameter is specified as ""; that means the gradreg.nsf database is on
the same Domino Web server as the database from which the formula is
being executed.

Figure 9-6:
The
@DbLookup
at work.

Figure 9-7 shows the result of the @DbLookup formula specified in Figure 9-6. Figure 9-8 shows the view from which the formula is pulling the values.

Figure 9-7:
The result
of the
@DbLookup
formula
shown in
Figure 9-6.

Figure 9-8:
The view
from
which the
@DbLookup
in Figure 9-6
is pulling
the values.

Security with Fields

Even though I devote an entire chapter to security, I think you should be aware at this point about the security you can have by using the Authors and the Readers field date types. The next few paragraphs are a brief summary of security with certain field types.

Authors field

The Authors field determines whether users listed as Authors in the database's ACL can edit documents (see Chapter 15 for more about the ACL). Users who have Author access in the ACL can read, create, and edit their own documents. How does the Domino Web server know what documents they created? You guessed it — the Authors field.

You have to create the Authors field; it isn't just part of the form by default. If you don't create an Authors field, people who have Author access in the ACL can't edit the documents that they create. Also, if you create an Authors field but don't put the author's name in it, he or she can't edit the document.

Users who have Editor access in the ACL can edit other people's documents, so the Authors field has no significance to them; it neither grants nor denies additional functionality. Users who have Reader access and below cannot edit documents under any circumstances, so they, too, do not have additional functionality granted or denied by the Authors field. Only users who have Authors access in the ACL are affected by the Authors field.

To add an Authors field to a form, simply select Authors from the Type drop-down list in the Properties for Field InfoBox (see Figure 9-9). The figure shows Author as the name for the field (typed in the Name text box), but don't let that throw you; you can name the field anything you want. The vital selection here in creating the field is what you select as the type (from the Type drop-down list box).

Figure 9-9:
Creating an
Authors
field.

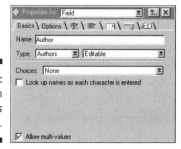

Readers field

The Readers field determines whether users can read documents. No matter what a user's access is in the ACL — even if it's Manager — if a document has a Readers field and the user isn't listed in it, the user cannot read the document.

To add a Readers field to a form, simply specify the Type as Readers in the Properties for Field InfoBox (see Figure 9-10).

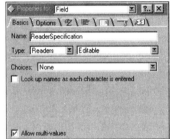

Figure 9-10:
Creating a
Readers
field.

Adding names and groups

You can create the Authors and Readers fields as Computed, and have a formula generate the name(s) or group(s), or you can create them as Editable and allow users to specify the names in them.

No, You Can't Eat the Editable Fields

A field can be Editable, which means users can input information into it, or it can be a variation of Computed, which means the Domino Web server generates the input via a formula.

The differentiation between editable and computed fields is that editable fields allow user input and computer fields don't. Both of them can execute calculations. The result of a calculation in an editable field, however, can be changed with user input.

Editable fields

You generally format most of the fields that you create on your Domino Web site as Editable, because you want your users to be able to input information. Editable fields do more than just let people input data, though. You can choose three types of formulas to execute in an Editable field, each of which makes data input and data storage easier:

- **Default Value:** When users first create a document, you can, for the purpose of saving users time and effort, have a default value formula input a value into the field.

  Suppose you have a project-tracking application that stores a project begin date and a project end date in each project document. I think it's safe to say that most of the time the project-begin date is the same as the date on which the document is created and the project-end date is 90 days later. If you create a Project Begin Date field that has a default value of today's date and a Project End Date field of 90 days from today, you save the user the time of entering the date and the effort of having to figure out the date 90 days from today.

  The fields are Editable so that, in the 10 percent of the cases in which the document is created that day but in which the project doesn't commence for another seven days, the author of the document can simply type over the inputted default value with the real project-begin date. If a project is to end 120 days from the start date, the author can simply replace the value in the field with the date 120 days from today.

- **Input Translation:** The Input Translation formula is a nice way to manipulate information in a field after the user submits a form. It allows you to format data, remove spaces or characters, or add characters.

  For example, if someone enters a telephone number in XXX-XXX-XXXX format, you can use the Input Translation formula to automatically reformat the number to (XXX) XXX-XXXX format to make it uniform with the other telephone numbers in the database.

- **Input Validation:** This formula allows you to validate what user enters. It is most commonly used to ensure that a user enters a value in a required field before letting him submit a document.

  For example, if you have an Input Validation formula that requires input into a field before the user can submit the document — say, a social security number — and a user tries to submit the document without specifying it, you can reject the submission and generate a message that tells the user that the document cannot be submitted until the field in question has a value.

To add one or all three of these formulas to an editable field:

1. **Choose View⊅Design to put the form in Design mode.**

   If you don't see the Design option in the View menu, choose View⊅Show⊅Design. The Design pane expands in the Navigation window.

2. **In the Design pane, click the Event drop-down list and select an event.**

   See Figure 9-11. In this chapter we cover only Default Value, Input Translation, and Input Validation. The other selections in this list, which relate to LotusScript, are not covered in this book.

3. **Type the formula into the Formula box.**

4. **Save the form by choosing File⊅Save.**

Computed fields

Domino recognizes three types of computed fields:

✔ **Computed:** Fields that are recalculated whenever a user opens or submits a document.

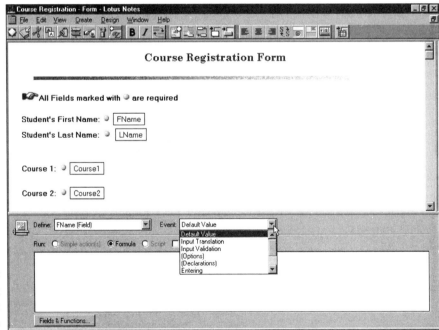

Figure 9-11:
Select an
event.

✔ **Computed for display:** Fields that are recalculated only whenever a user opens a document. Use this computed type of field when you need information, such as the current date, that does not need to be stored with the document. Computed for display fields can't display in columns.

✔ **Computed when composed:** Fields that are calculated only once, when the document is first created. Use this computed type of field when document information, such as when it was created or what sequence number it has, must be preserved.

Extra Help from Field Help

Each field has what is called *Field Help*. It's basically a text message at the bottom of the screen that gives users directions or help regarding what to enter in the field they're in while creating or editing a document with a Notes client. For example, if you're in a social security number field, the Field Help message at the bottom of the screen may read, "Enter social security number in this format XXX-XX-XXXX."

Now that I have explained Field Help, forget what I just told you; Field Help does not display a text message at the bottom of the screen when users view documents on Web browsers. They do something even better, though; they enable you to limit the size and length of a Text field, the number of rows of a Keywords field, and the size and text wrap setting of a Rich Text field.

Specifying field help

You specify Field Help in the Properties for Field InfoBox. To do so, follow these steps:

1. **Launch the Lotus Notes client.**

   The Lotus Notes Workspace, which displays the Domino Web server's databases as rectangular icons, appears.

2. **Click the icon for the database containing the form you want to edit.**

3. **Choose <u>V</u>iew⇨<u>D</u>esign.**

   The database opens. Refer to Chapter 6 if Design does not appear in the View menu.

4. **Click the Forms folder.**

   The names of the databases' forms appear in the view pane.

5. **Double-click the name of the form you want to edit.**

The form appears in edit mode.

6. **Double-click the field to which you want to add Field Help.**

The Properties for Field InfoBox appears (see Figure 9-12).

7. **Click the Options tab.**

8. **Type into the Help description box.**

9. **Save the form when you're finished.**

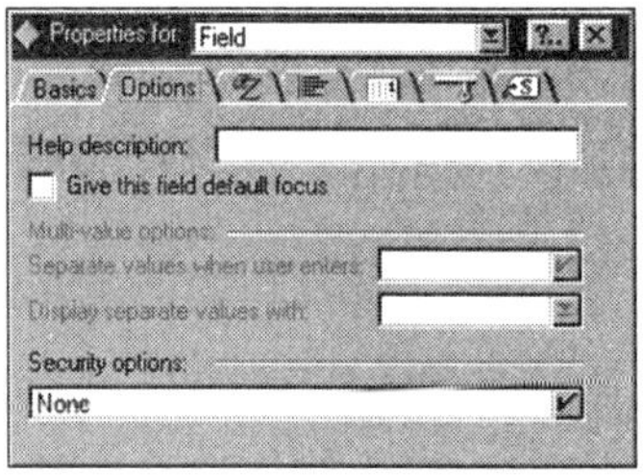

Figure 9-12:
The Options tab in the Properties for Field InfoBox.

Limiting the size and length of text fields

We all know what it's like to be in a hurry and run into one of our more "verbose" colleagues in the hallway. Wouldn't it be nice if it were socially acceptable to tell the person before he even opens his mouth, "You can talk to me, but I will have to cut you off and be on my way after you have used 50 characters, including punctuation. So don't be too animated; otherwise that'll cost you two exclamation points." (By the way, you used 207 characters to say that to him, so you can see what a nice, short conversation it will be.)

Well, you can limit the number of characters that people can type into a Text field, and you can control how many of those characters display. The Field Help shown in Figure 9-13 limits the number of characters that users can type into the field to 50 and displays 20 characters.

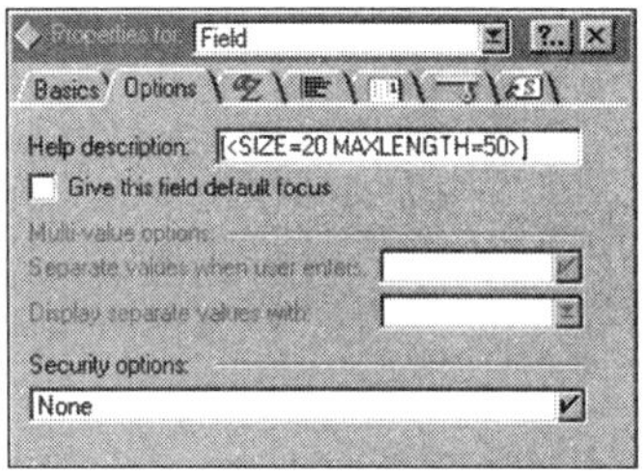

Figure 9-13:
Use the Help description to limit the number of characters that can be entered and displayed.

Limiting the display size of Rich Text fields

You can specify the size of the text box that appears for Rich Text fields. Figure 9-14 shows how to display a text box that is 5 rows long and 20 columns wide. Figure 9-15 shows the result of limiting the number of rows and columns of a text box for a Rich Text field.

Figure 9-14: Limit the number of rows and columns that a Rich Text field displays.

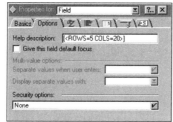

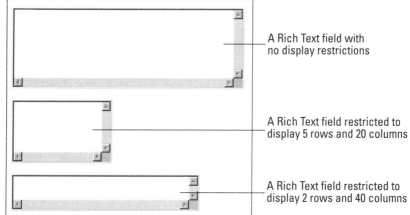

Figure 9-15: How Rich Text fields display with the Web browser.

A Rich Text field with no display restrictions

A Rich Text field restricted to display 5 rows and 20 columns

A Rich Text field restricted to display 2 rows and 40 columns

Controlling how text wraps in Rich Text fields

You can specify how text wraps in a Rich Text field. Figure 9-16 shows the syntax that enables text wrap in a Rich Text field. Figure 9-17 shows the result of wrapping text; instead of the text scrolling continuously to the right, it wraps to the next line. Notice that when you enable text wrapping, the default display size is quite a bit smaller than it is when text isn't wrapped. I recommend that in addition to specifying text wrap in the Field Help, you also specify a larger display size for the Rich Text field.

Figure 9-16:
How to wrap text in a Rich Text field.

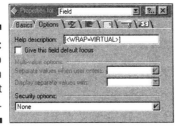

A Rich Text field that wraps text and displays in the default size when text wrap is enabled

A Rich Text field that wraps text and displays 5 rows and 50 columns

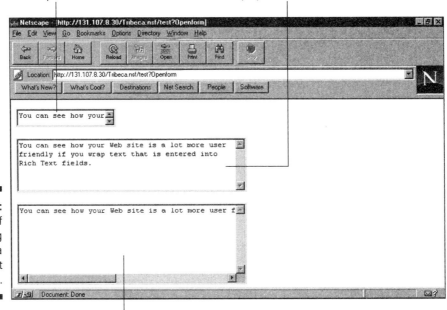

Figure 9-17:
Examples of wrapping text in a Rich Text field.

A Rich Text field that doesn't wrap text

Controlling how many rows display in a Keywords field

You can specify a maximum number of choices to display in a Keywords field. If choices exceed your specified maximum, a scroll bar appears so that users can scroll to their desired choices. Figure 9-18 shows the Field Help setting that displays three items from a Keywords list. Figure 9-19 shows a Keywords field that displays the default number of choices (which is one) and a Keywords field that displays three choices and a scroll bar users can use to view the other choices.

Figure 9-18:
To display three choices in a Keywords field.

Figure 9-19:
Keywords fields displaying one choice and three choices.

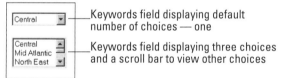

Keywords field displaying default number of choices — one

Keywords field displaying three choices and a scroll bar to view other choices

Chapter 10

A Web Site with a View

So you have lots of information that you want to present on your Domino Web site. How do you make it nice and orderly so that your friends, family, and customers can easily see what you have available and can read certain documents? The answer, in a word, is views.

Think of a *view* as a table of contents, a display of the documents in your Domino Web site. If users want to read a particular document, all they need to do is navigate to the correct view, click the link, and, like magic, the document shows up on-screen.

Look at Figures 10-1 and 10-2 to see how the exact same view looks a bit different on a Notes client than in a Web browser. Although the views do differ, the same information is available to the Notes client and the Web browser.

Views are an excellent and useful part of the Domino package. Views make navigating your Domino Web site a bit easier for the user and, depending on how you format the view, make your site look very professional. In this chapter, I discuss the care and feeding of views and one special view component, the column.

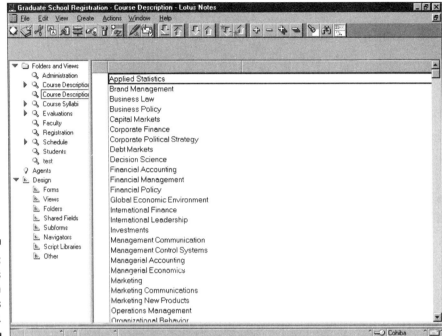

Figure 10-1:
A view as
seen with
a Notes
client.

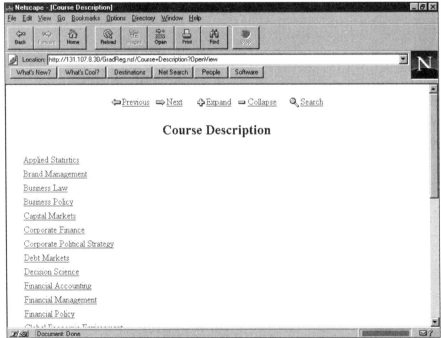

Figure 10-2:
A view as
seen with a
Web
browser.

You and Views

You have a lot of flexibility with the views you create on your Domino Web site. You can, for example, format the views and decide whether all the documents in the database or just a subset of documents will appear. You also can add and delete views quite easily, so that your site is always changing and never gets stale.

Creating views

Creating a view is a fairly straightforward matter. Just follow these steps:

1. **Choose <u>C</u>reate⬧<u>V</u>iew, or choose <u>C</u>reate⬧<u>D</u>esign⬧<u>V</u>iew.**

   The Create View InfoBox appears (see Figure 10-3).

2. **In the <u>V</u>iew name text box, type a name for your view.**

3. **Click the Sha<u>r</u>ed check box.**

   The InfoBox changes to display all the shared views in the database (see Figure 10-4).

   If you don't perform Step 3, and instead leave the default of Private, users will get an error when they try to open the view.

4. **Click the Add Condition button if you want to create a criterion that allows only certain documents to appear in the view.**

5. **Click <u>O</u>K.**

If, after creating the view, you decide that you want to change the name or the selection formula, you can do so by using the Create View InfoBox to change the name or the Design pane to change the selection formula.

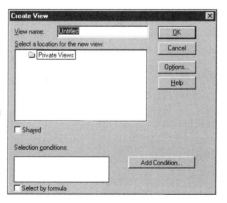

Figure 10-3:
The Create
View
InfoBox.

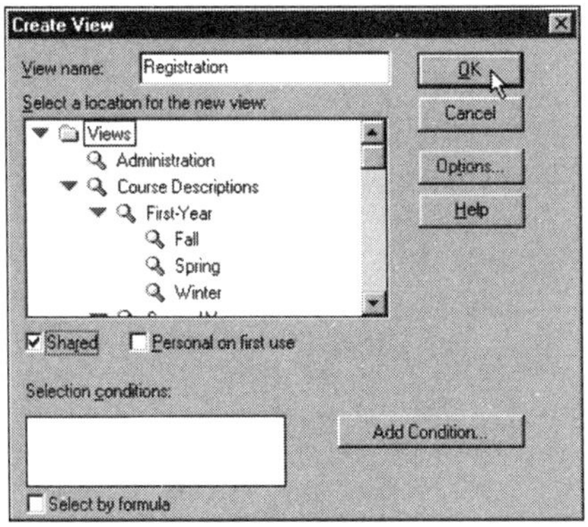

Figure 10-4:
The Create
View
InfoBox
filled in.

Formatting views

You can format a view to appear in a variety of ways to the user. To format a view, you must first put the view in Design mode by doing the following:

1. Choose View⇨Design.

If Design does not appear in the View menu, choose View⇨Show⇨Design.

2. Click the Views folder in the Navigation window.

All the views in the database appear in the View pane.

3. Double-click the name of the view in the View pane that you want to put in Design mode.

The view appears in Design mode (see Figure 10-5).

Click the Recalculate icon (shown in Figure 10-5) in the upper left-hand corner of the Design pane. After you click the icon, Domino displays the documents in the view (see Figure 10-6), and you can update the view anytime you make a column change or selection formula change. The Recalculation icon appears whenever you need to update the view; that is, whenever you have changed the view.

At this point, you can make changes to columns — which I discuss in the next section — and view properties via the View InfoBox.

To display the Properties for View InfoBox, do one of the following:

  ✔ Select Design⇨View Properties.

  ✔ Click the right mouse button and choose View Properties.

  ✔ Click the Design View Properties SmartIcon.

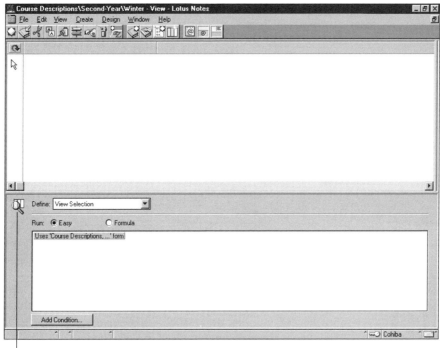

Figure 10-5:
A view in
Design
mode.

Recalculate icon

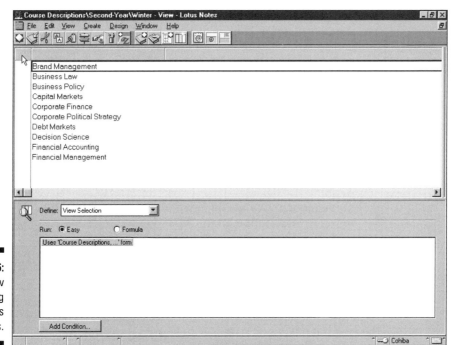

Figure 10-6:
A view
displaying
its
documents.

The Properties for View InfoBox (see Figure 10-7) enables you to change the view's properties. Bear in mind that many of these properties are relevant only if users access the views on Notes clients. Here are some of the relevant properties when designing a view for use on a Domino Web site:

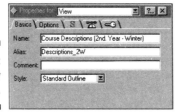

Figure 10-7:
The View
InfoBox.

✔ **Name:** The name that displays at the top of the view.

✔ **Alias:** Another name for the view for programming purposes; the user does not see it.

I highly recommend that you specify an alias, especially anytime you need to program the view's name into a formula or a URL. By using an alias, you leave open the option to change the name of the view that the user sees without having to change every formula or URL in which you have specified the view name.

For example, if you convert the application to another language or face a situation in which the view name changes often (such as one in which you have a view of the month's current contracts and you want "January Contracts" to display in January, "February Contracts" in February, and so on), using an alias would ensure that you avoid an unnecessary, and therefore rather annoying, inconvenience.

✔ **Background color:** One of the few formatting properties you can change in the View InfoBox that Web browsers recognize. Look for this selection in the Options tab.

✔ **Security:** A list (that you can create) that specifies who may look at the documents in a particular view. Check out the security (key) tab for this option. You can include in the security list any entry in the database's Access Control List (ACL) that has an access level of reader or above. By default, all the entries in the ACL that have an access level of reader or above are included in the security list. Refer to Chapter 15 for more information on the ACL.

Selecting documents for views

Consider a scenario in which you are building a graduate school's course registration application. The school offers 50 different courses throughout the year but only certain ones in any given term. You want to create a view that displays just the ten courses offered in the Winter term. You can do so by using a formula or a *selection condition.* The selection condition specifies that only documents meeting a certain criteria are displayed in the view. Some examples of possible criteria are

- ✔ All documents modified between January and June
- ✔ All documents created by Tim Whatley
- ✔ All customer accounts assigned to Dianne DeConn
- ✔ All records created with the Engineering Report form

Specifying a selection condition is a simple task. Do the following:

1. **Put the view in Design mode.**

   See Steps 1–3 in the section "Formatting views," earlier in this chapter.

2. **Choose View Selection from the Define drop-down list.**

   You then see something like Figure 10-8.

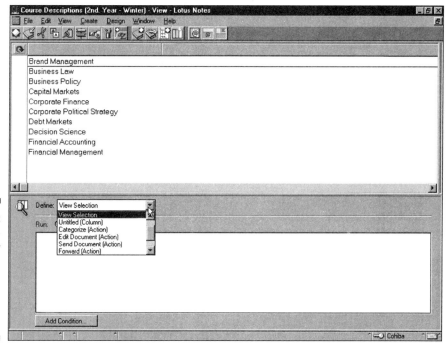

Figure 10-8:
Choose
View
Selection
from the
Define
drop-down
list.

3. **Click the Easy button in the Run section of the Design pane.**

4. **Click the Add Condition button.**

   The Search Builder InfoBox appears (see Figure 10-9).

5. **Choose a condition from the Condition drop-down list.**

   See Figure 10-10 for an idea of what your screen should look like now.

6. **Specify the criteria you want in the Search for documents field.**

   For example, if you select the By Date condition, you can specify a criterion of a date before which all selected documents must be created, or a date after which all selected documents must be created. If you specify the By Field condition, you can specify criteria of the name of a field and the value that the field must contain for the document to be selected. If you specify the By Author condition, you can specify a criterion of a certain person's name by which all selected documents must be created.

7. **When you're finished, click OK.**

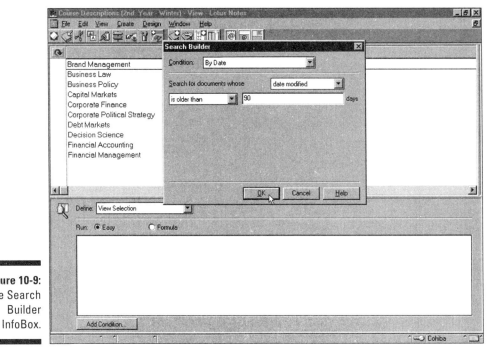

Figure 10-9:
The Search
Builder
InfoBox.

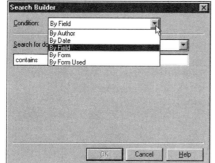

Figure 10-10:
The
Condition
drop-down
list.

Call Them Columns

When you open a view on a Domino Web site, you see documents in a column. The first column provides the hypertext links that open the documents.

You can sort columns to display the documents in ascending or descending order, or you can categorize them to group similar documents on top of each other. The information displayed in a column representing a document can be a number of different things, such as:

- ✔ The information in a single field or multiple fields
- ✔ The result of a formula or concatenation
- ✔ The result of HTML tags

A column representing a document cannot display other types of information, such as:

- ✔ The information in a rich text field
- ✔ The information in an encrypted field

Adding columns

You can add columns to a view in just a few steps. To add a column

1. Put the view into Design mode.

You see something like what's in Figure 10-11. If you don't know how to put the view in Design mode, refer to Steps 1–3 in the section on formatting views.

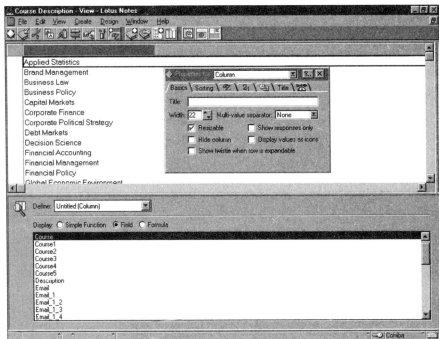

Figure 10-11:
A view in
Design
mode.

2. Choose Create➪Insert New Column or Create➪Append New Column.

Choose Insert New Column if you want to create a new column directly before the column where the cursor is located. Choose Append New Column if you want to create a new column after all the existing columns in the view, regardless of where the cursor is located.

3. Click one of the Display radio buttons in the Design pane.

You can choose any one of the three options listed below. For more about each option, see the section "Display options explained" later in this chapter.

- **Simple Function:** You choose this button to easily display the document's creation date, its author's name, its last modification date, and other bits of information (see Figure 10-12).

- **Field:** This button enables you to choose a field to display from a list of all the fields in the database.

- **Formula:** Choose the Formula button to specify a formula with which to produce the field's result.

4. Press Ctrl+S to save your modifications.

Display options explained

Step 3 in the preceding "Adding columns" section introduces the display options. A necessary part of adding a column to a view is determining what the column displays. Whether you select Simple Function, Field, or Formula as the display option, the sky is pretty much the limit as to the information that you can display in a column.

You don't need to have programming knowledge to create a column that displays information; you can select from a list a number of simple functions that will display information in a column. Just click the Simple Function in the Display section of the Design pane and pick an item from the list that appears (see Figure 10-12).

You can also add a column that shows the user a field from the database. Just like with the Simple Function button, the Field radio button does all the hard work for you. You can simply pick from the list of all the fields in the database (refer to Figure 10-11). Once again, you do not need programming knowledge to create a column that displays field information.

So you say you want a column to include a formula? Okay, now you need to know some programming. You can specify @Functions, concatenation, and HTML in columns by selecting the Formula button.

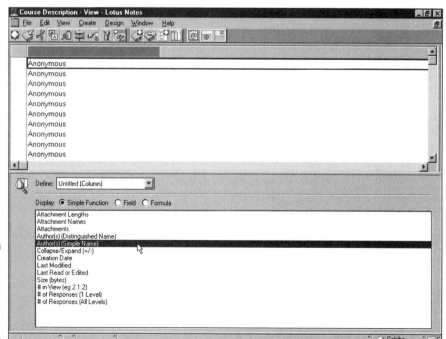

Figure 10-12:
Simple
Functions
for column
display.

In the example shown in Figure 10-13, I have *concatenated,* or placed together, the Course field, a slash character, and the Term field, and Figure 10-14 shows the result: The two fields display together with a slash between them.

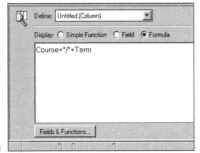

Figure 10-13:
Formula for
column
display.

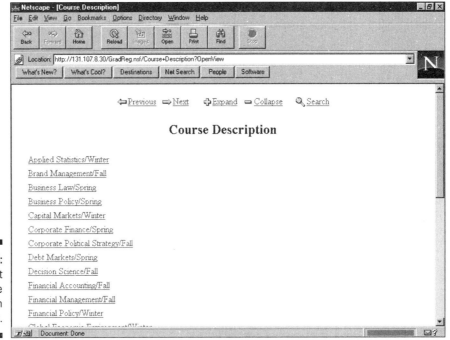

Figure 10-14:
The result
of the
column
formula.

In the preceding example, I concatenated two text values. But what if I want to concatenate the Course field with a numeric field that specifies the price of the course (say, the Price field)? Do you think the following would work?

```
Course+"/"+Price
```

You are absolutely correct — if you answered "No." Before I can concatenate the two fields, I must convert the *Price* field to a text string, like this:

```
Course+"/"+@Text(Price)
```

As a matter of fact, if I want the information in the price field to display as currency, with two decimal points, I would specify the optional format-string, like so:

```
Course+"/"+@Text(Price;"C")
```

Sorting

Whether a column displays text, numbers, or dates, you can sort the column in ascending or descending order. To sort a column, follow these steps:

1. **Put the view in design mode.**

   If you don't know how to put the view in Design mode, refer to Steps 1–3 in the section on formatting views.

2. **Click the column that you want to sort.**

3. **Choose** <u>D</u>esign⇨<u>C</u>olumn Properties.

   The Column InfoBox appears.

4. **Click the Sorting tab.**

5. **Click either Ascending or Descending.**

6. **Save the form when finished by choosing** <u>F</u>ile⇨<u>S</u>ave.

Categorizing

You may decide that, rather than simply sorting the documents, you want to group them first. For example, you may have all the graduate courses a school offers listed in a sorted column but decide you would like to group all the courses based on the term in which they are offered (see Figure 10-15). To group a column and then sort it, do the following:

1. **Click the column that you want to sort.**
2. **Choose Design⇨Column Properties.**

   The Column InfoBox appears.
3. **Click the Sorting tab.**
4. **Click either Ascending or Descending.**
5. **Click Categorized for type.**

Formatting

The Column InfoBox allows you to change much of the formatting properties for the column. You can change the color of the font, the size of the font, or the font's attributes — bold, italicized, underlined, or strikethrough. You can also format the way numbers and time appear.

A couple of exceptions apply to the first column of the view, because it's the hypertext link. You cannot change its color, nor can you elect to forgo underlining the word.

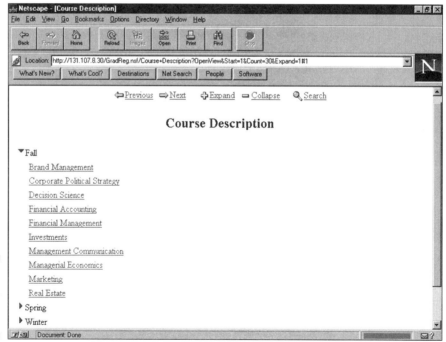

Figure 10-15:
A
categorized
view.

Generally speaking, you should be careful about underlining text. On the Web it is universally understood that underlined text represents links, so you run the risk of confusing your users if you underline text.

One other nifty property that the Column InfoBox allows you to specify is whether to use icons to represent values. Instead of simply displaying text in a view, you may want to display icons to give your users visual cues. For example, you may want a thumbs-up icon to indicate an approved document and a thumbs-down icon for one that isn't approved. Figure 10-16 displays all the possible icons. To specify an icon, follow these steps:

1. **In the Column InfoBox, choose the Display values as icons option.**

2. **Specify an appropriate column formula using a value from 1 to 172, depending upon the desired icon.**

   For example, the formula @If(Status="Approved";83;84) displays the thumbs-up icon (which is mapped to the number 83 — see Figure 10-16) if a document's Status field contains the value "Approved." If a document's Status field does not contain the value "Approved," the thumbs-down icon (which is mapped to the number 84) appears.

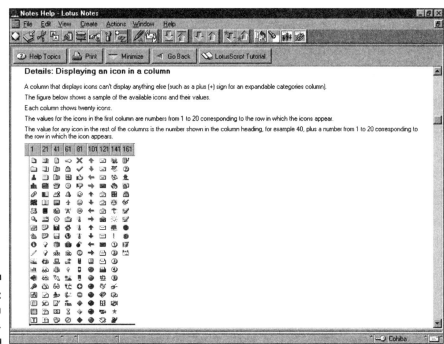

Figure 10-16:
Column
icons.

Chapter 11

Lights, Camera, Actions

- -

In This Chapter

▶ Creating action buttons

▶ Examples of action buttons

▶ Copying action buttons among forms and views

▶ Controlling the use and display of action buttons

- -

*A*ction buttons allow visitors to your Domino Web site to navigate through the site (or other sites on the Web) and execute commands such as creating or deleting a document.

You define specific actions buttons to a particular view or form. You can certainly share them among forms and views, but the fact that they are specific allows you to create buttons that just have an importance at a particular time. For example, if I am in edit mode in a document, I don't want an Edit button that puts the document in edit mode; I don't want the clutter. The Edit button should only appear to your users when they are in read mode.

Action buttons appear as icons and text at the top of the form or view in what is called the button bar (see Figure 11-1).

Figure 11-1:
The action
button bar.

Breaking Old Habits

 If you're accustomed to developing applications that only Lotus Notes clients access, and you rely on allowing your users to navigate and execute commands via menus, you need to gently rewire your brain. Web browsers don't have menus for navigating and executing commands, and just about everybody who'll be accessing your Web server will do so with their Web browsers. Get used to your users needing to click on text links, image maps, or action buttons to get things done on your server.

Web browsers also don't support buttons in forms (aside from the submit button and the button used for attaching files, which are both Notes-supplied buttons). So you have to use action buttons to give your forms button functionality.

Creating Actions

The action buttons that you create appear in the button bar at the top of either a view or a document. Creating action buttons is easy.

Creating a form action

Adding action buttons to your forms allows your users not only to execute commands, but to navigate to other parts of the site or to other sites on the Web when the users are creating, editing, or reading documents. Again, although your users can use action buttons with a Web browser, you can't create them with one; you have to use the Lotus Notes client to create them. To create an action button, do the following:

1. **Launch the Lotus Notes client.**

   The Lotus Notes Workspace, which displays the Domino Web server's databases as rectangular icons, appears.

2. **Click the icon for the database containing the form to which you want to add the action button**

3. **Choose <u>V</u>iew⇨<u>D</u>esign.**

   The database opens. Refer to Chapter 6 if Design does not appear in the View menu.

4. **Click the Forms folder in the Navigation pane.**

   All the forms in the database appear in the View pane.

5. **Double-click the name of the form to which you want to add an action button.**

The form appears in Design mode.

6. **Choose View⇨Action Pane.**

The Action pane appears, displaying the names of all the actions associated with the form. You don't have to do this step to create an action, but I recommend it so that you can make sure that an action button which performs the desired task hasn't already been created.

7. **Choose Create⇨Action.**

The Properties for Action InfoBox appears, and you see Untitled in the Action pane (see Figure 11-2).

8. **Type the title of the action in the Title box and then click the green check mark to confirm the new title.**

The title appears on the action button that users see in their Web browsers and in the list of actions in the Action pane.

9. **Click the drop-down arrow next to the Button Icon box and select an icon.**

10. **If Lotus Notes clients will be used to view the form, click the Include action in Action menu check box.**

For Notes clients, checking this box makes the action appear in their menus. If your users will use the form only through a Web browser, *don't* check the box; see the next step.

11. **Click the Include action in button bar check box.**

If this box is not checked, Web browsers don't display the action button.

12. **In the Position text field, type the position number where you want the new action button to appear in the action button bar.**

For example, if you want the action button to be the third one in the action button bar (which appears at the top of a form or view) type **3**.

Several of the actions listed in the Action pane may not appear on the action bar, either because they execute a formula that Web browsers don't support, or because the Include action in button bar check box hasn't been checked. All the action buttons have an assigned position number, but not all buttons will appear on the action button bar when viewed from a Web browser, so you may get unexpected results when specifying positions.

For example, an action button that you specify to be in position five may actually display first if the action buttons specified for positions one through four can't display in the action button bar for one of the previously stated reasons.

Action InfoBox   Action Pane

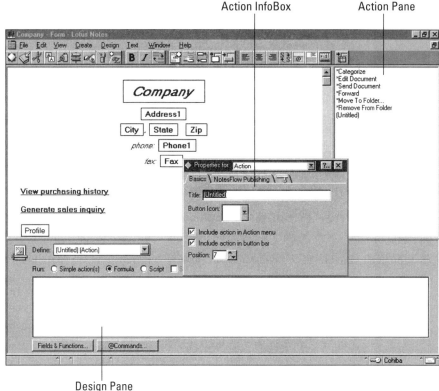

Figure 11-2:
A form in
Design
mode
displaying
the Action
pane and
the Action
InfoBox.

Design Pane

13. In the Design pane, click the Formula radio button.

This selects Formula as the Run option. Actions created with the other Run options — Simple action(s) and Script — do not translate to Web browsers.

14. Type the action's formula in the formula window of the Design pane, and click on the green check mark to confirm the formula.

See Figure 11-3. Click the Fields & Functions button to bring up a listing of the fields in the database and of all the @Functions. Click the @Commands button to get a listing of the @Commands. Keep in mind that some @Commands in the list don't translate to Web browsers.

System actions, Simple actions, LotusScript actions, and actions that use unsupported @Commands don't translate to the Web browser, meaning they don't show up on Web browsers. Certain @Commands, such as @Command([EditClear]), are supported and can appear in forms, but not in views. Unsupported action buttons don't appear in the Web browser, which alleviates a major headache for you — you don't have to worry about buttons that don't do anything sneaking onto your Web document.

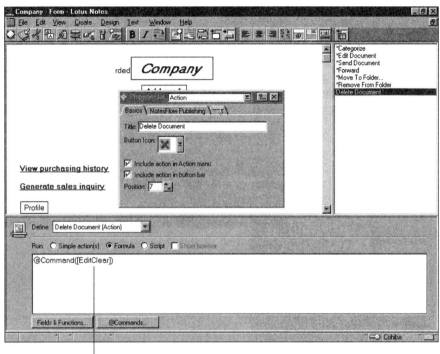

Figure 11-3:
An action
button's
formula.

Formula that executes when users click the action button

Creating a view action button

You create a view action button in almost the same way you create a form action button (see the section immediately prior). The only differences are: In Steps 2 and 3, you click the Views folder in the Navigation pane to display the views in the database, and then you double-click in the View pane on the name of the view to which you want to add an action.

The Action bar on a Lotus Notes client displays only a certain number of action buttons (the number varies depending on the length of the action buttons' titles). If you create more action buttons than can fit on the action bar, users of Lotus Notes clients simply won't see them. Web browsers, on the other hand, display all the action buttons; they display in the Action bar and their text wraps so that more buttons can fit on the action bar. Keep in mind, however, that if you run into a case where you are displaying a ton of action buttons, you're shirking your responsibility to be a clutter-free developer. You won't make many friends if you create a cluttered interface for your users!

System actions

The Action pane includes six predefined actions, called *system actions* (see Figure 11-4), which work great in an environment in which only Lotus Notes clients access the server. Your whole reason for reading this book and using the Domino Web server is to enable users with Web browsers to access your server, though. These system actions won't do you any good, because Web browsers don't support them; they simply don't show up on-screen when your Web browser users open views or documents that contain them.

Figure 11-4:
Web
browsers
don't
support the
system
actions.

*Categorize
*Edit Document
*Send Document
*Forward
*Move To Folder...
*Remove From Folder

You can, however, write a formula to create actions that perform the same functions as these system actions. For example, you can mimic the Edit Document system action by creating an action that executes the @Command([EditClear]) formula. Actions not specified in the following section, "Action Buttons in Action," are beyond the scope of this book.

Action Buttons in Action

As in any walk of life, when you develop a Domino Web site, you should always treat people the way you would want to be treated if your situations were reversed. I'm sure that when you visit a Web site, you expect to be treated to a clutter-free and easy-to-use environment. When you create actions, you can go a long way toward making friends if you keep the interface clutter-free by displaying only buttons that are relevant to your users' current activities.

For example, if your users are reading documents, it makes sense to display a button that allows them to edit the documents. After the user presses the button and puts the document in Edit mode, continuing to display the edit button is pointless. Why display an action button that puts a document in Edit mode within a document that's already in Edit mode? That's just needless clutter.

Here are some of the more popular buttons to include in your Web site. The sections following this list detail how to create these buttons.

- ✔ **Work with documents:** Include action buttons that let users create, edit, and delete documents. A save action button isn't necessary, because every document, by default, has a submit button (which performs the same function) embedded in it. Keep in mind that some of these buttons can appear only in forms; for example, you can't create an edit action button for a view.

- ✔ **Navigation:** Create action buttons that allow users to navigate to other views in the database, other databases on the Domino Web site, or other sites on the Web. You can do the same thing with hypertext links, but the buttons are so *snazzy!*

- ✔ **Search:** Create an action button that lets users execute a search of the entire database. Every view, by default, includes a link that executes a search in that particular view. If you want your users to be able to execute a search of the entire database, however, and that particular view doesn't include all the documents in the database, you need to create an action button that does include all documents. Also, if you want your users to be able to execute a search of a group of databases or all the databases on the Domino Web server, you need to create an action button for that search function.

- ✔ **Access other elements:** Create action buttons that enable users to open navigators, agents, and the database's help documents. See Chapter 6 for more about these elements.

Creating documents

Users of your Domino Web site can create documents with the touch of a button — if you go through the hassle of creating a Create Document button that uses a formula to create a document. The following formula allows you to create an action that creates a new document with the specified form:

```
@Command([Compose];"server";"database";"form")
```

For example, @Command([Compose];"";"sales.nsf";"Account Pro-file") creates a new document with the Account Profile form in the sales.nsf database on the current Domino Web server. @Command([Compose];"Account Profile") does the same thing if the button is being executed in the sales.nsf database.

Before users may use a Create Document action button, they must have at least Author access in the database's ACL. See Chapter 15 for more about the ACL and its levels of access.

Editing documents

You can put an Edit Document button on your Web site that permits the user to edit documents. The `@Command([EditDocument])` formula edits the document that is currently in Read mode. You can't use this formula in a view action.

Before users may use the Edit Document action button, they must have Editor access or higher in the database's ACL, or else have Author access and be specified in the document's Authors field. See Chapter 15 for more about the ACL and its levels of access.

Getting rid of documents

Create a Delete Document button if you want your Web site users to be able to delete entire documents. The `@Command([EditClear])` formula deletes the document that is currently in either Read or Edit mode. You can't use this formula in view actions.

As with so many of the neat buttons, the ACL restricts this function to certain users. Before users may use this action button, they must not only have Author access or above in the database's ACL, but the Delete documents check box in the ACL dialog box must also be enabled. See Chapter 15 for more about the ACL and its levels of access.

Insight into navigating in site

You can use `@Command([OpenView])` to create a button that navigates a user to another view in the same database; you need only supply the name of the view. For example

```
@Command([OpenView];"North East")
```

navigates the user to the North East view in the database.

If you've worked with Notes before, you may be familiar with using the following `@Command`:

```
@Command([OpenView];"ViewName";"Key")
```

where `Key` specifies the name of the document that the cursor highlights when a user opens the view. Be aware that the `Key` works only when the view is accessed with a Lotus Notes client; if you specify the `Key` argument in the formula, the action button doesn't appear in Web browsers.

Outta sight! — navigating outside site

To open another site on the Internet or another database on the server, you can use URL syntax used in conjunction with the @URLOpen formula. For example

```
@URLOpen("http://www.netvibes.com")
```

opens the www.netvibes.com Web site.

Where is that document?

Users can search the active view by clicking the Search hyperlink, at the top and bottom of every view, by default. If the view doesn't contain all the documents in the database, however, enabling users to do a search of all database documents requires you to create an action button.

The formula

```
@URLOpen("http://www.netvibes.com/policy.nsf/All+Documents/
         $SearchForm?SearchView")
```

presents users with the default search form they can use to search the All Documents view in the policy.nsf database of the www.netvibes.com Domino Web server. If you use this formula, create an All Documents view that displays all the documents in the Web site (and be sure to create a Full Text Index for each database). See Chapter 10 for more information about how to create the All Documents view; see Chapter 14 to find out about creating a Full Text Index.

You can create a button that enables the user to search a group of databases, or all the databases on the Domino Web server. Just use the following formula:

```
@URLOpen("http://131.107.8.30/searchsite.nsf/
         $SearchForm?SearchSite")
```

This formula presents users with a default search form that they can use to search a special full-text indexed database, called searchsite.nsf. The database includes specifications for groups of databases on the Domino Web server that can be searched as a group.

Accessing navigators, agents, and help documents

Your buttons can also perform more complex actions than just enabling searches or putting documents in Edit mode. You can use the `@Command([OpenNavigator])` formula to open certain elements. For example

```
@Command([OpenNavigator];"Real Estate")
```

displays the `Real Estate` navigator. As soon as users click the action button, the navigator is displayed to their Web browsers. They can then click the hotspots in the navigator to navigate through the Web site or execute commands.

The formula

```
@Command([ToolsRunMacro];"Process Inspections")
```

executes the `Process Inspections` agent. The agent runs on the server and can either process documents or execute commands, depending upon what the Web site developer has designed it to do.

This formula

```
@URLOpen("http://www.architecture.com/tribeca.nsf/
          $about?OpenAbout")
```

opens the About Database document in the `tribeca` database on the `www.architecture.com` Domino Web server, and

```
@URLOpen("http://www.architecture.com/tribeca.nsf/
          $help?OpenHelp")
```

opens the Using Database document in the `tribeca` database on the `www.architecture.com` Domino Web server. After either of the help documents display on users' Web browsers, the users can click the text links to either navigate through the site or execute commands.

Copying the Design of Action Buttons

I assume a couple of things about you. First, you consider your Domino Web site, and therefore the action buttons in your Domino Web site, to be exquisite works of craftsmanship. Second, you like to work efficiently and to use your time effectively, so that you don't have to spend as much time laboriously coding action buttons as you do learning and playing.

With these two assumptions in mind, I'll tell you something you'll like about action buttons; they can be shared among multiple forms and views. If you create a great action button, you don't have to re-create it manually in any other form or view in which you want to use it. You simply copy it to other forms or views.

Using the Clipboard

Using the Windows Clipboard is the easiest way to copy an action button from one form or view to another. If you're running Domino in Windows NT, follow these steps:

1. **Launch the Lotus Notes client.**

   The Lotus Notes Workspace, which displays the Domino Web server's databases as rectangular icons, appears.

2. **Click the icon for the database that contains the action button.**

3. **Choose View⇨Design.**

   The database opens. See Chapter 6 if Design does not appear in the View menu.

4. **Click the Forms (or Views, depending upon whether you are copying a form's action or a view's action) folder.**

   The names of the databases' forms (or views) appear in the view pane.

5. **Double-click the name of the form (or view) you want to edit.**

   The form (or view) appears in Design mode.

6. **Choose View⇨Action Pane.**

   The Action pane appears.

7. **Click the action that you want to copy.**

8. **Choose Edit⇨Copy, or click the Edit Copy SmartIcon.**

   You can't copy system actions to the Clipboard, but Web browsers don't support them anyway, so you're not out anything on that count.

9. **Press Esc to exit Design mode.**

10. **To put the form in Design mode, double-click the form or view to which you want to paste the action.**

11. **Choose View⇨Action Pane.**

    The Action pane appears with the cursor in it — a necessary ingredient to pasting the action.

12. Choose Edit⇨Paste.

The pasted action appears in the Action pane. The Paste option is grayed out if you don't have the cursor positioned in the Action pane.

Although any action button that you paste from a form to a view appears in the Action pane, some action buttons that appear in the action button bar of a form do not appear in the action button bar of a view.

13. Press Ctrl+S to save the form or view.

Controlling Action Button Use and Display

You can prevent people from using action buttons and seeing action buttons. You may have an application that only allows people in a certain department or people who are above a certain management level to be able to click on an action button and create a document. While you're at it, since only certain people can use the action button, you may as well make sure that only those certain people can see the action button. The last thing your users need is to have a button displaying on their Web browsers that doesn't do anything when they click on it.

Who can use action buttons?

The security model you set up in the Access Control List (ACL) works with action buttons. For example, you could use action buttons in the design of a Human Resources database with an ACL that enables members of the Human Resources department to read and create documents while the rest of the employees in the company can only read the documents.

If you're an HR manager, you should be thrilled because only you are allowed to create documents in the corporate HR intranet site. If you're an employee in another department, though, you should be sad, because now you're going to have to forget about finding that security hole that would allow you to create a document in the company's Human Resources database declaring your birthday as a company holiday, or a new policy that reimburses employees 100 percent of the cost of their family vacations.

Anyhow, what's pleasing to developers is that, if a document has a Create Document action button, and some users do not have Author access in the ACL, an authentication dialog box prompts for their names and passwords (see Figure 11-5). If they have access to create documents and they specify the correct password, they are authenticated to create documents. If they do not have the ability to create documents, another dialog box (see Figure 11-6) tells them that they aren't authenticated (or in this case *authorized*, which is basically the same thing).

Figure 11-5:
The Authentica-tion dialog box.

Figure 11-6:
Oops! You don't have access.

When are action buttons seen?

As a developer of a Domino Web site, you can hide an action button based on certain conditions. For example, you can display an action button that lets a user who's reading a document switch it into Edit mode, but which vanishes as soon as they click it and enter Edit mode. You can also create a formula that hides the button from certain people or members of certain groups.

To specify hide options for an action button:

1. **Double-click the form or view to put it into Edit mode.**

2. **Choose View⇨Action Pane.**

   The Action pane appears.

3. **Double-click the name of the action.**

   The Properties for Action InfoBox appears (see Figure 11-7) .

4. **Click the Hide tab.**

   The Hide tab looks like a rolled-up window shade. The tab holds all hiding options for an action.

5. **Click the appropriate Hide check box.**

   You can choose any or all of the options listed next to Hide action when document is. Check the Previewed for reading box or Previewed for editing box if you don't want the user to see the action button when he or she is previewing the document for reading or editing, respectively (keep in mind that these options only affect your users who are accessing the information with Lotus Notes clients, because no way exists to preview a document with a Web browser). Check the Opened for reading box or Opened for editing box if you don't want the user to see the button when he or she has opened the box for reading or editing, respectively.

6. **If you click the Hide action if formula is true radio button, type a formula in the formula box.**

   Use the @Username formula to hide the button if the user must be someone in particular. Keep in mind that all Web users have the name Anonymous unless they have logged in. To force users to log in, assign No Access to Anonymous in the ACL; that way, all users have to specify their name and password when they enter the database. In this situation, the Domino Web server knows who people are. (See Chapter 15 to find out how to get the Web user's name from the log.)

In Figure 11-7, the formula @UserName="Mike Summers" hides the button from Mike Summers and displays it for everyone else. To display the button for Mike Summers and hide it from everyone else, the formula would read @UserName!="Mike Summers". You can also create groups in the Public Address Book, and can make sure users are members of a group.

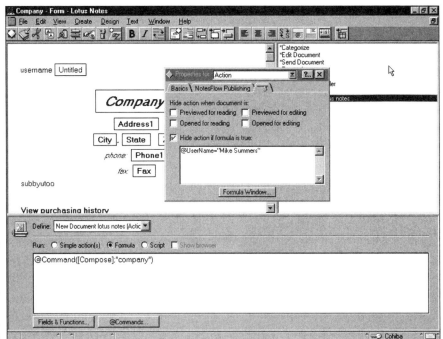

Figure 11-7:
The Properties for Action InfoBox.

Chapter 12

Navigators as Good as Columbus

*W*hen you think of top-notch navigators, you should think of Christopher Columbus and the Domino Web server. "What?" you say, "Christopher Columbus a top-notch navigator? Didn't he find America only because he couldn't find his way to his intended destination of Asia?"

To the contrary, Christopher Columbus is one of history's most effective navigators. Aided only by a compass, an *astrolabe* (an instrument that determines your distance from the equator by calculating the altitude of the sun, moon, and stars), and the belief that the Earth is round, he set out to find a westward route to China. And he would have succeeded, had a little continent called America not been in his way. So Columbus was a great navigator and were it not for his navigation skills, not only would the Spanish monarch Isabella never have had the opportunity to try sweet potatoes and plantains (which Columbus brought back to Spain with him), but this book may never have been written.

You can create navigators just as good as Christopher Columbus on your Domino Web server.

What Are Navigators?

Navigators are image maps (or pictures with areas called *hotspots* that are designed to do something when users click them) that enable users to maneuver through and execute commands in your Domino Web site, or to maneuver to other sites on the Web.

Using navigators, you can enable your users to do the following:

✔ Maneuver to databases, views, documents, and other navigators in your Domino Web site

✔ Open a URL to a different site on the Web

✔ Use a form to create content on your Domino Web site

✔ Execute agents on the Domino Web server

Designing Navigators

Before you can create a navigator for your Domino Web server, you must create an image. Unfortunately, you can't create images in Lotus Notes. Consequently, designing a navigator takes a couple of distinct steps that involve separate applications. First you create an image in an application other than Lotus Notes. Then you start up Lotus Notes and use that image to create your navigator.

Preparing the image

I can't give you much information on creating an image for use as a navigator. Several whole books deal with the topic of creating images. I can offer one piece of advice, though: Create navigator images no larger than the size of a standard Web browser window — about 640 pixels (9.0 inches) wide by 405 pixels (5.5 inches) long.

The general steps that you must complete before you do anything in Notes to create the navigator are:

1. **Create an image with a graphics editor.**

   Figure 12-1 shows an image in Microsoft Paint, just one of many graphics applications that you can use to create your image.

2. **Save the image.**

   Technically (if you're using Windows NT or X Windows in UNIX) you can skip saving the image to a file and just copy the image to the Clipboard without saving it. You don't have to save the image to be able to use it on your Domino Web site. All the same, though, you really ought to save it. You never know when you may need your image to create other navigators, or to edit the first or any other navigator you create using the image.

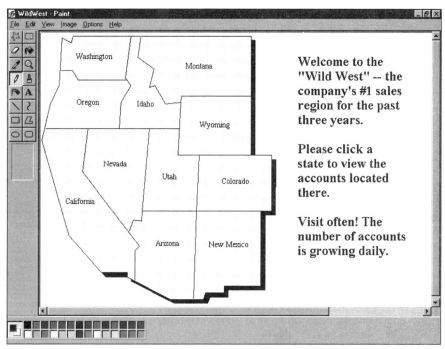

Figure 12-1:
An image in
Microsoft
Paint.

3. **Copy the image to the Windows Clipboard in Windows NT or the X Windows Clipboard equivalent in UNIX.**

In the graphics application you use to create the image, choose Edit⇔Copy to copy the image to the Clipboard. Any image that you can copy to the Clipboard can be used as a Domino Web site navigator.

Creating a new navigator

Regardless of how you ready an image to use as a navigator, you must first have it in the Clipboard before you can use it in your Domino Web site. After you copy the image to the Clipboard, you're ready to commence creating the navigator in Lotus Notes. Follow these steps:

1. **Launch the Lotus Notes client.**

The Lotus Notes Workspace, which displays the Domino Web server's databases as rectangular icons, appears.

2. **Click the icon for the database in which you want to create the navigator.**

3. Choose View⇨Design.

The database opens. If you don't see Design in the View menu, choose View⇨Show⇨Design.

4. Choose Create⇨Design⇨Navigator.

The navigator builder window appears (see Figure 12-2).

5. Choose Create⇨Graphic Background.

The image you copied to the Windows Clipboard appears as the navigator's background.

Although you can choose Edit⇨Paste to get the image in the Clipboard to appear as the navigator's background, I strongly discourage you from doing so. In order for the Domino Web server to convert the navigator to a Web image map, the graphic you paste from the Clipboard must align to the absolute upper-left corner of the navigator builder window. Choosing either Create⇨Graphic Background or Edit⇨Paste initially pastes the graphic into that position, but if you choose Edit⇨Paste you can inadvertently move the graphic out of that

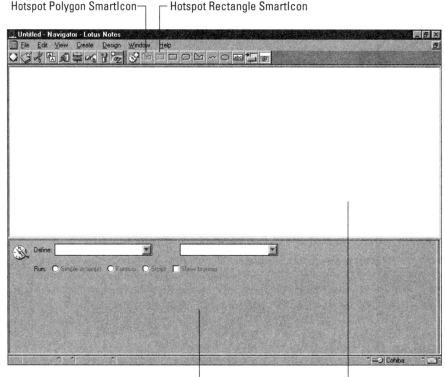

Figure 12-2:
A new
navigator in
Design
mode.

position while you are working in design mode. Graphics that you add by choosing Create➪Graphic Background, on the other hand, cannot be moved at all.

Users receive the error message shown in Figure 12-3 when they open a navigator in which you have failed to make sure that the image is aligned with the absolute upper-left corner of the navigator builder window.

Figure 12-3: Possible result for the user if you paste an image into a navigator.

6. **Choose Create➪Hotspot Rectangle or choose Create➪Hotspot Polygon.**

   This step enables a region of the image as a hotspot. The cursor becomes a crosshair in the Navigator builder window, so decide which type of hotspot you want to use.

   - **Rectangular hotspot:** Use this type of hotspot if you want to enable a rectangular region of the image as the hotspot. Users with Web browsers can click any part of the rectangle to execute the hotspots formula.

   - **Polygonal hotspot:** Yes, "polygonal" is a word! And it has nothing to do with marrying more than one person at the same time. It is an adjective used to describe a figure that is bounded by three or more straight lines. Use the polygon hotspot when you need to draw a freehand shape that could have an unlimited number of connected lines. If your image is a map of the United States and you want to let users click individual states to open views specific by state, this is a perfect time to use the polygon hotspot. Although Colorado and Wyoming are pretty close to being perfect rectangles, your users are going to have a tough time opening views to the other 48 states if you don't draw a freehand polygon hotspot around their borders.

7. **Place your cursor on the region in the image where you want the hotspot and draw it.**

   If you're drawing a rectangular hotspot, hold the mouse button down and drag the cursor (see Figure 12-4); the hotspot appears when you let go of the mouse button. If you're creating a polygonal hotspot, click the mouse button where you want the hotspot to begin and move the cursor in a straight line to the next angle in the polygon, click the mouse button again, and so on, until the hotspot you have drawn borders the region.

8. **After you draw the hotspot, double-click with the mouse to enable the hotspot.**

   The hotspot then appears as a thick red outline. At the same time, the Properties for Hotspot InfoBox appears, and the Design pane changes so you can create a formula. (Make sure the Basics tab of the InfoBox is forward; you can safely ignore the HiLite tab. Web browsers don't support the settings in that tab, which allow you to specify when and how the hotspot's border appears.) Figure 12-5 shows a completed rectangle hotspot, Figure 12-6 a completed polygon hotspot.

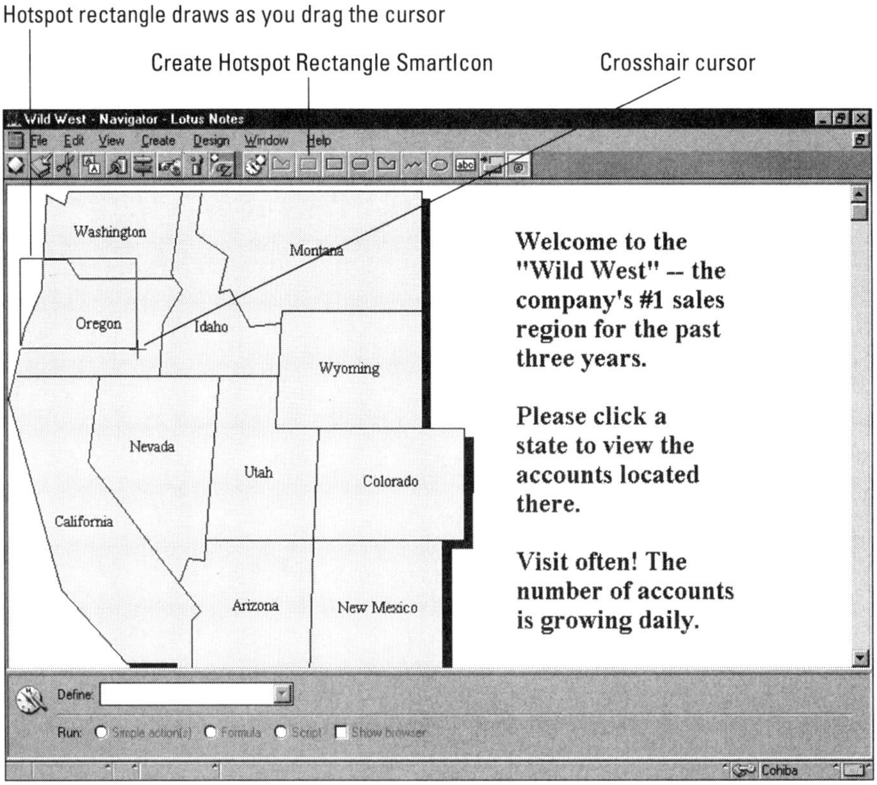

Hotspot rectangle draws as you drag the cursor

Create Hotspot Rectangle SmartIcon

Crosshair cursor

Figure 12-4: Drag cursor to create a rectangular hotspot bordering Oregon.

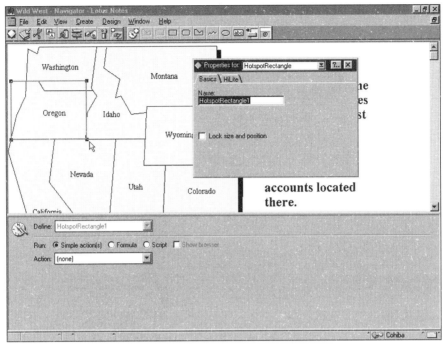

Figure 12-5:
A rectangle
hotspot.

Figure 12-6:
A polygon
hotspot.

9. **Type the hotspot's name in the Name text area of the Properties for Hotspot InfoBox.**

10. **Click the Lock size and position check box.**

    Enabling this check box prevents against inadvertently moving the hotspot to another region on the image.

11. **Select either the Simple action(s) radio button or the Formula radio button as the Run option in the Design pane.**

    Web browsers don't support the Script option.

12. If you selected the Simple action(s) radio button, choose an action from the Action drop-down list.

Figure 12-7 shows the Action drop-down list. You can create a simple action that opens a navigator, opens a view, opens a URL, or opens a link to another database, view, or document. The only choice in the Simple action(s) drop-down list that Web browsers don't support is `Alias a Folder`. Figure 12-8 shows an example of a simple action that opens the Oregon Accounts view.

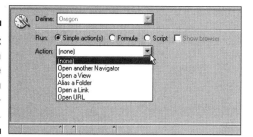

Figure 12-7:
Select a simple action from the drop-down list.

Figure 12-8:
The simple action opens a view called Oregon Accounts.

13. If you selected the Formula radio button, specify a formula in the formula window.

Figure 12-9 shows the formula equivalent of the simple action (shown in Figure 12-8) that opens the Oregon Accounts view.

Figure 12-9:
The formula opens a view called Oregon Accounts.

Mouse pointing at hotspot

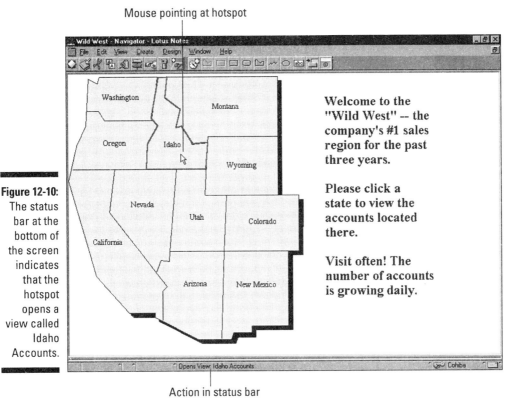

Figure 12-10:
The status
bar at the
bottom of
the screen
indicates
that the
hotspot
opens a
view called
Idaho
Accounts.

Action in status bar

14. Press Ctrl+S to save the navigator.

After you create the hotspots in the navigator, you can test what each
hotspot does. Choose Design➪Test Navigator to put the navigator in Test
mode. As you move the cursor around in the navigator, the status bar
indicates what each hotspot does. For example, when you roll the cursor
over the Idaho hotspot, the status bar indicates that the hotspot opens the
Idaho Accounts view, as shown in Figure 12-10.

Editing an existing navigator

As you work on your Domino Web site, you end up editing existing navigators in addition to creating new ones. For example, after your company
expands into markets in other regions, you have to create a new navigator
for your intranet site that includes an image of the new region. To edit an
existing navigator, follow these steps:

1. **Launch the Lotus Notes client.**

   The Lotus Notes Workspace, which displays the Domino Web server's databases as rectangular icons, appears.

2. **Click the icon for the database that contains the navigator you want to edit.**

3. **Choose View▷Design.**

   The database opens. If you don't see Design in the View menu, refer to Chapter 6.

4. **Click the Navigators folder.**

   The names of the database's navigators appear in the View pane.

5. **Double-click the name of the navigator you want to edit.**

   The navigator appears in Edit mode.

After you add the image to the navigator, you can add nothing more, except hotspots. Although the navigator drawing tools include options for adding rectangles, rounded rectangles, ellipses, polygons, lines, text, and buttons, Web browsers don't support any of these features. If you want to draw anything on an image, you must do it in your graphics editing program.

Opening Navigators

After you create the navigator, how do you and your users open it on a Web browser? You can do this a number of ways. One way is to have it automatically open as the site's home page. Another way is to click an action button, text link, or a hotspot in another navigator. And a third way is to type the Domino-specific URL syntax for opening a navigator in your Web browser.

Look! No hands!

If you want the navigator to act as your Home Page, have the navigator open automatically when users first open the database:

1. **Launch the Lotus Notes client.**

   The Lotus Notes Workspace, which displays the Domino Web server's databases as rectangular icons, appears.

2. **Click the icon for the database that you want the navigator to automatically open.**

3. **Choose File▷Database▷Properties.**

   The Properties for Database InfoBox appears (see Figure 12-11).

Figure 12-11:
Specify
in the
Database
InfoBox a
navigator
that you
want to
automatically
open.

   4. **Click the Launch tab.**

   5. **Choose Open designated Navigator in its own window from the On Database Open drop-down list.**

   6. **In the Navigator drop-down list, choose the navigator that you want to automatically open.**

      You can close the InfoBox by clicking the X icon in its upper-right corner. You don't need to save the setting; as soon as you select the navigator name from the drop-down list, it is enabled.

   This setting immediately takes effect. The next person to open the database is presented with the navigator you just specified as the Home Page.

Clicking an action button

You can open the navigator through an action button, in either a view or a form. To create a button that executes a navigator:

   1. **Launch the Lotus Notes client.**

      The Lotus Notes Workspace, which displays the Domino Web server's databases as rectangular icons, appears.

   2. **Click the icon for the database to which you want to add the action button.**

   3. **Choose View➪Design.**

      The database opens. If you don't see Design in the View menu, refer to Chapter 6.

   4. **Click either the Forms folder or the Views folder, depending on whether you are creating an action button in a form or a view.**

      The names of the forms (or views) in the database appear in the View pane.

5. **Double-click the name of the form (or view) to which you want to add the action.**

   The form (or view) appears in Edit mode.

6. **Choose Create➪Action.**

   The Properties for Action InfoBox appears (see Figure 12-12).

7. **Type a name for the button in the Title text area and select an icon for the action button from the Button Icon drop-down list.**

8. **In the Design pane, click the Formula radio button of the Run option.**

9. **Type the** @Command([OpenNavigator];"*navigatorname*") **formula in the formula window.**

   Figure 12-12 shows the formula window in the Design pane.

10. **Press Ctrl+S to save the form or view.**

Using the sample shown in Figure 12-12 creates an action button that, when the user clicks it, the Wild West navigator appears.

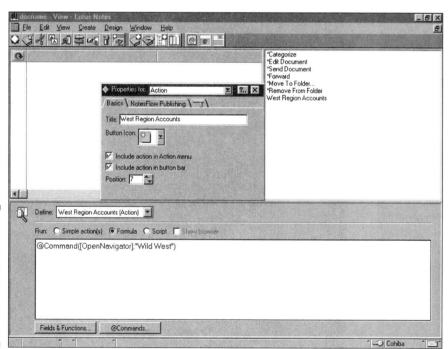

Figure 12-12:
The action
button you
create
opens a
navigator
called Wild
West.

Clicking a text link

You can have the navigator open through a text link on a document. To create a text link that opens a navigator, follow these steps:

1. **Launch the Lotus Notes client.**

   The Lotus Notes Workspace, which displays the Domino Web server's databases as rectangular icons, appears.

2. **Click the icon for the database to which you want to add the text link.**

3. **Choose View➪Design.**

   The database opens. If you don't see Design in the View menu, see Chapter 6.

4. **Click the Forms folder.**

   The names of the database's forms appear in the View pane.

5. **Double-click the name of the form to which you want to add the text link.**

   The form appears in Edit mode.

6. **Type the text that you want to function as the link, and then highlight it.**

7. **Choose Create➪Hotspot➪URL Link.**

   The URL Link Object InfoBox appears (see Figure 12-13).

8. **Type the Domino-specific URL syntax for opening a navigator in the formula window.**

   The syntax is

   ```
   http://servername/databasename/
           navigatorname?OpenNavigator
   ```

9. **Press Ctrl+S to save the form.**

Now when the user clicks the text you just created, the navigator appears. In the example URL, `http://131.107.8.30/Tribeca.nsf/Wild+West?OpenNavigator` (see Figure 12-13), the link opens a navigator called Wild West.

Notice that the plus sign (+) replaces any spaces in the navigator name.

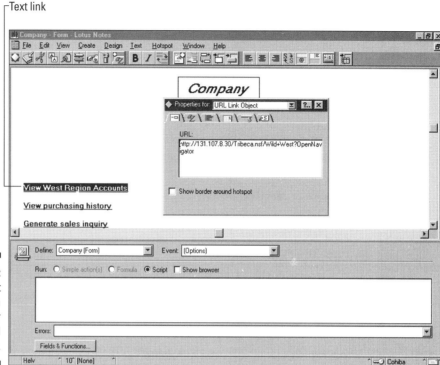

Text link

Figure 12-13:
This text
link opens a
navigator
called Wild
West.

Typing a URL

You can open a navigator by specifying the Domino-specific URL syntax in your Web browser. Also you can use this URL syntax in a navigator's hotspot formula to enable a navigator to open another navigator. The syntax is

```
http://servername/databasename/navigatorname?OpenNavigator
```

The URL `http://131.107.8.30/tribeca.nsfWild+West?OpenNavigator` (shown in Figure 12-14) opens the Wild West navigator in the `Tribeca.nsf` database on the Domino Web server that has an IP address of `131.107.8.30`. You can specify the name of the server instead of the IP address.

Notice that a plus (+) sign replaces any space that appears in the navigator name.

Figure 12-14:
The Wild
West
navigator
URL.

Location: http://131.107.8.30/Tribeca.nsf/Wild+West?OpenNavigator

Part III
How to Win Accolades and Influence People

 By Rich Tennant

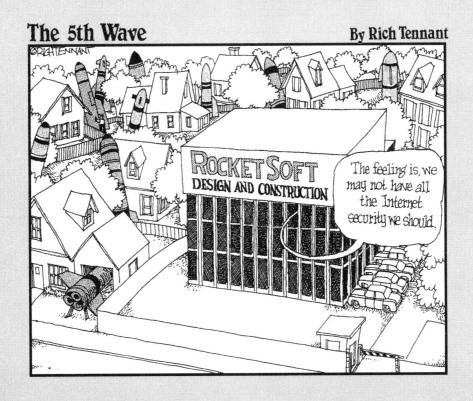

ROCKET SOFT DESIGN AND CONSTRUCTION

"The feeling is, we may not have all the Internet security we should."

In this part . . .

Developing a business Web site takes a lot of work. For employees inside the corporation and clients outside, the site must necessarily be useful, must be fully functional, and must be secure. For all the users to be impressed, the site must look good while it provides those necessities.

Domino takes some of the more onerous site-building tasks by the horns and wrestles them to the ground. For example, setting up good, responsible, and thorough security throughout your entire site is a breeze with Domino. This next group of chapters covers the heavy-duty functions of Domino. Master these and you'll be the topic of discussion during the next corporate board meeting — or at the very least, your manager won't snarl at you for a few days.

Chapter 13

Secret Agents

*A*gents are background processes you create to run on your server. They can make changes to documents and can execute actions such as mailing, moving, or deleting documents. You decide whether you want users to manually execute agents from their Web browsers or whether you want the server to automatically execute them when a particular condition is met. If you decide on the latter, you must determine just what conditions must be met to trigger the agent's execution. You could, for example, have an agent execute when a document is mailed in to the server, whenever a document is created or modified, or when a period of time (hour, day, week, or month) expires.

Don't be confused by the name of this chapter; agents are "secret" only in the sense that they are your "secret weapon" against any competitors not running their Internet or intranet sites on a Domino Web server. Agents on the Domino Web server can do some powerful things. For example, agents can automatically archive documents that are a certain age, they can send reminder e-mail messages to people who have not taken action on a document, they can send an e-mail warning to people when inventory is low or when an account has gone beyond its credit limit, and they can search for information that matches a profile you set up and e-mail you the results.

If you implement a workflow scheme with your Internet or intranet site, the agents are the brains and muscles that enable the workflow to happen without user intervention.

If you're a LotusScript guru, you're going to have a good time designing agents. Of all the features on your Domino Web server that you can use formulas to execute (action buttons, text links, navigators, fields, columns, and so on), agents are the only ones you can use LotusScript to create formulas for, because agents are the only LotusScript-programmable feature that can benefit users of Web browsers.

Working with Agents

You probably find yourself creating agents from scratch, not so much because you view yourself as an artist who must create an original masterpiece, but because you are either doing different things with your Internet or intranet site than your peers are, or are doing the same thing differently. Although most of your work might be different from that of others, nothing is wrong with tweaking someone else's work if you have the opportunity and permission. Knowing how to create agents from scratch and knowing how to edit existing agents are necessary skills in creating a really far-out Domino Web site!

Creating a new agent

I know society is moving toward being paperless, but when it comes to application development such as making an agent, I think you'll find that you benefit greatly from sitting down with a piece of paper and pencil (with your computer turned off) and jotting down what you want the agent to do and how you want it to do it. Say this five times fast: "The flow of a flowchart's flow doesn't slow the flow of the mind's flow." I'm confident that the time you spend to create a flowchart for the agent is time you'll be glad you spent.

After you jot down what the agent does and how you want it to do it, you're ready to create. Follow these steps to make an agent:

1. **Launch the Lotus Notes client.**

   The Lotus Notes Workspace, which displays the Domino Web server's databases as rectangular icons, appears.

2. **Click the icon for the database in which you want to create the agent.**

3. **Choose View⇨Agents.**

   The database opens with the Agents folder active, displaying the database's agents in the View pane.

4. **Choose Create⇨Agent.**

   A new agent appears in Design mode (see Figure 13-1).

5. **Type a name for the agent in the Name text area.**

   Your users accessing the database with Web browsers won't see the name, but you should still give it a name that describes its purpose. A good name for your agent makes future design enhancement or troubleshooting a bit easier.

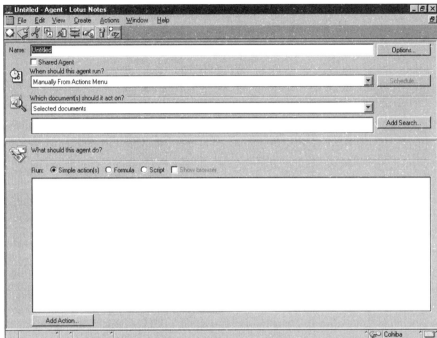

Figure 13-1:
An agent in
Design
mode.

6. Click the Shared Agent check box.

If you don't check this option, your users get an error when they try to execute the agent (see Figure 13-2).

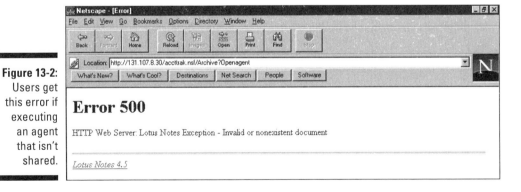

Figure 13-2:
Users get
this error if
executing
an agent
that isn't
shared.

Error 500

HTTP Web Server: Lotus Notes Exception - Invalid or nonexistent document

Lotus Notes 4.5

7. **Select a Web-supported choice from the When should this agent run? drop-down list.**

   The choices are:

   - **Manually From Actions Menu** or **Manually From Agent List:** Web browsers don't support actions menus, and your users won't find any agent lists on their Web browsers. You can select either of these run options if people are executing the agent by clicking an action button, text link, or navigator hotspot, or if they're typing the Domino-specific URL that executes agents. (See Chapters 5, 11, and 12 for more information on URLs, action buttons, and navigators, respectively.)

   - **If New Mail Has Arrived:** Select this run option if you want the agent to execute any time that a document is mailed in to the database.

   - **If Documents Have Been Created or Modified:** Select this run option if you want the agent to execute when users either create or modify documents. Click the Schedule button to specify a range of dates in which you want to enable the agent and whether to enable it on weekends.

   - **If Documents Have Been Pasted:** Web browsers don't support this option.

   - **On Schedule Hourly:** Select this option if you want the agent to execute once every 30 minutes, hour, two hours, four hours, or eight hours. Click the Schedule button to specify the time increments at which you want the agent to run, a range of times in the day in which to enable the agent, a range of dates in which to enable the agent, and whether to enable the agent on weekends.

   - **On Schedule Daily:** Select this option if you want the agent to execute once every day at a specific time. Click the Schedule button to specify the time of day you want the agent to start, a range of dates in which to enable the agent, and whether to enable the agent on weekends.

   - **On Schedule Weekly:** Select this option if you want the agent to execute once every week on a specific day of the week and time. Click the Schedule button to specify the day of the week and the time of the day you want the agent to start, and a range of dates in which to enable the agent.

   - **On Schedule Monthly:** Select this option if you want the agent to execute once every month on a specific date and time. Click the Schedule button to specify the date and the time of the day when you want the agent to start, and a range of dates in which to enable the agent.

- **On Schedule Never:** Select this option if you want to disable the agent. You may find this option convenient if you're troubleshooting and just want to temporarily disable the agent.

8. Choose a Web-supported choice from the Which document(s) should it act on? drop-down list.

This is the first of two steps for specifying what documents you want the agent to act upon when it executes. The selections differ, depending on the choice you make in Step 7 concerning when to enable the agent to run. If you specify that the agent run whenever new mail arrives, the agent runs only on newly received mail documents. If you specify that the agent run if anybody creates or modifies documents, the agent runs only on the newly created or modified documents. If you specify that the agent run manually, you can choose any of the following six options concerning which documents it can act upon. If you specify that the agent run on a scheduled basis, you can choose from only the first two of these six options.

- All documents in database

- All new and modified documents since last run

- All unread documents in view

- All documents in view

- Selected documents (not supported by Web browsers)

- Run Once (@Commands may be used)

9. Click the Add Search button.

This is the second of the two steps for specifying what documents you want the agent to act upon when it executes. The Search Builder dialog box appears (see Figure 13-3). The Search Builder dialog box enables you to create search criteria in a graphical interface. You can create criteria that tells agents to select documents based on date created or modified, the value in a particular field, the form used to create them, or specific words or phrases. Figure 13-4 shows an example of criteria, specified in the Search Builder dialog box, that instructs the agent to act upon documents created more than 30 days ago.

10. In the Design pane, click the Formula radio button or the Script radio button as the Run option.

Although Web browsers do support a few of the simple actions, such as Modify Field, they don't support most of them. When users select an unsupported simple action, they receive an error. Fear not, though; you can reproduce all the simple actions that Web browsers *do not* support by using formulas.

11. Type the formula in the formula window of the Design pane.

12. Press Ctrl+S to save the agent.

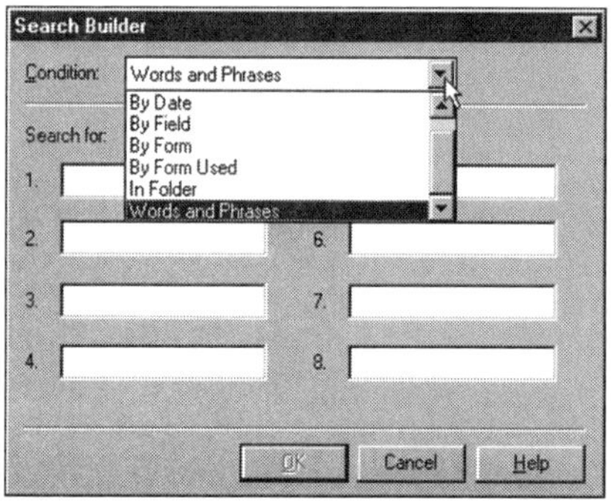

Figure 13-3:
You can
further
define what
documents
the agent
acts on.

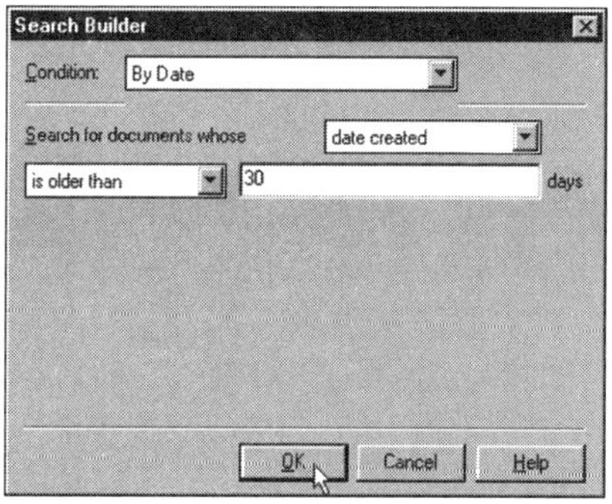

Figure 13-4:
The Search
Builder
dialog box.

Editing an existing agent

Your Domino Web site evolves and grows over time, so in addition to creating new agents, you need to edit existing ones. To edit an existing agent, follow these steps:

1. **Launch the Lotus Notes client.**

    The Lotus Notes Workspace, which displays the Domino Web server's databases as rectangular icons, appears.

2. **Click the icon for the database that contains the agent you want to edit.**

3. **Choose View⬎Agents.**

    The database opens.

4. **Click the Agents folder.**

    Normally the Agents folder is already selected by default. The names of the database's agents appear in the View pane.

5. **Double-click the name of the agent you want to edit.**

   The agent appears in Edit mode.

6. **Make desired edits.**

   For example, you can change when the agent should run or on what documents it should act upon, or change what the agent does by changing its formula.

7. **Save the agent.**

Running Agents on Doc Open and Save

As discussed in the previous section, you can create agents that users execute manually by clicking an action button, text link, or navigator hotspot, or by typing the Domino-specific URL in their Web browsers. You can also create agents that the Domino Web server automatically executes based on a schedule, or whenever users mail, create, or modify documents. You can also create agents that the Domino Web server automatically executes when users open or save a document.

Run before the starting gun

When users open a document, the Domino Web server converts the Lotus Notes document to HTML and sends it to users' Web browsers. You can specify that an agent run between the time the document is requested by a Web browser and when it is actually displayed to the Web browser — and you are correct if you think that this time period is only about a split second. Developers commonly specify this type of execution if they want to perform a process or computation that can only be done with LotusScript. Because the Domino Web server only supports LotusScript in agents and not in, say, action buttons or text links, using LotusScript with agents is a way you can have a LotusScript formula execute on a specific document.

To specify an agent that can execute LotusScript (as well as non-LotusScript) formulas between the time the document is requested by a Web browser and actually displayed to the Web browser, follow these steps:

1. **Create a field, and name it $$QueryOpenAgent.**

   I discuss creating a field in Chapter 9. After you name the field, you should see a screen like the one in Figure 13-5.

Figure 13-5:
Create the
$$QueryOpen
Agent field.

2. From the Type drop-down list boxes, choose Text and Editable.

Text and Editable are the default values for new fields.

3. In the Design pane, type the name of the agent (enclosed in quotes) for the field's Default Value.

Although the name of the agent is not case-sensitive, the name you put in the default field must exactly match the name of the agent in every other way — number of characters, punctuation, and spaces. The name of the agent in Figure 13-6 is "UpdateAccountLog."

4. Save the form by choosing File⇨Save.

Now that the form is saved, the agent you specified in Step 3 executes any time that a user opens a document created with the form.

Figure 13-6:
Specify the
agent's
name
enclosed in
quotes as
the field's
Default
Value.

When you're creating the agent that is specified in the $$QueryOpenAgent field, make sure that the following are true:

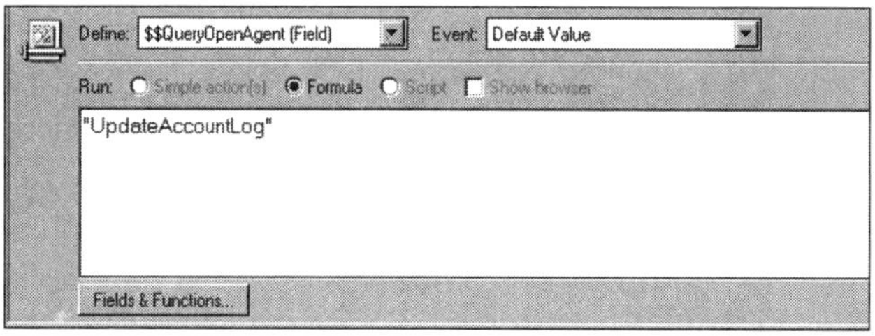

✔ You typed the agent's name as the exact name specified in the $$QueryOpenAgent field's default value (Figure 13-7).

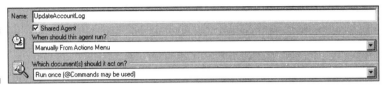

Figure 13-7:
The Agent.

✔ You selected the Shared Agent check.

✔ You chose Manually From Actions Menu from the When should this agent run? drop-down list.

✔ You chose Run once (@Commands may be used) from the Which document(s) should it act on? drop-down list.

Run after the finish line

To save a document to the server's hard drive, users click the Submit button that Domino automatically puts on an editable document. If you want to use the values in the document to perform another operation, for example, you can specify that an agent run after the user clicks the Submit button but before the document actually saves to disk.

If you want an agent to execute when a user saves a document, the name of the field must be $$QuerySaveAgent, you must enclose the name of the agent that you want to execute in quotes, and you must specify the agent as the field's default value. Be sure to follow the same rules for creating the field (except the name of the field) and agent as detailed in the section "Run before the starting gun."

If you're using Input Translation and/or Input Validation formulas in conjunction with a $$QuerySaveAgent field that contains LotusScript, be sure to include a refresh at the beginning of the agent's LotusScript formula. You want to do that because the QuerySave event occurs before the Input Translation and Input Validation formulas calculate. If you do not refresh these calculations before the QuerySave event occurs, the QuerySave event could process incorrect or incomplete information.

Other Ways to Run Agents

You can create a number of ways for an agent to execute. You can make it so the Domino Web server executes the agent automatically or users execute it by clicking on an action bar, text link, navigator hotspot, or by typing the URL. This section covers the different ways you can design an agent to execute.

Automatic execution

When creating the agent, if you specify that the server automatically execute agents when certain conditions are met, your job is done; the agents run from here to eternity every time the conditions you designate are met. Neither you, as the designer, nor your users visiting the site with Web browsers need to do anything to execute the agents. The conditions you can specify as times when agents should execute automatically are as follows:

- ✔ When a document is mailed in to the database
- ✔ When a document has been created or modified
- ✔ Once every 30 minutes, hour, two hours, four hours, eight hours, day, week, or month (refer to the section "Creating a new agent" earlier in this chapter for the steps to create a time-specific agent)

Clicking an action button

You can have the agent execute when users click an action button in a view or in a form. To create a button that executes an agent, do the following:

1. **Launch the Lotus Notes client.**

    The Lotus Notes Workspace, which displays the Domino Web server's databases as rectangular icons, appears.

2. **Click the icon for the database that you want the button to appear in.**

3. **Choose View⇨Design.**

    The database opens. If Design does not appear in the View menu, refer to Chapter 6 for help.

4. **Click the Forms folder or the Views folder, depending on whether you are creating an action button in a form or a view.**

    The names of the database's forms (or views) appear in the View pane.

5. **Double-click the name of the form (or view) to which you want to add the action.**

    The form (or view) appears in Edit mode.

6. **Choose Create⇨Action.**

    The Properties for Action InfoBox appears.

7. **In the Properties for Action InfoBox, type a name for the action in the Name text field and select an icon for the action button from the Button Icon drop-down list.**

8. **Click the Formula radio button for the Run option in the Design pane.**

9. **Type** `@Command([ToolsRunMacro];"`*agentname*`")` **in the formula window.**

   Figure 13-8 shows how to run an agent called ArchiveDocs.

10. **Press Ctrl+S to save the form (or view).**

Figure 13-8:
The action
button
opens an
agent
called
ArchiveDocs.

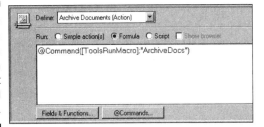

Clicking a navigator hotspot

You can have an agent execute when users click a hotspot in a navigator. To create a navigator and hotspot that executes an agent, follow these steps:

1. **Copy an image to the Windows Clipboard (in Windows NT) or the X Windows Clipboard equivalent (in UNIX).**

   Because you can't create images in Notes, you must create or import an image in your desired graphics application that you want as your navigator. After you have created the image and copied it to the Clipboard, you can begin the Notes-specific steps for creating the navigator.

2. **Launch the Lotus Notes client.**

   The Lotus Notes Workspace, which displays the Domino Web server's databases as rectangular icons, appears.

3. **Click the icon for the database that you want the button to appear in.**

4. **Choose View⇨Design.**

   The database opens. If Design does not appear in the View menu, refer to Chapter 6 for help.

5. **Choose Create⇨Design⇨Navigator.**

   The navigator appears in Design mode.

6. **Choose Create⇨Graphic Background.**

   Choosing Graphic Background opens the navigator builder window and pastes the image currently stored in the Clipboard into it.

7. Choose Create⇨Hotspot Rectangle or Create⇨Hotspot Polygon.

The cursor appears as a crosshair when it's in the navigator builder window. You use the crosshair cursor to draw the hotspot.

8. Click and drag to draw the hotspot with the crosshair cursor and click once when you're finished drawing.

The InfoBox for the hotspot appears after you draw the hotspot.

9. Click the Formula radio button for the Run option in the Design pane.

The formula window appears.

10. Type `@Command([ToolsRunMacro];"agentname")` **as the formula in the formula window.**

Figure 13-9 shows an action button that runs an agent called ArchiveDocs.

11. Press Ctrl+S to save the navigator.

Figure 13-9:
The action
button
opens an
agent
called
ArchiveDocs.

Clicking a text link

You can have the agent execute when users click a text link in a document. To create a text link that executes an agent:

1. Launch the Lotus Notes client.

The Lotus Notes Workspace, which displays the Domino Web server's databases as rectangular icons, appears.

2. Click the icon for the database that you want the button to appear in.

3. Choose View⇨Design.

The database opens. If Design does not appear in the View menu, refer to Chapter 6 for help.

4. Click the Forms folder.

The names of the database's forms appear in the View pane.

5. **Double-click the name of the form to which you want to add the text link.**

   The form appears in Edit mode.

6. **Type the text that you want to function as the link, and highlight it.**

7. **Choose Create⇨Hotspot⇨URL Link.**

   The Properties for URL Link Object InfoBox appears.

8. **In the URL window of the Properties for URL Link Object InfoBox, type in the Domino-specific URL syntax for executing agents.**

   The syntax is:

   ```
   http://servername/databasename/agentname?OpenAgent
   ```

   Figure 13-10 shows an example of a text link that executes the ArchiveDocs agent in the `accttrak.nsf` database. Notice that the IP address of the Domino server was used in place of the server name.

9. **Press Ctrl+S to save the form.**

Figure 13-10:
This text
link
executes an
agent
named
ArchiveDocs.

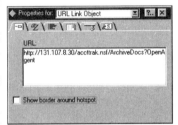

Typing a URL

You can have an agent execute when a user specifies a Domino-specific URL syntax in a Web browser. The syntax is:

```
http://servername/databasename/agentname?OpenAgent
```

The URL shown in Figure 13-11 executes the ArchiveDocs agent in the `accttrak.nsf` database on the Domino Web server that has IP address of `131.107.8.30`. You can specify the name of the server instead of the IP address.

Figure 13-11:
URL that
executes an
agent
named
ArchiveDocs.

Location: http://131.107.8.30/accltrak.nsf/ArchiveDocs?OpenAgent

Popular Agents

Now that you know the nitty-gritty about making agents, I want to offer you some specific examples of ways you can use agents.

Keep tabs on the sales force

Say you have a sales force automation intranet site, and all sales leads are tracked in the database. Say you also have a workflow process that enables the flow of documents through the sales qualification process.

You could use an agent that reminds you when you need to take action on a lead. If you manage a group of sales reps, you can have an agent that, if a lead has been in the database for three days and has not been acted upon (that is, has not been modified in some way), first sends a message to your mail file alerting you that a certain rep hasn't taken action on a particular lead. The agent then sends a message to the sales rep alerting him that he needs to take action. Lastly, if the rep still hasn't attended to the lead after five days, the agent sends you another message alerting you of that fact.

If you would rather not receive a message to your mail file, you could opt to have the lead flagged in the database as a way to alert you.

Don't let them slide too far

You could have an accounts receivable agent that alerts you when a particular account exceeds a dollar value of credit, or that alerts you when an account has been overdue for a certain number of days.

Working with documents

You can create agents that do any of a number of things to your documents.

You can create agents that change the values in your documents or append additional data to the values already present in fields. You can create agents to delete documents that contain a certain value or have been in the database for a certain period of time. You can create an agent that archives documents after a certain period of time.

Workflow

The most common use of agents involves using them to deal with workflow. Say you have an approval process application that requires an employee to get his manager and vice president to sign off on something. In that sort of situation, you wouldn't want the document requesting the vice president's approval to appear on her desk until after your manager has given his approval. After all, why even present the idea to the vice president if your manager wouldn't approve it?

You could create a workflow process that sends the document to your vice president immediately after your manager signs off on it. You would create an agent that enables this workflow. As soon as a field, say the manager's status field, changes from pending to approved, the agent sends the document to your vice president.

If you don't want the document mailed to your manager and vice president, you might create an agent that displays the document in a view that only the vice president can see. As soon as the vice president approves the document, it appears in that view.

Chapter 14
The Search Goes On!

. . . .

In This Chapter

▶ Executing a search

▶ Incorporating search buttons and links

▶ Designing a single view or single database search

▶ Designing a multiple database search

. . . .

So you have great information at your Domino Web site. Excellent! Now, how do you make that information easily accessible? You could, for one, allow the user to execute a search for documents matching criteria the user specifies.

Consider a scientific research intranet site that has 5,000 documents from which a scientist is trying to find information on a particular subject, say "Helminthosporium dematioideum." Domino may not know that Helminthosporium dematioideum is a fungus (just wait until the *next* release), but it does know that 34 of the 5,000 documents contain information on Helminthosporium dematioideum, and if the scientist searches on this text string, Domino returns those 34 documents.

Say your Internet site lists all your products. Instead of forcing consumers to read each document to find the product (and possibly give up and take their business elsewhere if it takes too long), you can allow them to simply execute a search for the product. Users can search a single view in a database, a single database, a group of databases, or all the databases on the Domino Web server.

In this chapter, I explain how you can make your Domino Web server seek out specific information contained in your Notes database. Visitors to your site will appreciate the power of a Domino search engine, and you'll appreciate how Lotus made this process so easy.

Creating Searches

Users who view your Domino Web site via Web browsers can execute searches by typing a URL, clicking an action button, or clicking a link. If you want to create action buttons or links, you must be familiar with search URLs, because they are the code behind those action buttons and links.

Search URLs explained

You can use two types of search URLs for users to search your Domino Web site: the SearchView URL and the SearchSite URL. Each type works best in specific situations.

The SearchView URL

The SearchView URL enables users to search a single view. Its syntax is:

```
http://Host/Database/View/
          [$SearchForm]?SearchView[ArgumentList]
```

- ✔ **Host:** The name of the Domino Web server (for example, www.cabanawear.com).

- ✔ **Database:** The name of the target database of the search.

- ✔ **View:** The name of the target view of the search.

- ✔ $SearchForm: An optional parameter that tells the server to display the Full Text Search window so that the users can create a search.

- ✔ ?SearchView: An action that tells the Domino Web server to search the view that the user specifies (in the specified database).

- ✔ ArgumentList: An optional parameter that Domino ignores if the user specifies $SearchForm. If the user doesn't specify $SearchForm, however, and does specify ArgumentList, Domino displays the Search Results window instead of the Full Text Search window, listing the documents that match the search criteria specified in the ArgumentList. The syntax of the ArgumentList is:

  ```
  &Query=Search String;Search Order;Search
           Thesaurus;Search Max;Search Word Variants
  ```

  - • Search String: Specify the word or phrase you are searching for.

  - • Search Order: Specify the value 1, 2, or 3, where 1 is for a "Relevance" sort, 2 is for an "Oldest first" sort, and 3 is for a "Newest first" sort. The default is 1.

- Search Thesaurus: Specify TRUE or FALSE, where TRUE indicates to find word variations as defined by the thesaurus and FALSE to find exact matches only. The default is FALSE.

- Search Max: Specify the maximum number of matching documents to display. The default is 0, which indicates to display all matching documents.

- Search Word Variants: Specify TRUE or FALSE, where TRUE says to find variants of the search word or phrase, and FALSE to find only the exact word. TRUE is the default.

Here is an example of a search URL that uses all of the ArgumentList components:

```
http://www.maltisse.com/sales.nsf/accounts/
        ?SearchView&Query=Bartley;1;TRUE;15;TRUE;
```

This URL searches the accounts view in the sales.nsf database on the www.maltisse.com Domino Web server. The ArgumentList components specify, reading left to right, to search for the string "Bartley," to sort the results by relevance, to use the thesaurus, to return no more than 15 documents, and to search word variants.

If you want to set up a search that encompasses all the documents in an entire database, use the SearchView URL to search a view that displays all the documents in the database.

The SearchSite URL

The SearchSite URL enables you to search a group of databases or all the databases on the Domino Web server. Its syntax is:

```
http://Host/Database/[$SearchForm]?SearchSite[ArgumentList]
```

The syntax of the SearchSite URL differs in only two ways from the syntax of the SearchView URL:

- ✔ The SearchSite URL does not have a view component.
- ✔ The ?SearchSite action tells the Domino Web server to search a group of databases instead of a view.

The SearchSite URL uses the same arguments as the SearchView URL.

Search buttons in view and forms

You can create a search action button in a view or in a form. Your users click these buttons to execute a search. To create a search action button in a view or form, follow these steps:

1. **Launch the Lotus Notes client.**

   The Lotus Notes Workspace, which displays the Domino Web server's databases as rectangular icons, appears.

2. **Click the icon for the database to which you want to add a search button.**

3. **Choose View⇨Design.**

   The database opens. Refer to Chapter 6 if Design does not appear in the View menu.

4. **Click the Views (or Forms, depending upon whether you are creating the action button in a view or form) folder.**

   The names of the databases' views (or forms) appear in the view pane.

5. **Double-click the name of the view (or form) in which you want to create the action button.**

   The view (or form) opens in Design mode.

6. **Choose Create⇨Action.**

   The Properties for Action InfoBox and the Action pane appear (see Figure 14-1).

Action InfoBox   Action pane

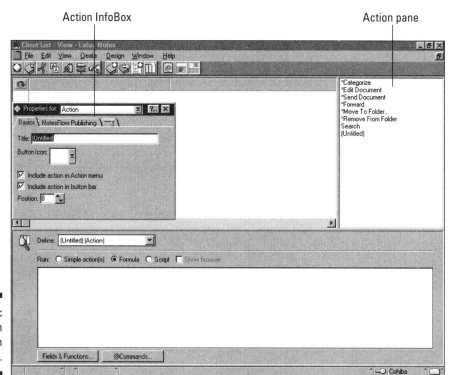

Figure 14-1:
A view in
Design
mode.

7. **Replace** (Untitled) **in the Title box of the Properties for Action InfoBox with the name you want your users to see in the action button.**

8. **Choose an icon from the Button Icon drop-down list.**

   Your users will see this icon in the action button.

9. **Make sure that the Include action in button bar check box remains checked (the default).**

   Otherwise your users won't see the button.

10. **In the Design pane, select the Formula radio button as the Run option.**

11. **Type the search URL in the formula window of the Design pane.**

    You must enclose the search URL in quotes and put it in the @URLOpen @Function in the formula window; otherwise you get an error when trying to save the formula. For example, rather than simply typing

    ```
    http://www.cabanawear.com/sales.nsf/Client+List/
          $SearchForm?SearchView
    ```

    into the formula window, you type

    ```
    @URLOpen("http://www.cabanawear.com/sales.nsf/
          Client+List/$SearchForm?SearchView")
    ```

Notice that the name of the view specified in the preceding example, Client List, includes a space in it. You must replace this space with a plus sign (+), as in Client+List, or users get an error when they click the action button.

Figure 14-2 shows the formula for an action button called Search, and Figure 14-3 shows what the button looks like to users with Web browsers.

Search links in standard views

All *standard* views (that is, ones that you haven't customized) include a default search link (as shown in Figure 14-4). These default search links search only the view in which they appear. You may decide that the default search link suits your users' needs perfectly, in which case you don't need to design an action button or a link.

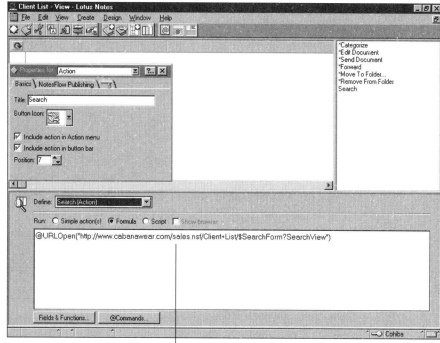

Figure 14-2:
A search action button in design mode.

Search action button formula

Search action button

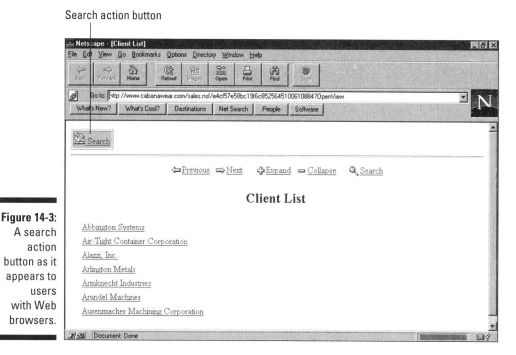

Figure 14-3:
A search action button as it appears to users with Web browsers.

Search link

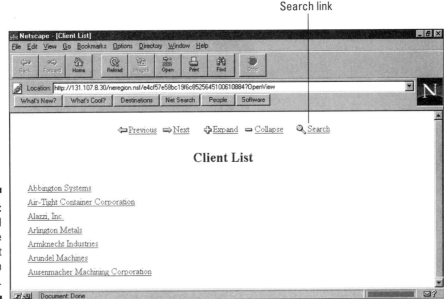

Figure 14-4:
All standard
views have
default
search
links.

Search links in forms

Creating action buttons isn't the only way to enable your users to execute searches; you can also enable text links. To create a search text link, follow these steps:

1. **Launch the Lotus Notes client.**

   The Lotus Notes Workspace, which displays the Domino Web server's databases as rectangular icons, appears.

2. **Click the icon for the database containing the form to which you want to add a text link.**

3. **Choose View⇨Design.**

   The database opens. Refer to Chapter 6 if Design does not appear in the View menu.

4. **Click the Forms folder in the Navigation pane.**

   The forms in your database display in the View pane.

5. **Double-click the label box for the form in which you want to create the search link.**

   The form opens in Design mode.

6. **Type the text you want to serve as the link in the form and highlight it as shown in Figure 14-5.**

7. **Choose Create⇨Hotspot⇨URL Link.**

The URL Link Object InfoBox appears (see Figure 14-6).

8. **Type the search URL into the URL formula box.**

Unlike with the action button, you don't have to enclose the URL in quotes or use it in conjunction with @URLOpen. Simply specifying the URL as follows works fine:

```
http://www.cabanawear.com/sales.nsf/Client+List/
          $SearchForm?SearchView
```

9. **Press Ctrl+S to save the form.**

Highlighted text to be the search link

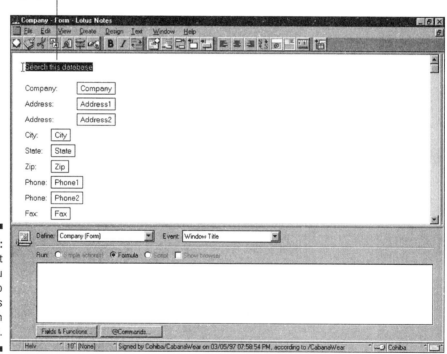

Figure 14-5:
Highlight the text you want to function as the search link.

URL formula box

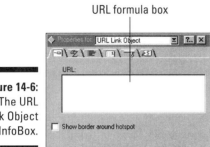

Figure 14-6:
The URL
Link Object
InfoBox.

Figure 14-7 shows how the form looks in a Web browser. Notice how the mouse cursor changes from an arrow to a hand with a pointing finger when it's on the search link.

Searching a single database

I mention at the beginning of this chapter that you can search a single database, but how? After all, the SearchSite URL searches a group of databases, and the Searchview URL searches a specific view in a database.

Search link   Mouse pointer

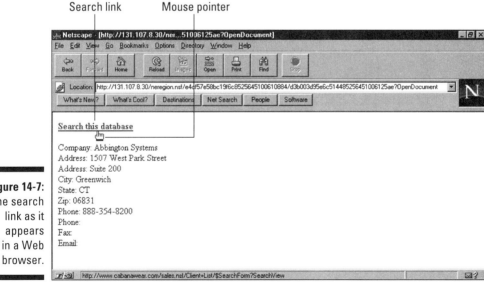

Figure 14-7:
The search
link as it
appears
in a Web
browser.

Well, all you need to do is create a view within the database you want to search that displays all the documents in the database, and then use the SearchView URL to search that view. In essence, then, you are searching the entire database. Refer to Chapter 10 for more information on creating a view that includes all documents.

Designing Searches for a View or Database

After you create a search action button or a link, your next step is to prepare the database to be searchable. As I mention in the last section, to search a database, you must first have a view that displays all the documents in the database. If you haven't created such a view within the database, see Chapter 10 to find out how.

In order for the Domino Web server to find documents, you must create a Full Text Index for the database, either when you first create the database or after you or someone has already created it. The Full Text Index is comprised of a group of files created on the Domino Web server's hard drive. These files index the words contained in documents and attachments in the Domino Web site. The Full Text Index can be continually updated so that as new documents or attachments are added to the site, they are included in the Full Text Index.

Creating the Full Text Index when you first create the database

When you create the database, simply select the Create full text index for searching check box in the New Database dialog box (see Figure 14-8), which is specified in Step 7 of the following list.

To create a database with a Full Text Index, follow these steps:

1. **Launch the Lotus Notes client.**

   The Lotus Notes Workspace, which displays the Domino Web server's databases as rectangular icons, appears.

2. **Choose File⇨Database⇨New.**

   The New Database dialog box appears.

Figure 14-8:
You can
create the
Full Text
Index when
you first
create the
database.

3. **Specify the server name in the Server text box.**

   Click the down arrow and scroll until you find the server name that you want.

   The default for the Server text box is Local; keep that as the server name if you want to store the database on the machine you work on. Otherwise, type in the name of the server where you want to store the database.

4. **In the Title text box, type in your database title.**

   The database title is the name users see when they view the list of databases on your Domino Web server.

5. **In the File Name text box, type in the filename and directory under which you want to store the database.**

6. **Set the size limit for the database and do not specify that the database be encrypted.**

   The database encryption feature is not supported by the Domino Web server; it is only for users accessing the database with Lotus Notes clients.

7. **Select the Create full text index for searching check box.**

8. **Click the Template Server button and, from the scroll box, select a template name on which to base the design of your new database.**

   The template server defaults to "Local," which indicates the hard drive of the machine on which you are working. When the "Show advanced templates" check box is selected both the default templates and the templates that are specified as advanced appear in the scroll box. This is a confusing option, because none of the templates that ship with the software are marked as "advanced," so if you select this check box you don't notice a change in the scroll box.

9. **When you're finished, click OK.**

Creating the Full Text Index after the database has been created

If you want to create a Full Text Index for a database that already exists, or if you want to update or delete an existing Full Text Index for a database, follow these steps:

1. **Launch the Lotus Notes client.**

   The Lotus Notes Workspace, which displays the Domino Web server's databases as rectangular icons, appears.

2. **Click the icon for the database for which you want to create the Full Text Index.**

3. **Choose File➪Database➪Properties.**

   The Properties for Database InfoBox appears (see Figure 14-9).

Figure 14-9:
The
Properties
for
Database
InfoBox.

4. **Click the Full Text tab.**

5. **Click the Create Index button.**

   The Full Text Create Index dialog box appears (see Figure 14-10).

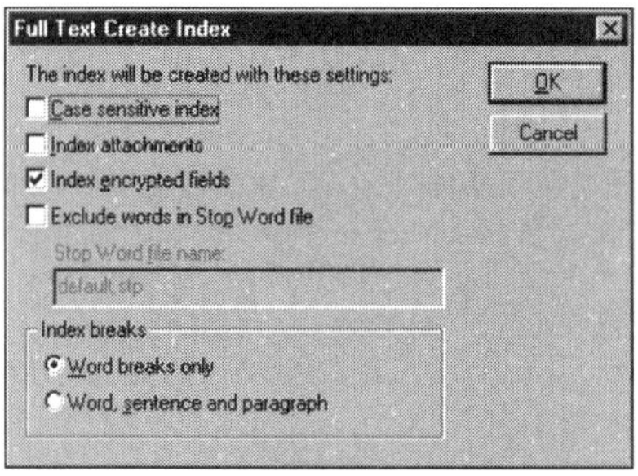

Figure 14-10:
The Full
Text Create
Index dialog
box.

The Full Text Create Index dialog box presents the following options:

- **Case-sensitive index:** Click this check box to index words once for each case occurrence; for example, to make separate index entries for "Street" and "street."

- **Index attachments:** Click this check box to index words in files that are attached to documents.

- **Index encrypted fields:** Click this check box to index words in encrypted fields.

- **Exclude words in Stop Word file:** Click this check box to specify words (appearing in the Stop Word file) to specifically *not* index. For example, if you include words in the Stop Word file such as "the," "and," "or," "a," and so on, Domino doesn't index those words.

- **Word, sentence and paragraph:** If you select this radio button, users can execute *proximity operators*. For example, users can restrict their search to find only documents with the words "red" and "bicycle" in the same paragraph or in the same sentence.

- **Word breaks only:** If you select this radio button, a search finds all matches to the search item, regardless of where in the document the word appears, or the proximity of the word to other words included in the search criteria.

6. **Click OK.** The new database and its Full Text Index are created.

Designing Searches for a Group of Databases

You can enable users to search a group of databases or all the databases on your Domino Web server by creating a Search Site database and using the SearchSite URL. The Search Site database is only utilized when searching a group of databases; it is not necessary when searching a single database or a view within a database. You may want to create multiple Search Site databases on your Domino Web server if you have different databases that belong to distinct groups or categories. For example, the sales department may want all of their databases to belong in one search group, and Human Resources may want all of their databases to belong in another search group.

Creating the Search Site database

When you create a Search Site database, you need to base its design on the Search Site template (`srchsite.ntf`). To create the Search Site database:

1. **Launch the Lotus Notes client.**

   The Lotus Notes Workspace, which displays the Domino Web server's databases as rectangular icons, appears.

2. **Choose File➪Database➪New.**

   The New Database dialog box appears (see Figure 14-11).

Figure 14-11:
The New Database dialog box.

3. **Click the Server drop-down list and choose the server on which to store the database.**

4. **Click the Title text box and type in the title of the database.**

5. **Click the folder icon next to the File Name text box and choose the file name of the database you want.**

6. **Click the Create full text index for searching check box.**

7. **Click the Template Server button to select the name of the server where the Search Site template is located.**

   The default, Local, signifies the machine at which you are working.

8. **Select the template called Search Site from the scroll box at the bottom of the New Database dialog box.**

   The Search Site template's file name is `srchsite.ntf`, which appears next to the About button.

9. **Click OK.**

   The Search Site database is created.

Preparing a database to be searchable

Decide what databases you want to include in the search group. After you make that decision, you're ready to specify which databases on the Domino Web server are to be included in site searches. Follow these steps:

1. **Select a database that you want to include in the database group.**

2. **Choose File⇨Database⇨Properties.**

   The Properties for Database InfoBox appears (see Figure 14-12).

Figure 14-12:
The
Database
InfoBox.

3. **Click the Design tab.**

4. **Check the Include in multi database indexing check box.**

   Individual databases included in a site search don't have to be full text indexed, but if you want searches to include their documents, you need to enable this check box. This setting takes effect immediately; you do not have to do anything else to save it.

If you need to check this box for a number of databases, don't go to the database InfoBox for each database. Instead, go to the Server Administration Panel and take care of the matter globally by following these steps:

1. **Choose Files⇨Tools⇨Server Administration.**

2. **Click the Database Tools button.**

   The Tools to Manage Notes Databases dialog box appears (see Figure 14-13).

3. **Click the databases for which you want to enable multi-database indexing.**

   To select more than one database, press the Ctrl key as you click the databases.

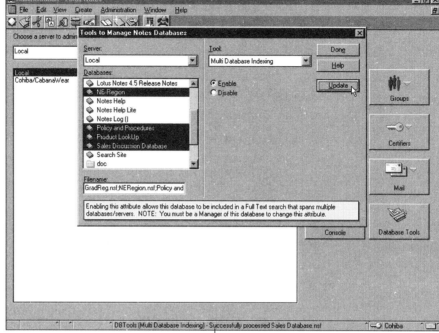

Figure 14-13:
Specify
Multi
Database
Indexing to
index a
group of
databases
easily.

Status bar message

4. In the Tool drop-down box, choose Multi Database Indexing.

5. Click the Enable radio button.

6. Click the Update button.

A message box announces that the databases were successfully processed. The status bar also displays a message that the indexing of the
databases was successfully processed.

7. Click Done.

Configuring the Search Site database

To configure the Search Site database, you must create a document for the
databases included in the search group. Follow these steps:

1. Choose Create➪Search Scope Configuration.

The Multi-Database Search Configuration document appears (see Figure
14-14).

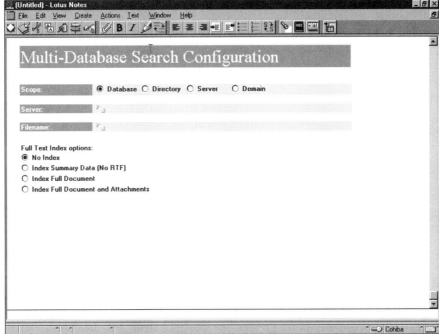

Figure 14-14:
The Multi-
Database
Search
Configuration
document.

2. **Choose a scope for the search.**

   You have four options (as radio buttons): Database, Directory, Server, or Domain. I assume that you specify a server in the following steps, but I also cover what happens if you choose Domain.

3. **Type the name of the server in the Server field.**

   If you selected the Domain radio button in Step 2, you are presented with a Domain field instead of a Server field. Type the name of the domain in that field.

4. **Type the name of the filename in the Filename field.**

   If you selected the Directory radio button in Step 2, you are presented with a Directory field instead of a Filename field. Type the name of the directory in that field.

5. **Choose a Full Text Index option.**

   You have four Full Text Index options:

   - **No Index:** Databases specified in the scope aren't indexed.

   - **Index Summary Data (No RTF):** Only data that appears in views is indexed, which means text in attachments or in rich text fields is not indexed.

- **Index Full Document:** Only data that appears in views and in rich text fields is indexed. Text in attachments is not indexed.

- **Index Full Document and Attachments:** Data that appears in views, rich text fields, and attachments is indexed.

6. Create a full text index the Search Site database.

See "Designing Searches for a View or Database" earlier in this chapter.

You don't need to make sure the individual databases included in the scope are full text indexed, but you do need to make sure that the Search Site database is. Also, make sure that the Include in multi database indexing check box is selected for each individual database.

Chapter 15

Security

*U*sing the tools that Domino provides, you can create a very comprehensive security model for your Domino Web server. You can grant or deny access to different parts of the site. You can determine what those people to whom you grant access can do; for example, you can allow some people to read and create documents, and others only to read documents. And you can implement *SSL (Secure Sockets Layer) security,* which is a protocol that activates authentication when communicating over the Internet.

When granting or denying access to information on the Web site, think of the security model as a series of doors. You can give somebody a key to the first door, which represents access to the actual Web server. After users open the server door, they face a bunch of other doors; these doors represent the individual databases on the server. You can give them keys to all the doors, or just give certain people keys to certain doors. When users open any of the database doors, they face another group of doors; and these doors represent individual documents in a database. Again, you can give them keys to all the doors, or just give certain people keys to certain doors.

At this point, you may be thinking about installing a retina or fingerprint scan device at the doors so that people's keychains don't tear holes in their pockets — but wait, another set of doors awaits. Finally, when users open any of the document doors, they face another group of doors; and these doors represent individual fields in a database. That's right; you can give them keys to all the doors, or just give certain people keys to certain doors.

You utilize the database's Access Control List (ACL) to determine what those users to whom you give access to a database can do in the database; namely, whether they can read, create, edit, or delete documents.

Database Security

If I may refer to the analogy of the keys from the introduction to this chapter, I present the information in this section under the assumption that you have given people the first key — the one that gives them access to the Web server. Determining whether somebody can access a Web server exceeds the scope of this book, though, because server access involves firewalls, protocols, hardware, and security software.

So, now that users can access your Domino Web server, how do you determine what databases they can access and what they can do in those databases? In an acronym — ACL. Each database has an Access Control List (ACL), a list of the individuals or groups that can access the server and what they can do on the server.

To view a database's ACL, follow these steps:

1. **Launch the Lotus Notes client.**

   The Lotus Notes Workspace, which displays the Domino Web server's databases as rectangular icons, appears.

2. **Click the icon for the database that has the ACL you want to view.**

3. **Choose File⇨Database⇨Access Control.**

   The Access Control List dialog box appears (see Figure 15-1).

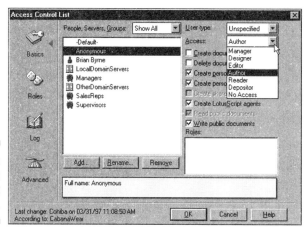

Figure 15-1:
The Access
Control List
(ACL).

Understanding the ACL

The ACL lists individuals and groups specified in the server's Public Address Book, each of which is assigned one of the following seven levels of access:

- **No Access:** Users can't access the server.

- **Depositor:** Users can create documents but can't read them. This level of access is most commonly given in a ballot database, where people can submit a vote but can't see what or who other people voted for.

- **Reader:** Users can read documents but can't create them.

- **Author:** Users can read, create, and edit their own documents.

- **Editor:** Users can do everything Author access allows, plus they can edit other people's documents.

- **Designer:** This level of access applies only to users who use Lotus Notes clients to access the database, not to those who use Web browsers to access it. Users who have this level of access can do everything Editor access allows, plus they can make design changes to the database.

- **Manager:** This level of access applies only to users who use Lotus Notes clients to access the database, not to those use Web browsers to access it. Users who have this level of access can do everything Designer access allows, plus they can do things like make changes to the ACL and replication settings.

The ability to delete documents is not inherent in any of the seven levels of ACL access. None of the levels, including Manager, grant the ability to delete documents, by default. In the ACL, you can choose to grant the ability to delete documents to users who have Author access of above. To grant the ability to delete documents, click the Delete documents check box in the Access Control List dialog box (see Figure 15-2).

You must have Manager level access in a database's ACL to make changes to the ACL. Also, you must make changes on a Lotus Notes client; you can't make changes to the ACL with a Web browser.

Assigning an access level

You can assign a level of access for people accessing the database with Web browsers in a couple of different ways.

Check box to allow document deletion

Figure 15-2:
Granting
the ability to
delete
documents.

Without using the ACL

Without even touching the ACL, you can quickly assign a maximum access level for all users who use Web browsers to access the database. You make this global assignment through the Access Control dialog box that can be brought up in the Lotus Notes workspace. This assignment can limit settings in the ACL.

For example, if a user has Manager access in the ACL and you set the global maximum level to Author for all users who use Web browsers to access the database, then that Manager user only has Author access to the database. The setting, however, can't grant access not allowed through the ACL. For example, if a user has Reader access assigned through the ACL and the global maximum access is set to Manager, then that Reader user still only has Reader access in the database.

To make such an assignment, follow these steps:

1. **Launch the Lotus Notes client.**

   The Lotus Notes Workspace, which displays the Domino Web server's databases as rectangular icons, appears.

2. **Click the icon for the database that has the access level you want to set.**

3. **Choose File⇨Database⇨Access Control.**

   The Access Control List dialog box appears.

4. **Click the Advanced icon.**

   The Access Control List dialog box changes to show different options.

5. **Click the Maximum Internet browser access drop-down list.**

   A drop-down list of access levels appears (see Figure 15-3).

6. **Choose a level of access from the list.**

7. **Click the OK button.**

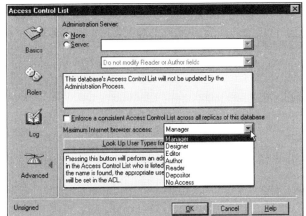

Figure 15-3:
Select a
level from
the drop-
down list.

Setting Web browser access in this manner overrides the ACL. For example, if you set the maximum browser access to Reader, a user who is assigned Manager access in the ACL only has Reader access when she accesses the database with a Web browser. (Of course, she still has Manager access when she accesses the database on a Lotus Notes client.)

Using the ACL

The best way for you to assign a level of access to the database for people using Web browsers is through the ACL, because you can assign different levels of access to different groups and individuals. To use the ACL for assigning access levels for all those who are using browsers, follow these steps:

1. **Launch the Lotus Notes client.**

   The Lotus Notes Workspace, which displays the Domino Web server's databases as rectangular icons, appears.

2. **Click the icon for the database that has the ACL you want to set.**

3. **Choose File➪Database➪Access Control.**

   The Access Control List dialog box appears.

4. **Click the Add button.**

   The Add User dialog box appears.

5. **Type the name** Anonymous **into the text field in the Add user dialog box and click OK.**

   The Add User dialog box closes and Anonymous appears in the People, Servers, Groups list of the Access Control List dialog box (see Figure 15-4).

   Domino uses the name Anonymous to identify anyone who uses a Web browser to access the server.

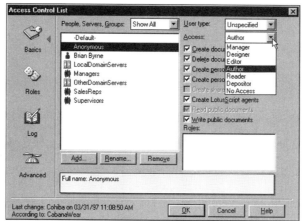

6. **Highlight Anonymous from the list and click the Access drop-down list box.**

7. **Select a level of access.**

8. **Click the OK button.**

Unless users authenticate (which is covered in the next section), the Domino Web server knows them as "Anonymous." If you do not specify an access level for an Anonymous entry in the database's ACL, Web browser users have whatever access was assigned to the Default entry when the database was built.

Forcing user authentication

Authentication is the process in which users must enter their names and passwords before they can access a database or perform actions such as creating or deleting documents on the server.

Users must authenticate when they try to do something that the access level assigned to Anonymous doesn't permit. If you assign to Anonymous (the name that Domino recognizes as meaning every user accessing the server through the Web browser) the No Access access level in the ACL, an authentication dialog box prompts users trying to access the database (see Figure 15-5). On the other hand, if you assign to Anonymous the Reader access level in the ACL, users can access the database and read documents without having to authenticate. However, those users meet up with the authentication dialog box as soon as they try to do something that Reader access doesn't permit, such as create a document.

In the authentication dialog box, users must enter a correct name and password, and that name must have the access in the database's ACL to do what the user is trying to do. For example, a particular database's ACL has only two entries in it: Anonymous, which is assigned Reader access, and the user name Brian Byrne, which is assigned Author access. When the user Brian Byrne accesses the database and starts to read documents, the Domino Web server considers him to be "Anonymous." As soon as he tries to do something more than read documents (which is the level of access assigned to Anonymous) he is prompted to enter his name and password. If he enters Brian Byrne and the correct password in the authentication dialog box, the user can now create documents, because his individual name has Author access in the ACL. If other users try to create documents, they cannot authenticate because their names aren't specified in the ACL.

Figure 15-5:
The
authentica-
tion dialog
box.

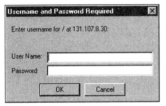

To authenticate with the server, users must specify a name that is stored in the database's ACL, and the password for that name. Passwords are stored in a *person document* in the Public Address Book. A person document is a document stored in the Public Address Book that contains information specific to an individual user.

For example, if No Access is assigned to Anonymous and someone using a browser tries to access a database, a dialog box appears, prompting the user for a name and password. Before the user can access the database, three things must happen:

✔ The name she types must match one that is listed in the ACL.

✔ That matching name in the ACL must have assigned to it the access level required for accessing the database.

✔ The password she types must match the password that is stored in the Public Address Book for the name she typed.

Assigning a password to a name

Before a user can authenticate with a Domino Web server, he must have a name and password, which is contained in his person document in the server's Public Address Book. The developer must, therefore, create a person document in the book before the user can authenticate. To create a person document, follow these steps:

1. **Launch the Lotus Notes client.**

   The Lotus Notes Workspace, which displays the Domino Web server's databases as rectangular icons, appears.

2. **Click the icon for the Public Address Book.**

3. **Choose Create⇨Person.**

   A new person document appears (see Figure 15-6).

4. **Type the name of the user in the fields of the Name section.**

5. **Type a password into the HTTP password field.**

6. **Press the Save icon to save the new person document.**

After you save the person document, the password is encrypted so that nobody else can see it, including you (see Figure 15-7).

Users who have Lotus Notes User IDs should note that the password used to authenticate with a Domino Web server is not the same password as the one associated with the ID. If you're a user who does not have a Lotus Notes User ID, what I just told you can be forgotten because it doesn't affect you.

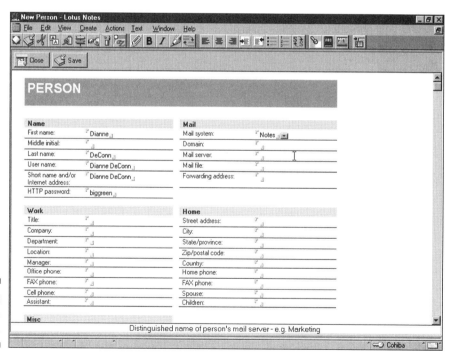

Figure 15-6:
The person
document.

Figure 15-7:
The
password is
encrypted.

Name	
First name:	Dianne
Middle initial:	
Last name:	DeConn
User name:	Dianne DeConn
Short name and/or Internet address:	Dianne DeConn
HTTP password:	(BF1F72F22EB62A2DFECBAB 5295D670D6)

Creating group documents

In addition to being able to specify "Anonymous" as well as individual names in the ACL for assigning access, you can specify a group name that includes the names of users. I strongly recommend that you manage your ACL in this manner. When people move in and out of groups (such as, using an intranet example, when people get promoted, move into different departments, or leave the company), removing their names from a single group document in the Public Address Book is much easier than adding or removing their names in the ACLs of countless databases. To create a group document, do the following:

1. **Launch the Lotus Notes client.**

   The Lotus Notes Workspace, which displays the Domino Web server's databases as rectangular icons, appears.

2. **Click the icon for the Public Address Book.**

3. **Choose Create⇨Group.**

   A new group document appears (see Figure 15-8).

4. **In the Group name field of the Basics section, type the name of the group.**

5. **Choose Multi-purpose from the Group type drop-down list.**

6. **Type a description of the group in the Description field.**

7. **Click the drop-down list button next to the Members field.**

   The Names dialog box appears (see Figure 15-9).

   You also can type the names into the field, but you must type the names in the group document exactly as they appear in the person document. Therefore, I strongly recommend that you select the names from the Names dialog box to eliminate spelling errors (and if you type them, you eventually *will* get spelling errors).

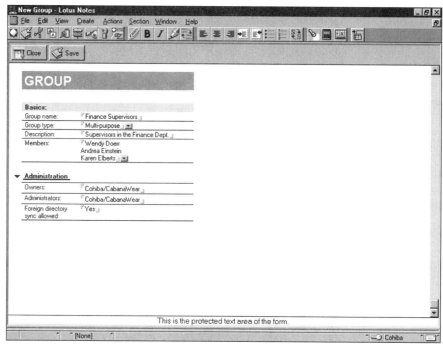

Figure 15-8:
The group document.

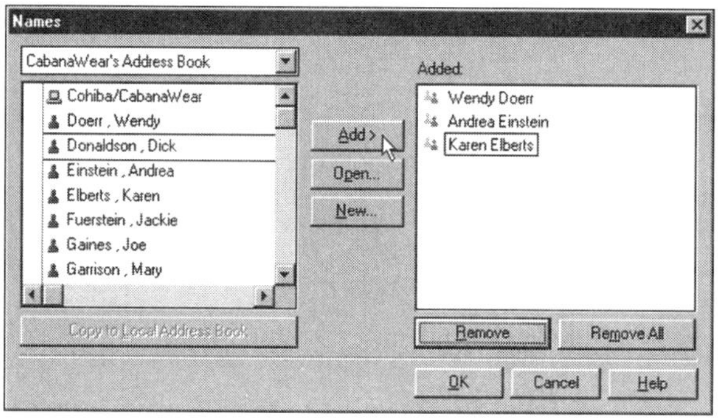

Figure 15-9:
Select names that you want to include in the group.

8. **In the left-hand side of the Names dialog box, click the name of a user or another group.**

These names and groups are the ones listed in the server's Public Address Book.

9. **Click the Add button.**

The name you selected in Step 8 now appears on the right-hand side of the dialog box. You can repeat this step to add several names. All the names in the right-hand side of the box are included in the group.

10. Click OK.

The names you selected appear in the Members field of the group document. (Refer to Figure 15-8 to see what I mean.)

11. Save the group document.

Document Security

Whenever users access the Domino Web server and a database on it, you have control over which documents they can edit and see. Actually, you can set up these controls to work automatically by using the tools that come with Domino.

If your users don't have access to the server and a database on it, read the section "Database Security" earlier in this chapter.

Controlling which documents users can edit

Users who have Author access can read, create, and edit documents that they originate. How does the Domino Web server know whether they created the document? Through the existence of a special field — called, strangely enough, an *Authors* field — that has a data type of Authors. The field can be Editable or Computed. (See Chapter 9 for more information on field data types.) You can allow users to type their names into the field or you can create a formula that automatically enters their names into the field.

More than one name can appear in the Authors field. Anybody who has Author access in the database's ACL and whose name appears in the Authors field of the document can edit a document in the database, regardless of whether they created it.

You, as the Domino Web site designer, can create an Authors field on a form so that users can edit the documents that they create. To create an Authors field on a form:

1. Launch the Lotus Notes client.

The Lotus Notes Workspace, which displays the Domino Web server's databases as rectangular icons, appears.

2. Click the icon for the database that contains the form to which you want to add the Authors field.

3. Choose View⇨Design.

The database opens in Design mode. If Design doesn't appear in the View menu, refer to Chapter 6 for help.

4. Click the Forms folder.

The names of the database's forms appear in the View pane.

5. Double-click the name of the form to which you want to add the Authors field.

The form appears in Edit mode.

6. Click once on the area of the form where you want the field to appear.

The cursor is now positioned where the field is to be added.

7. Choose Create⇨Field.

The Properties for Field InfoBox appears (see Figure 15-10).

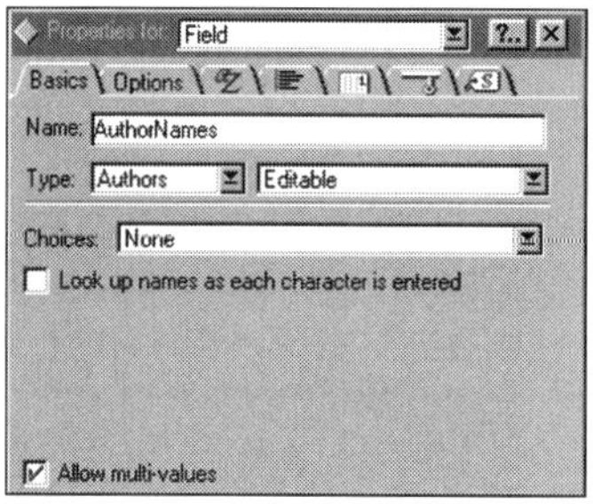

Figure 15-10: Creating an Authors field.

8. Type a name for the field in the Name text box.

You can call it anything you want; the name has no bearing on the field's function.

9. Click the leftmost Type drop-down list and select Authors.

10. In the rightmost Type drop-down list, choose Editable, Computed, or Computed when composed, as appropriate.

Do not select Computed for display because the value in this type of computed field is not stored with the document (see Chapter 9 for more information on the types of computed fields).

- If you select Editable, ignore the Choices field and don't check the Look up names as each character is entered check box.

- If you select Computed, or Computed when composed, type @UserName in the formula window to calculate the user's name. By specifying this formula, the Domino Web server automatically fills the user's name into the field when the user composes a document.

11. **Click the Allow multi-values check box if you want to let your users enter more than one name in the field.**

12. **Press Ctrl+S to save the form.**

Controlling which documents users can see

Regardless of a user's access level in the ACL, you can control whether he or she can read individual documents. Even if users have Manager access, you can prevent them from seeing individual documents. All you have to do is create a Readers field on the form. If a document has a Readers field, only the people who are specified in it, individually or through a group, can read the document.

To create a Readers field on a form, follow these steps:

1. **Launch the Lotus Notes client.**

   The Lotus Notes Workspace, which displays the Domino Web server's databases as rectangular icons, appears.

2. **Click the icon for the database that contains the form to which you want to add the Readers field.**

3. **Choose View⇨Design.**

   The database opens in Design mode. If Design does not appear in the View menu, refer to Chapter 6 for help.

4. **Click the Forms folder.**

   The names of the database's forms appear in the View pane.

5. **Double-click the name of the form to which you want to add the Readers field.**

   The form appears in Edit mode.

6. **Click once on the area of the form where you want the field to appear.**

   The cursor is now positioned where the field is to be added.

7. **Choose Create⇨Field.**

   The Properties for Field InfoBox appears.

8. **Type a name for the field in the Name text box of the Properties for Field InfoBox.**

   You can call it anything you want; the name has no bearing on the field's function.

9. **In the leftmost Type drop-down list, choose Readers.**

10. **Select Editable, Computed, or Computed when composed.**

    Do not select Computed for display. See the steps under "Controlling which documents users can edit" earlier in this chapter for more details.

    If you select Editable, ignore the Choices field and don't check the Look up names as each character is entered check box. If you select one of the two computed selections, type `@UserName` in the formula window to calculate the user's name.

11. **Click the Allow multi-values check box if you want to let your users enter more than one name in the field.**

12. **Press Ctrl+S to save the form.**

Controlling Security within a Document

The last level of security is within the document. You can create areas within a document that only certain people can edit or that only certain people can see.

Controlling editing of a section

You can control whether users can edit specific parts of a document, by creating a section that has controlled access.

1. **Put the form to which you want to add the section in Edit mode.**

   Follow Steps 1 – 5 of the section on "Controlling which documents users can see" earlier in this chapter.

2. **Click and drag with the mouse to highlight the lines in the form that you want to include in the controlled-access section.**

3. **Choose Create⇨Section⇨Controlled Access.**

   The Properties for Form Section InfoBox appears (see Figure 15-11).

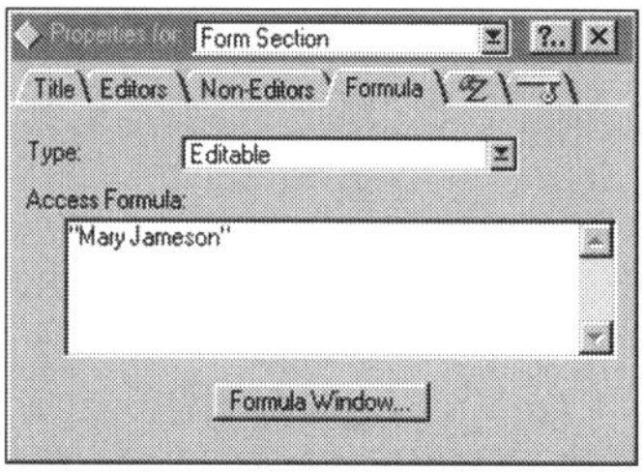

Figure 15-11:
The Form
Section
InfoBox.

Properties for Form Section

Title \ Editors \ Non-Editors \ Formula \

Type   Editable

Access Formula:
"Mary Jameson"

Formula Window...

4. **Click the Formula tab.**

5. **Choose Editable from the Type drop-down list.**

6. **In the Access Formula scroll box, type within quotation marks the name of the person or group you want to have edit access to the section.**

7. **Press Ctrl+S to save the form.**

Controlling reading of a section

To control who can read part of a document, you can hide lines based on a formula criterion.

1. **Put the form that includes the lines you want to hide in Edit mode.**

   Follow Steps 1 – 5 of the section on "Controlling which documents users can see" earlier in this chapter.

2. **Click and drag with the mouse to highlight in the form the line(s) you want to hide.**

3. **Choose Text⇨Text Properties.**

   The Properties for Text InfoBox appears (see Figure 15-12).

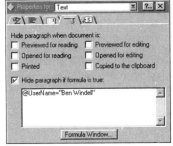

Figure 15-12:
The
Properties
for Text
InfoBox.

4. **Click on the Hide When tab.**

5. **Click the Hide paragraph if formula is true check box.**

6. **In the formula window, type the formula syntax**

   ```
   @UserName=<usersname>
   ```

   where the `<usersname>` variable is the name of the person enclosed in quotes who can read the hidden line(s). For example: `@UserName="Ben Windell"`.

7. **Press Ctrl+S to save the form when you're finished.**

Chapter 16

Show Me the $$
(Customizing Tools)

*T*he default look of the views generated by the Domino Web server is nice and intuitive, but you can do better. For that matter, you can even improve the look of your navigators and the format in which they display search results.

This chapter's title, "Show Me the $$," has a double meaning — neither of which has anything to do with Tom Cruise, Cuba Gooding, Jr., or their hit movie *Jerry Maguire*. First of all, the chapter title refers to how you can customize the look of views, navigators, and search results using a number of fields and forms that begin with $$ (for example, $$ViewBody, $$ViewList, $$NavigatorBody, $$ViewTemplateDefault, $$NavigatorTemplateDefault, and $$SearchTemplateDefault).

Second, the title refers to how customizing your views, navigators, and search results could very well have an impact on the company's bottom line. Let's face it — the more interesting and appealing your Web site, the more often people are apt to visit and tell their friends and family to visit. The more people visit your site, the more stuff they buy from you now (in the case of a commerce site) or in the future (in the case of a marketing site). Moreover, the more people who visit your site, the more money you save or bring in. Though it's not readily apparent, that statement is true because you are communicating more effectively with your suppliers or successfully getting your employees to work and share ideas more efficiently.

Money, either making it (earning it, not counterfeiting it, I said!) or saving it, is probably one of the reasons you're thinking about using Domino to build a Web site or improve an existing site; you could say that you want your Domino Web site to show you the money. The information in this chapter goes a long way toward bringing you a few steps closer to that goal.

Customizing Views

Your users rely heavily on the views in your Domino Web site. Views are what gives users the listings, often chronological or alphabetical, of the documents or content in the site. Considering that views are one of the most often used and relied upon elements of the site, spending time planning and implementing their customization makes a lot of sense.

What's wrong with the default views

The views that the Domino Web server generates by default do a pretty good job of listing documents and showing links that make it easy for users to open documents. These views offer some nice default links that allow you to expand, collapse, and search the view. Plus, they give you the ability to create customized actions buttons.

You may be asking, "Well then, why should I change the default views?" My answer is: Because you are creative and you can do better. Figure 16-1 shows a default view, including its name, action buttons, links to execute certain commands, and links to open documents.

Figure 16-2 shows some of the things you can do to customize the same view. You can add many things that the standard default view does not offer, such as graphics, tables, fields, text, and navigators.

Stepping through customization

Customization of views may not seem very intuitive at first, but you can actually do it easily. To customize a view, you create a form through which the view appears. You must give the form itself one of these two names:

- **$$ViewTemplateDefault:** If you want all the views in the database to appear through this one form

- **$$ViewTemplate for <*viewname*>:** If you want just the view specified as the <*viewname*> variable to appear through this form

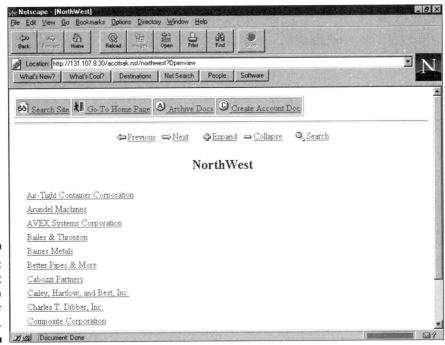

Figure 16-1:
A default
Domino
Web server
view.

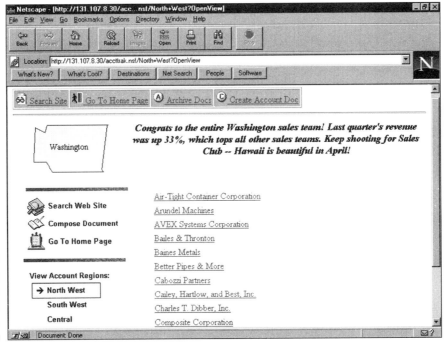

Figure 16-2:
A
customized
view.

When users request to open a view, the Domino Web server follows three procedures in succession to determine how to display the view. For example, if you request to open a view called Reference, Domino follows these steps:

1. It looks for a form called $$ViewTemplate for Reference. If Domino finds that form, it displays the Reference view through the form. If it doesn't find the form, it goes on to the next step.

2. It looks for a form called $$ViewTemplateDefault. If Domino finds that form, it displays the Reference view through the form. If it doesn't find the form, it goes on to the next step.

3. It looks for the Reference view, and when Domino finds that view, it displays the view in the view's standard, noncustomized format.

As discussed earlier in this chapter, you can display graphics, tables, fields, text, and navigators in a customized view. Basically, you create a form and name it either $$ViewTemplateDefault or $$ViewTemplate for *<viewname>*, add whatever elements you want to add (graphics, tables, fields and/or text) to it, and then add a special field to the form through which the view appears. The form that you create must contain one of the following fields through which the view appears:

- ✔ **$$ViewList:** Displays a list of the views in a database
- ✔ **$$ViewBody:** Displays the view specified in the field's Default Formula

Note: You can have only one $$ViewBody field per form.

If you want a navigator to appear with the view, you can also include the following fields:

- ✔ **$$NavigatorBody:** Displays the navigator specified in the field's Default Formula
- ✔ **$$NavigatorBody_*n*:** Displays more than one navigator with a view

If you want multiple navigators to appear, append an underscore and a number to $$NavigatorBody.

Before you go any further, compare Figure 16-3 to Figure 16-2. Figure 16-3 shows the form (in Edit mode on a Lotus Notes client) that was used to create what appears on the Web browser shown in Figure 16-2. Notice that a graphic of Washington state is pasted onto the form, text is typed and formatted on the form, the $$NavigatorBody field is used to display a navigator, and the $$ViewBody field is used to display the documents from a view.

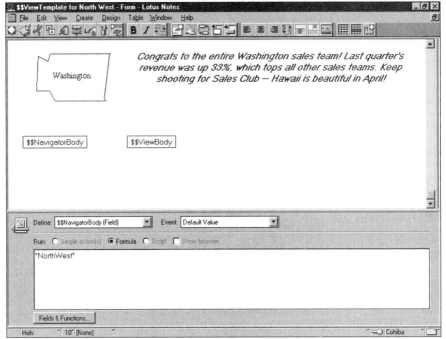

Figure 16-3:
The view in
Design
mode.

Customizing all views

If you want all the views in a database to appear in the same customized format, you need to create only one form, called $$ViewTemplateDefault. When users click an action button, a text link, or a navigator hotspot, or type a Domino-specific URL, to open a particular view, the view displays through the $$ViewTemplateDefault form. To create the form, do the following:

1. **Launch the Lotus Notes client.**

   The Lotus Notes Workspace, which displays the Domino Web server's databases as rectangular icons, appears.

2. **Click the icon for the database to which you want to add the $$ViewTemplateDefault form.**

3. **Choose View➪Design.**

   The database opens. If Design does not appear in the View menu, choose View➪Show➪Design.

4. **Choose Create➪Design➪Form.**

   The new form appears in Design mode.

5. **Add to the form the text and graphics that you want to appear when users open a view.**

6. **Choose Create⇨Table.**

   The Create Table InfoBox appears (see Figure 16-4). I recommend that before you add fields to the form, you add a table; you can space the fields a lot better on the form if you add them to the cells of the table. For example, if you want the documents in a view to appear directly to the right of a navigator, put the navigator field in the left column of a table and the view field in the right column of the table.

Figure 16-4: The Create Table dialog box.

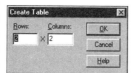

7. **In the InfoBox, type the number of Rows and Columns for the table that you want to appear on the form, and click OK.**

   The table appears on the form.

8. **Position the cursor in the table cell where you want to add a field by clicking once in the appropriate cell.**

   The documents in a view appear through this field.

9. **Choose Create⇨Field.**

   A field named Untitled is added to the form, and the Properties for Field InfoBox appears.

10. **Type the name of the field in the Name text box.**

   You can name the field either $$ViewBody or $$ViewList. Figure 16-5 shows how fields with these names appear to a Web browser. The $$ViewList field generates a list of the links to the other views in the database. The $$ViewBody field generates a list of the links to documents.

   You can have only one field (per form) that generates a list of the links to documents. Although I don't know why you may need to, you can create multiple fields that generate a list of links to the other views in the database. All you have to do is name them $$ViewList, $$ViewList_1, $$ViewList_2, and so on. By the way, you can use this naming convention with the $$NavigatorBody field (discussed later in this chapter in "Customizing Navigators") to have multiple fields (per form) that display navigators.

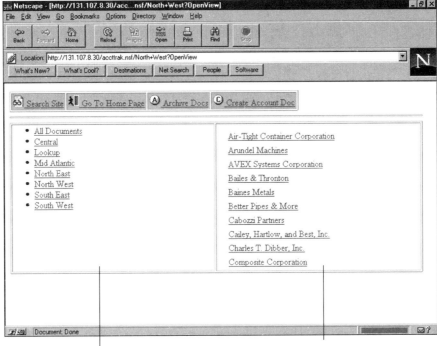

Figure 16-5:
How a Web
browser
displays the
$$ViewList
and
$$ViewBody
fields.

Result of a field named $$ViewList   Result of a field named $$ViewBody

11. **In the two Type drop-down lists, choose the Text data type and choose Editable as the field type.**

    I ask you to choose Editable, which is the default field type, just to keep the steps flowing easy. Note that any of the Computed options also work. Figure 16-6 shows the Properties for Field InfoBox.

12. **Disregard the field's Default Value formula in the Design pane.**

    If you name the field $$ViewList, the listing of the database's views always appear, regardless of the formula. If you name the field $$ViewBody, the documents from the view being opened always appear, regardless of the formula.

13. **Position the cursor in the table cell where you want to add a navigator.**

    (This table became apparent in Step 7, in case you're keeping track.) If you aren't adding a navigator to the form, you can skip Steps 13 to 19 and save the form now. One of the reasons for customizing a view, however, is to add not only text and graphics but also navigators to it. I include these steps in case you would like to add a navigator.

Name the field $$ViewBody $$ViewBody field   Table cell in which field is added

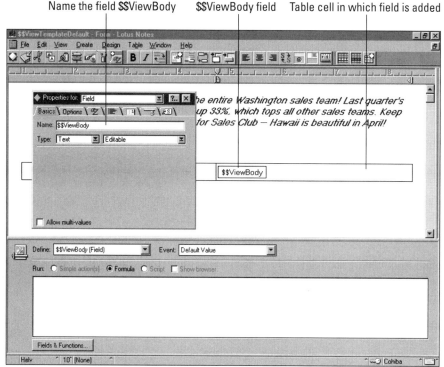

Figure 16-6:
The
$$ViewBody
field.

14. Choose Create➪Field.

Performing this step adds a field named `Untitled` to the form.

15. Type in $$NavigatorBody as the field name in the Name text box of the Properties for Field InfoBox.

You can have only one $$ViewBody field per form, but if you want to have multiple navigators appear in a customized view, simply name additional navigator fields $$NavigatorBody_1, $$NavigatorBody_2, and so on.

16. In the two Type drop-down lists, choose the Text data type and choose Editable as the field type.

I ask you to choose Editable, which is the default field type, just to keep the steps flowing easy. Note that any of the Computed options also work.

17. In the Design pane, type the name of a navigator and enclose it in quotes, or type a formula that generates the name of a navigator, in the formula window for the Default Value.

Figure 16-7 shows "MainNavigator" as the navigator name in the formula windows.

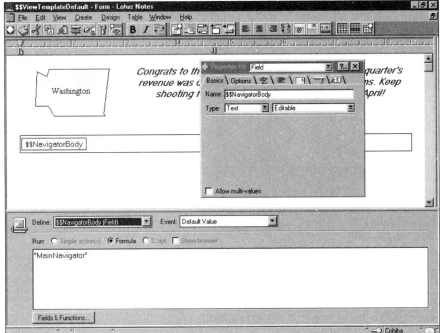

18. Choose <u>D</u>esign⇨Form <u>P</u>roperties.

The Properties for Form InfoBox appears (see Figure 16-8).

19. Type the name $$ViewTemplateDefault **in the Form name text box.**

20. Press Ctrl+S to save the form.

Displaying the name of the view

When you display views through the $$ViewTemplateDefault form, the view name doesn't appear. If you want, you can add a field to the form that displays the view name. To do so, follow these steps:

1. **Double-click the $$ViewTemplateDefault form to put it into Design mode.**

2. **Position the cursor where you want the view name to appear by clicking once in the desired area.**

3. **Choose Create⇨Field.**

   Performing this step adds a field named Untitled to the form, and the Properties for Field InfoBox appears.

4. **In the two Type drop-down lists, choose the Text data type and choose Editable as the field type.**

   I ask you to choose Editable, which is the default field type, just to keep the steps flowing easy. Note that any of the Computed options also work.

5. **In the field's Design pane, type @ViewTitle in the formula window for the Default Value.**

   See Figure 16-9.

6. **Press Ctrl+S to save the form.**

Figure 16-9:
Type
@ViewTitle
for the
field's
Default
Value.

Customizing individual views

If you have a $$ViewTemplateDefault form in your database and a user opens any of the views in the database, the database appears through that form, unless you have individually customized the view. You can individually customize a view by following the same steps you follow to create a $$ViewTemplateDefault form (in "Customizing all views" earlier in this chapter), except that you must give the form a different name.

The naming syntax for a form that customizes an individual view is $$ViewTemplate for *viewname,* where the *viewname* variable is the name of the view. For example, if you want to customize just the view named Reference, you create a form and call it $$ViewTemplate for Reference.

When you name the form, do not add or remove any of the spaces in the naming syntax defined in the last paragraph. Notice that $$ViewTemplate doesn't have a space in between the *w* and the *T,* but spaces do occur before and after the word *for.* If you inadvertently add or remove a required space, the view doesn't appear through the form as you would expect.

Customizing Navigators

Just as you can customize the way a view appears, you can customize the way a navigator appears.

"Wait a minute," you say, "The information in the previous section is quite helpful in finding out how to customize a view, but Chapter 12 deals exclusively with creating and customizing navigators." Please note that, although you can add text and graphics to a navigator, you must use a graphics editor sotware package to do so. When you customize a navigator by having it display through a form, you can have not only customized text and graphics, but also tables, fields, and views, appear with your navigator.

When users request to open a navigator, the Domino Web server follows three procedures in succession to determine how to display the navigator. For example, if you request to open a navigator called Sitemap, Domino follows these steps:

1. It looks for a form called $$NavigatorTemplate for Sitemap. If Domino finds the form, it displays the Sitemap navigator through the form. If it doesn't find the form, Domino goes on to the next step.

2. It looks for a form called $$NavigatorTemplateDefault. If Domino finds the form, it displays the Sitemap navigator through the form. If it doesn't find the form, Domino goes on to the next step.

3. It looks for the Sitemap navigator and, when Domino finds the navigator, it displays the navigator in its standard, noncustomized format.

Customizing all navigators

If you want all the navigators in a given database to appear in an identical customized format, you need to create one form only, called $$NavigatorTemplateDefault. When users click an action button, a text link, or a navigator hotspot, or type a Domino-specific URL, to open a particular navigator, that navigator displays through the $$NavigatorTemplateDefault form. To create the form, follow these steps:

1. **Launch the Lotus Notes client.**

   The Lotus Notes Workspace, which displays the Domino Web server's databases as rectangular icons, appears.

2. **Click the icon for the database to which you want to add the $$NavigatorTemplateDefault form.**

3. **Choose View⇨Design.**

   The database opens. If Design does not appear in the View menu, refer to Chapter 6 for help.

4. **Choose Create⇨Design⇨Form.**

   The new form appears in Design mode.

5. **Add the text and graphics that you want to appear when users open a navigator.**

   See Chapter 12 for the details on how to add text and graphics to a navigator.

6. **Position the cursor where you want to add the field through which the navigator appears.**

   Adding tables and inserting the fields into the cells of the table helps space the fields on the form. To avoid unnecessary repetition, I don't include the steps for adding a table here. See the section "Customizing all views" in this chapter for steps on adding a table.

7. **Choose Create⇨Field.**

   A field named Untitled is added to the form, and the Properties for Field InfoBox appears.

8. **Type $$NavigatorBody in the Name text box.**

   Although you can have multiple navigators appear when you customize a view, by adding fields called $$NavigatorBody_1, $$NavigatorBody_2, and so on, you can't have different navigators appear on $$NavigatorTemplateDefault or $$NavigatorTemplate for *navigatorname* forms. If you specify multiple fields with them, Domino ignores their formulas and the same navigator displays in each of the fields.

9. **In the two Type drop-down lists, choose the Text data type and choose Editable as the field type.**

   I ask you to choose Editable, which is the default field type, just to keep the steps flowing easy. Note that any of the Computed options also work.

10. **Disregard the field's Default Value formula in the Design pane.**

    The navigator that appears to your users through the field is the one that they request to be opened. You cannot override this.

11. **Click once in the table cell to position the cursor where you want to add a navigator.**

    If you aren't adding a view to the form, you can skip Steps 12 – 17 and save the form now, but one of the reasons for customizing a navigator is to add not only text and graphics but also views, so I include these steps.

12. **Choose Create⇨Field.**

    A field named Untitled is added to the form and the Properties for Field InfoBox appears.

13. **Type $$ViewBody in the Name text box.**

14. **In the two Type drop-down lists, choose the Text data type and choose Editable as the field type.**

    I ask you to choose Editable, which is the default field type, just to keep the steps flowing easy. Note that any of the Computed options also work.

15. **In the Design pane, type the name of a view and enclose it in quotes, or else type a formula that generates the name of a view, in the formula window for the Default Value.**

16. **Choose Design⇨Form Properties.**

    The Properties for Form InfoBox appears.

17. **Type $$NavigatorTemplateDefault in the Name text box.**

18. **Press Ctrl+S to save the form.**

Customizing individual navigators

If you have a $$NavigatorTemplateDefault form in your database, any time the user opens any navigator in the database, the navigator appears through that form — unless you have individually customized the navigator. You can customize a navigator by following the same steps you follow to create the $$NavigatorTemplateDefault form (see the "Customizing all navigators" section in this chapter), except that you must give the form a different name.

The naming syntax for a form that customizes an individual navigator is $$NavigatorTemplate for *navigatorname*, where the *navigatorname* variable is the name of the navigator. For example, if you want to customize just the navigator named Sitemap, you create a form and call it $$ViewTemplate for Sitemap.

It is essential that when you name the form, you do not add or remove any of the spaces in the naming syntax that I introduce in the last paragraph. Notice that $$NavigatorTemplate doesn't have any spaces between the *r* and the *T*, but that spaces do occur before and after the word *for*. If you inadvertently add or remove a required space, the view doesn't appear through the form the way you would expect.

Customizing Search Forms and Results

Your users find the ability to search a Domino Web site very useful. Your users also find your customization of the search form and search results very desirable. Customized search forms and search results allow you to tailor them to the different audiences that access your Domino Web site. You may want to add your corporate logo, personalized text, or personalized searching options.

When users execute a search in a view without a custom search form, they get the Domino Web server's default search form (see Figure 16-10).

Full Text Search

Search for the following word(s):

[   ] [Search]

Limit results to: [All ▾]

Sort results by: ⦿ Relevance
                    ○ Oldest first (by date)
                    ○ Newest first (by date)

Word options: ☐ Find exact word matches only
                    ☐ Find word variations as defined by thesaurus

Figure 16-10:
The default
search
form.

A better search form

You can create a customized search form simply by creating a new form with the necessary fields and text and then naming the form $$Search. Figure 16-11 shows an example of a customized search form.

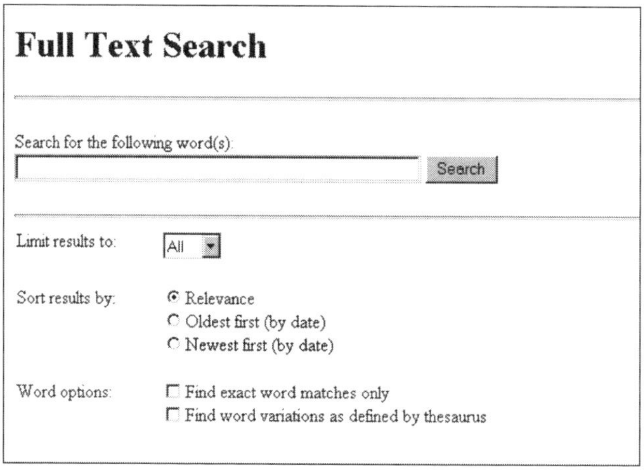

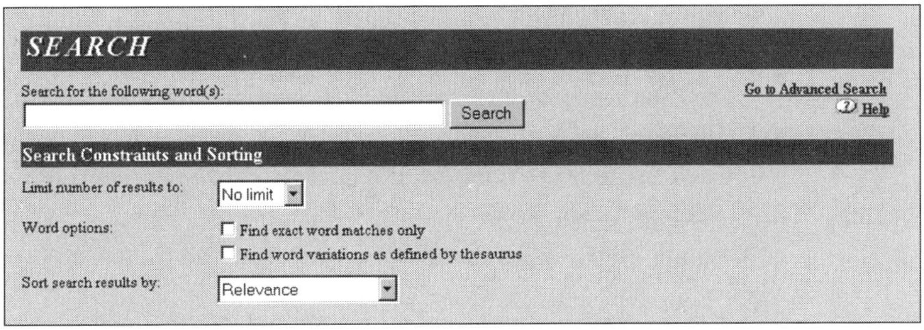

Figure 16-11:
A
customized
search
form.

```
SEARCH

Search for the following word(s):                                    Go to Advanced Search
[                                          ]  [ Search ]                    (?) Help

Search Constraints and Sorting

Limit number of results to:    [No limit ▼]

Word options:                  ☐ Find exact word matches only
                               ☐ Find word variations as defined by thesaurus

Sort search results by:        [Relevance              ▼]
```

The Search Site Template (`srchsite.ntf`), located on your Domino Web server, contains a number of search forms you can use in your database. To use search forms from the template, do the following:

1. **Create a database based on the** `srchsite.ntf` **template file.**

   See Chapter 6 for an explanation of how to create such a database.

2. **Copy a form to the Windows Clipboard.**

3. **Paste the form into your database.**

   Chapter 8 has information on pasting forms from the Clipboard into your database.

4. **Rename the form to $$Search.**

Getting better results

When you execute a search of a view in a database, the results display in the format of the view searched. If you want, you can have the results returned in a customized format. To create a customized search results form:

1. **Launch the Lotus Notes client.**

   The Lotus Notes Workspace, which displays the Domino Web server's databases as rectangular icons, appears.

2. **Click the icon for the database in which you want to create a customized search results form.**

3. **Choose View⇨Design.**

   The database opens. If Design does not appear in the View menu, refer to Chapter 6 for help.

4. **Choose Create⇨Design⇨Form.**

   The new form appears in Design mode.

5. **Add the text and graphics that you want to appear with the search results.**

   See Chapter 8 for information on how to add text and graphics to the form.

6. **Click the form to position the cursor where you want to add a field.**

   The field that you are about to add is the one through which the search results appear when users view the form with their Web browsers.

7. **Choose Create⇨Field.**

   A field named Untitled is added to the form, and the Properties for Field InfoBox appears.

8. **Type a name for the $$ViewBody in the Name text box.**

9. **In the two Type drop-down lists, choose the Text data type and choose Editable as the field type.**

   I ask you to choose Editable, which is the default field type, just to keep the steps flowing easy. Note that any of the Computed options also work.

10. **Disregard the field's Default Value formula in the Design pane.**

    The search results appear in the field regardless of what the formula specifies.

11. **Choose Design⇨Form Properties.**

    The Properties for Form InfoBox appears.

12. **Type $$SearchTemplateDefault in the Name text box.**

13. **Press Ctrl+S to save the form.**

Customizing search results for a specific view

You can create a customized search results form that works with a specific view. For example, if you execute a search of a view named Accounts, you can have the results present differently than if you execute a search of a view named Sales Reps.

The naming syntax for a form that displays the search results for a specific view is $$SearchTemplate for *viewname*, where the *viewname* variable is the name of the view with which the search results form is associated. For example, if you want to create a search results form that customizes the results when users do a search of a view called Accounts, name the search results form $$SearchTemplate for Accounts.

View Customization in Action

This entire chapter deals with the nuts-and-bolts issues of how to customize views. To close the chapter, I want to illustrate how a customized view can help those using your Domino Web site. And one of the best examples I can think of is using your own handmade view to provide your users with an intuitive graphical menu for moving around the site.

One really nice use of a customized view is to display a navigator along with the view. You create the navigator to show the user which view is selected. The North West view shown in Figure 16-12 is customized with a form ($$ViewTemplate for North West) that displays the document links in the middle of the view and a navigator on the left. Notice that the navigator is designed to show a highlight around the text North West and an arrow pointing at it to indicate that North West is the selected view.

Figure 16-13 shows a different view, called South West, that is customized using a form called $$ViewTemplate for South West. Notice that the customized view looks identical to the one in Figure 16-12, except that it displays a navigator (and documents of course) designed with an arrow and a highlight around the text South West.

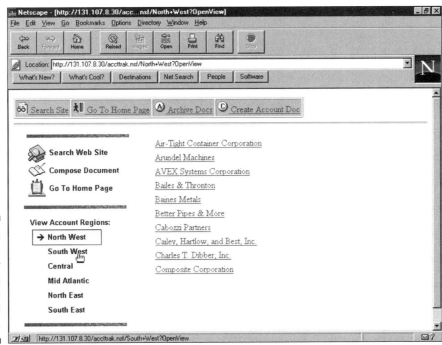

Figure 16-12:
The navigator indicates the selected view.

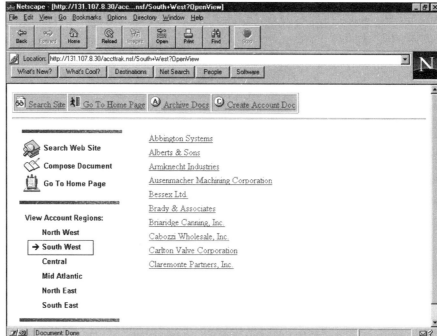

Figure 16-13:
The
navigator
indicates
the
selected
view.

Making subtle changes in different navigators to indicate which view is selected can make using your Domino Web site considerably more intuitive for your users, as this example demonstrates.

Chapter 17

Let's Get Attached

. . . .

In This Chapter

▶ Enabling users to attach and detach files

▶ Attaching and detaching files

▶ Uses for attaching and detaching files

. . . .

*T*he ability to transfer files is one of the most useful aspects of the Internet. A good bit of the information you need to share with customers or fellow employees isn't suitable for viewing in a Web site. For example, displaying software executables, spreadsheets, or word processing documents on your Web site just doesn't make sense. You want your customers and fellow employees to simply download these types of files to their hard drives and then either install them (in the case of software executables) or work with them using the appropriate software package.

With most server software, if you want people to be able to download files from your server, you have to set up an *FTP (File Transfer Protocol)* server. In other words, if you want people to download files from your Web site, you have to set up both a Web server and an FTP server.

The Domino Web server, on the other hand, allows users to both download and upload files, so you don't have to set up an FTP server. All you (as the developer) have to do is add an action hotspot that lets users attach files to documents. The users can simply type the name of the file they want, or select it from a dialog box, to attach it to a document in a special field, and then save the document. And users download files even easier.

Setting Up File Attaching for a Database

The Domino file-attachment default setting prohibits users from attaching files to a document. You must create on the form an action hotspot that allows users to attach files.

Visitors to your Web site can attach files to a document only if they're using a Web browser that supports file attaching. Netscape Navigator supports this function.

Enabling a form to allow file attaching

To edit an existing form so that users can attach files, do the following:

1. **Launch the Lotus Notes client.**

   The Lotus Notes Workspace, which displays the Domino Web server's databases as rectangular icons, appears.

2. **Click the icon for the database that contains the form to which you want to enable file attaching.**

3. **Choose View⇨Design.**

   The database opens. If Design does not appear in the View menu, refer to Chapter 6 for help.

4. **Click the Forms folder.**

   The names of the database's forms appear in the View pane.

5. **Double-click the name of the form to which you want to enable file attaching.**

   The form appears in Edit mode.

6. **Position the cursor at the location in the form where you want to add the file-attaching action hotspot and type descriptive text to let users know where to attach a file.**

   Make the description as intuitive as possible for your users; for example, "Attach File."

7. **Highlight the text and choose Create⇨Hotspot⇨Action Hotspot.**

   The Properties for HotSpot Button InfoBox appears (see Figure 17-1).

8. **Type** `@Command([EditInsertFileAttachment])` **in the hotspot's formula window.**

9. **Press Ctrl+S to save the form.**

I explain more about how users can attach files later in the chapter, but right now I want to call your attention to Figure 17-2, which shows what users get when they view a document in edit mode to which files can be attached. The line on which you added the action hotspot appears in a document in edit mode as the descriptive text that you typed in, a field in which users can type the name and path to the file they want to attach, and a Browse button that lets users select the file graphically from a dialog box. A user can select a file from this dialog box instead of typing in the path and name of the file.

Highlighted text   HotSpot Button InfoBox

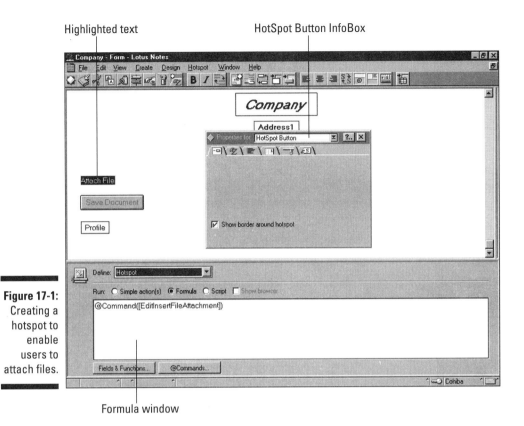

Figure 17-1:
Creating a
hotspot to
enable
users to
attach files.

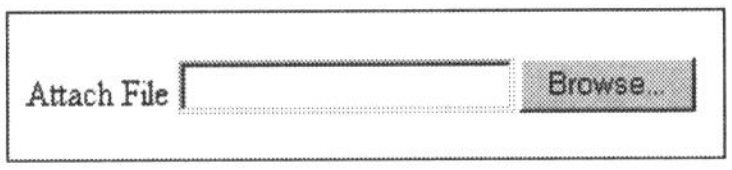

Formula window

Figure 17-2:
The
attachment
hotspot as it
appears in
the Web
browser.

Giving users access to work with attachments

Users must have at least Reader access in the database's Access Control List (ACL) before they can download attached files, and they must have at least Editor access in the database's ACL before they can attach files and delete attached files. See Chapter 15 for more information about the ACL and other security functions.

To set user's access level for a database, follow these steps:

1. **Launch the Lotus Notes client.**

   The Lotus Notes Workspace, which displays the Domino Web server's databases as rectangular icons, appears.

2. **Click the icon for the database in which you want to change the ACL.**

3. **Choose File⇨Database⇨Access Control.**

   The Access Control List dialog box appears (see Figure 17-3).

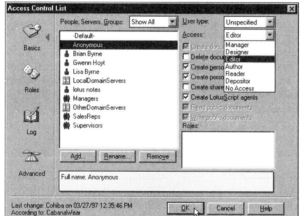

Figure 17-3:
Granting access so users can work with attachments.

4. **Click the Add button.**

   The Add User dialog box appears.

5. **Type the name of a user or group that contains the names of users and click OK.**

   You can use "Anonymous" in the ACL to specify everyone who accesses the Domino Web server with a Web browser but doesn't *authenticate*, which means provide a name and password when they open the database. See Chapter 15 for more about the ACL and authentication.

6. **Highlight the name of the person or group you just added and click the Access drop-down list.**

7. **Choose an access level.**

   You must select Reader or a higher level if you want to allow users to view and download attachments. (Actually, you must select Reader or higher to let them see any bit of the database, not just attachments.) You must select Editor or a higher access level if you want to let users attach files and delete attached files.

If you have experience with the Lotus Notes ACL, you probably know that you, the developer, have to check an additional check box before your users can delete documents. Realize that deleting documents and deleting attachments are not the same thing; that check box doesn't affect whether users can delete attachments. As far as deleting attachments goes, the Domino Web server does not differentiate between deleting an attachment and deleting text in a field.

8. Click the OK button.

Easing the editing

Users must have a document in Edit mode before they can attach files to it. Your best bet for enabling your users to put a document in Edit mode is to create an action button. Follow these steps:

1. Launch the Lotus Notes client.

The Lotus Notes Workspace, which displays the Domino Web server's databases as rectangular icons, appears.

2. Click the icon for the database that contains the form to which you want to add the action button.

3. Choose View⇨Design.

The database opens. If Design does not appear in the View menu, refer to Chapter 6 for help.

4. Click the Forms folder.

The names of the database's forms appear in the View pane.

5. Double-click the name of the form to which you want to add the action button.

The form appears in Edit mode.

6. Choose Create⇨Action.

The Action pane and the Properties for Action InfoBox appear (see Figure 17-4).

7. Type a name for the action in the Name text box, and choose an appropriate icon from the Button Icon drop-down menu.

Users will see this name and icon on the action button.

8. Type `@Command([EditDocument])` **in the action button's formula window.**

9. Press Ctrl+S to save the form.

Action InfoBox   Action pane

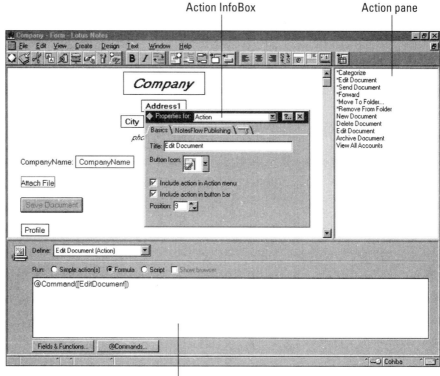

Figure 17-4:
Creating an
Edit action
button.

Formula window

A Look through the User's Eyes

You can see that enabling a form so that users can attach files to it isn't too hard. The steps a user must take to attach and detach files isn't too complicated, either.

This section of the chapter is primarily information about how visitors to your Domino Web site use the file-attaching function that you, the developer, set up. Even though this information doesn't pertain directly to developing a Domino site, it is useful to know what steps visitors must take to use the functions you enable.

Downloading attached files

Downloading attached files is accomplished with a few mouse clicks. Even if your browser doesn't support attaching files, you can view, delete, and detach attached files. To detach a file attachment, follow these steps:

1. **Open the document that contains the attachment.**

2. **Right-click the file attachment, which you can see at the bottom of the document.**

   Figure 17-5 shows a document that has an attachment. In Netscape Navigator, which I use as an example in this list, you get a pop-up menu of choices.

3. **In Netscape Navigator, choose Save Link As.**

   The Save As dialog box appears (see Figure 17-6). (Other browsers that support saving attachments have a similar function somewhere. Check your browser's documentation to find out what they've named the Save Link As function.) You see a graphic depiction of your computer's directory structure.

4. **Click the folder to which you want to save the file.**

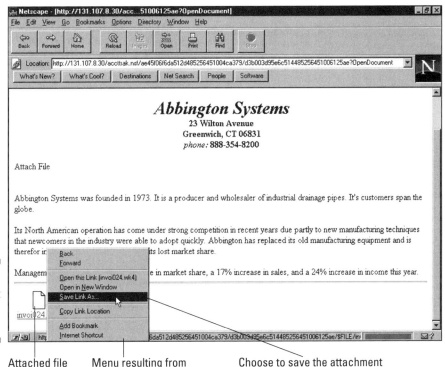

Figure 17-5:
A document
with an
attachment.

Attached file   Menu resulting from   Choose to save the attachment
                 right-clicking mouse   to your hard drive

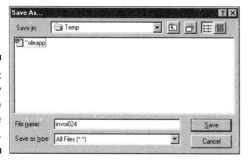

Figure 17-6:
Specify
where to
save the
file.

5. In the File name text box, type a name for the file you're saving.

6. Click the Save button.

You now have a copy of the file on your hard drive. Depending on the type of file, you can execute it, work with it in the appropriate software package, or do whatever else you want with it. It's a copy of the file that was — and still is — attached to the document on the Domino Web server, so whatever you do with the file you saved on your hard drive doesn't affect that original file on the server.

Viewing attached files

You may decide that rather than taking up space on your hard drive by downloading the file to it, you just want to view the information in the document and then be done with it. You can do that, too!

1. Follow Steps 1 and 2 under "Downloading attached files," prior to this section.

Notice also that, just like in the section referenced above, I use Netscape Navigator as an example browser in this series of steps.

2. In Netscape Navigator, choose Open this Link from the pop-up menu that appears when you right-click with the mouse.

Figure 17-7 shows the menu that opens when you right-click the attachment. The attachment appears in the application that's configured for viewing that type of file with your Web browser — if you have the application on your computer, of course. For example, if the attachment is a Microsoft Word file named Howdy.doc and you have a copy of the Word program on your computer, choosing Open this Link opens the file in Word.

You can bypass the above steps altogether by simply double-clicking the icon of the attached file. The browser then launches the viewer or application directly.

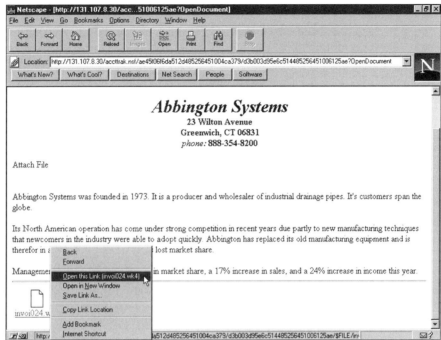

Figure 17-7:
Select this
option to
view an
attachment.

Deleting attached files

The power is yours! You can delete an attached file from a document, just
like you can delete text from fields in a document. When you delete a file
attachment, you must have at least Editor access to edit the document. To
delete a file attachment, do the following:

1. Put the document in Edit mode.

One of the easiest ways to put a document in Edit mode is to click an
edit action button in a document's action bar (see Figure 17-8).

Figure 17-8:
An example
of an edit
action
button in an
action bar.

2. Scroll to the bottom of the document to view the attachment icon.

3. Click the check box next to the name of the file attachment you want to delete.

See Figure 17-9.

4. Click the submit button.

In most cases, the submission message appears, letting you know that your save request was processed. *Note:* This message may not appear if the form's design has been customized using the $$Return field (see Chapter 18 for more information on the $$Return field).

Clicking the submit button deletes the file attachment from the document.

Attaching files

This section of the chapter is primarily information about how visitors to your Domino Web site use the file-attaching function that you, the developer, set up. Even though this information doesn't pertain directly to developing a Domino site, it is useful to know what steps visitors must take to use the functions you enable.

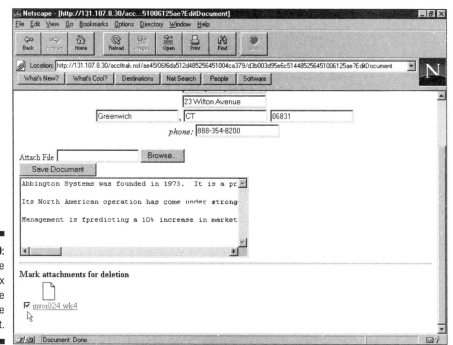

Figure 17-9: Click the check box to delete the attachment.

Attaching files, like deleting attached files, requires that you put the document to which you're attaching the file in Edit mode. You can attach any type of file to a document on a Domino Web server, although you must have a Web browser that supports attaching files, such as Netscape Navigator 2.0 or greater.

When you attach files, be aware that certain Web browsers don't support the ability to attach files and that some proxy servers do not fully support the attachment of binary files.

To attach a file to a document, follow these steps:

1. **Put the document in Edit mode.**

   The field where you can type the attachment name appears, as does the Browse button.

2. **In the attachment field, type in the path and name of the file you want to attach, or click the Browse button.**

   Clicking the Browse button opens the File Upload dialog box, which gives you a graphical representation of your computer's directory structure. You can use this dialog box to select the path and name of the file instead of typing it in (see Figure 17-10).

3. **If you click the Browse button, search your directory structure and click the name of the file you want to attach.**

   The name appears in the File name text box (see Figure 17-10).

4. **Click the Open button.**

   The File Upload dialog box disappears, and the path and name of the file your selected in the previous step appear in the attachment field.

5. **When the path and name of the file appear in the attachment box as shown in Figure 17-11, click the submit button.**

The Domino server doesn't tell you if you accidentally type the name of a nonexistent file or an incorrect directory structure, or if you simply incorrectly spell a file or directory name. The document appears to save correctly, which it does, but Domino doesn't attach the file you want to attach. Unfortunately, you probably will think Domino saved the file you wanted and that everything's fine. The only way you can know for certain that Domino has attached the proper file to the document is to open the document itself and check whether an icon for the file you submitted appears at the bottom of the document. So, to avoid running into the problem of files you expect to be attached not actually being attached, use the Browse button — or be extra careful when you type in the names of files.

The File Upload dialog box appears when users click the Browse button

Figure 17-10:
Attaching a file.

The Domino Web server adds this box and button

Figure 17-11:
The *Connects.nsf* file will be attached to the document.

You can attach only one file at a time, so if you want to attach multiple files to a document, you have to repeat the steps of typing the name of one file (or using the Browse button to find one file) and submitting one file over and over again until you have attached all the files you want to.

Uses for Attaching Files

This section gives you some examples of the many good reasons for allowing your users to attach and detach files.

Sharing spreadsheets and word processing documents

Say a visitor to your Web site has financial results in a spreadsheet or reports in a word processing document that he or she needs to share with other people. Converting those spreadsheets into HTML documents that Web browsers can view is just plain impractical. The file-attaching procedure that you can set up cures this problem. On a document so enabled, the user can attach files to a Web page and let other users download them and work with them in a spreadsheet or word processing program.

Suppose a user needs a group of people to collaborate on a particular spreadsheet before he or she can submit a final version of it. The user can save a lot of time and trouble by simply attaching the spreadsheet to a Web page. People can then detach the spreadsheet, update and edit it in their spreadsheet package, and then reattach it to the Web page so that others can add their input.

Selling content

You can create a commerce Web site where you can sell documents and software programs via your Domino Web site. You can attach files that customers can access and download to documents on the site.

Security obviously becomes a major concern here. You don't want some dishonest customer to download a product before paying for it. You can set up a process where customers submit their credit card information before you give them access to the document that contains the attachments.

Chapter 18

Don't Acquit the Default Submit (Message)

*W*hen you create or edit documents on a Domino Web server, you need a way to save the documents so that you and other users can access them later. So, how do you save documents on a Domino Web server? It's a snap — well, actually a click! All you need to do is click the submit button, which automatically appears at the bottom of every document currently being created or edited on a Domino Web server.

Clicking the submit button saves the document on the Domino Web server's hard drive. After you save the document, a message box appears and confirms that the document saved successfully. The document then becomes available to users who can access the server.

You may be asking, "If you automatically get a submit button at the bottom of every document currently being created or edited on a Domino Web server, what can I possibly gain from reading this chapter that discusses the submit button?" Let's just say that the default submit button and the message that Domino Web server generates to tell users the document was saved are a bit rudimentary — or at the very best, too generic.

This chapter covers all the neat ways you can customize the submit button and the message that informs users of a successful save.

Submitting Documents

If you don't customize either piece of the document submission process (the submit button or the message that confirms that the document saved successfully), users creating or editing documents on your Domino Web site see the Domino default submit button at the bottom of the document (see Figure 18-1).

When users click the submit button, the document saves to the Domino Web server and users receive the `Form processed` message (see Figure 18-2), which indicates that the document saved successfully.

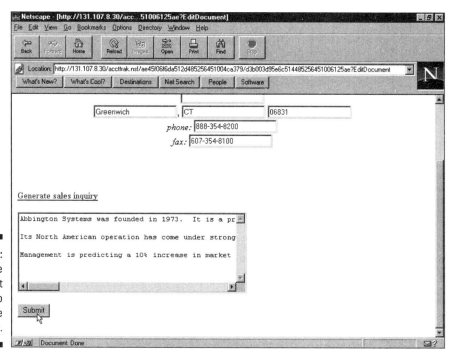

Figure 18-1: Click the submit button to save the document.

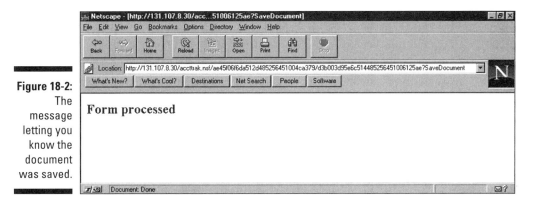

Figure 18-2:
The
message
letting you
know the
document
was saved.

Working with Buttons

If you're accustomed to developing applications that only Lotus Notes clients can access and which contain oodles of buttons in the forms, but you now want to create applications that Web browsers can access, I have some good news and some bad news.

The bad news first — Web browsers don't support buttons in forms (with some exceptions I discuss later). That's right. Sorry, but you did read that correctly. Not only do Web browsers not support buttons in forms, but they also don't even *display* them. (Actually, that's a good thing — you don't want to present users with something that doesn't even work.)

And let's not forget the good news — you can still provide the functionality that you are accustomed to providing through buttons on the form. You create action buttons in the action button bar instead of on the form. So in the end, you aren't losing any of your application's functionality. And that is good news! (See Chapter 11 for information on creating action buttons.)

A few exceptions exist to the "buttons don't display for Web browsers" rule. First of all, the Domino Web server displays two types of buttons: the submit button (which displays automatically) and the file attach button (which you set up to display — see Chapter 17). The other two exceptions to the rule really aren't exceptions; they're tricks you can use to get what look like Notes buttons to appear. You can paste an image that looks like a button from the Windows Clipboard or your operating system's equivalent and create a link that executes a command or navigates to another part of the Web. You can also use HTML to simulate a button.

Adding a Notes button

You may be wondering, "If Web browsers ignore buttons, why does this section cover adding them?" As I mention earlier in this chapter, the Domino Web server does put one browser-recognizable button on a document — the submit button, which automatically appears at the bottom of the document.

You can create a button that acts just like the submit button. If you want, you can create this button to appear in another part of the document, and to contain text other than *Submit.* If you go this route, the Domino Web server uses the button you create as the submit button and does not add its submit button to the bottom of the form.

Keep in mind that if you add any more Notes-specific buttons besides the submit button that you create, those buttons do not display on Web browsers.

To create your very own submit button that Web browsers can display, do the following:

1. **Launch the Lotus Notes client.**

   The Lotus Notes Workspace, which displays the Domino Web server's databases as rectangular icons, appears.

2. **Click the icon of the database that contains the form to which you want to add the button.**

3. **Choose <u>V</u>iew⇨<u>D</u>esign.**

   The database opens. If Design does not appear in the View menu, refer to Chapter 6 for help.

4. **Click the Forms folder.**

   The names of the database's forms appear in the View pane.

5. **Double-click the name of the form to which you want to add the button.**

   The form appears in Edit mode.

6. **Click the location in the form where you want to add the button.**

7. **Choose <u>C</u>reate⇨<u>H</u>otspot⇨<u>B</u>utton.**

   This action adds the button to the form. The Properties for Button InfoBox appears (see Figure 18-3).

8. **Type a label for the button in the Button label text box.**

   Don't bother typing a formula in the formula window of the Design pane, because the Domino Web server disregards anything you type. (In this instance, the button can only perform a save of the document.)

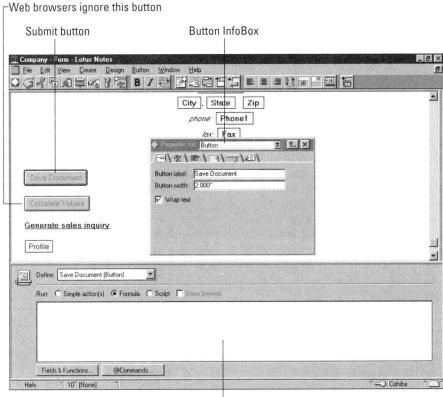

Web browsers ignore this button

Submit button

Button InfoBox

Formula window

Figure 18-3:
Adding a
button to a
form.

9. Press Ctrl+S to save the form.

Figure 18-4 shows the browser's view of the work shown in Figure 18-3. Compare Figure 18-4 to Figure 18-1. Notice how, instead of appearing at the bottom of the document, the submit button now appears where you added it? Also notice that the additional button, labeled Calculate Values in Figure 18-3, does not appear in the browser's view in Figure 18-4.

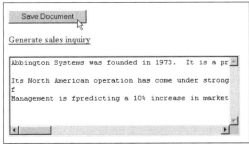

Figure 18-4:
The new
submit
button as
viewed with
a Web
browser.

Pasting in an image as a button

Before you paste into a form an image to use as a button, you must copy an image of a button into the Windows Clipboard or your operating system's equivalent. Unfortunately, you can't create a button in a Notes form and then copy it to the Clipboard. You must either create a form with a button and then do a Print Screen of the form or use a graphics editor to create an image that looks like a button.

Because creating a form with a button and then doing a Print Screen copies the entire screen, including the button, to the Windows Clipboard, you should paste the Print Screen into a graphics editor, cut the button from the graphic, and copy just the button to the Clipboard.

After you copy the button image to the Clipboard through whatever means, do the following:

1. **Double-click the form to which you want to add the button.**

   The form opens in edit mode.

2. **Click on the location in the form where you want to add the button.**

3. **Choose Edit⇨Paste.**

   This pastes the button from the Clipboard onto the form.

4. **Click the button on the form to highlight it.**

5. **Choose Create⇨Hotspot⇨URL Link.**

   The Properties for URL Link Object InfoBox appears.

6. **Type the URL in the formula window of the URL Link Object InfoBox.**

   You can specify a URL to navigate either to another part of the Domino Web site or to another site on the Web, or you can use the ?OpenAgent URL syntax to execute an agent. (See Chapter 5 for more information about this syntax and about Domino-specific URLs in general.)

7. **Press Ctrl+S to save the form.**

Adding a reset button with HTML

You can use HTML (HyperText Markup Language) to add buttons. Figure 18-5 shows an example of a special HTML button that resets field values. When users click this button, all the fields reset to their default values but the document doesn't save. I recommend including this button so that if users make a mistake, they can reset the field values without accidentally saving a document that has erroneous information.

The syntax to create the HTML reset button is:

```
[<INPUT TYPE ="Reset" VALUE="Button label"><BR>]
```

As Figure 18-5 indicates, all you need to do is type the HTML directly onto the form, just as you would if the HTML code were static text. The Domino Web server converts the HTML to a button. Refer to Chapter 20 for more information on incorporating HTML into a form. Notice that you must enclose the code in square brackets; otherwise, the Domino Web server interprets the HTML code as text and doesn't translate it.

Figure 18-6 shows the way the HTML reset button appears viewed on a Web browser. Notice that it looks the same as the submit button that was created through the the procedure covered in the "Adding a Notes button" section earlier in this chapter.

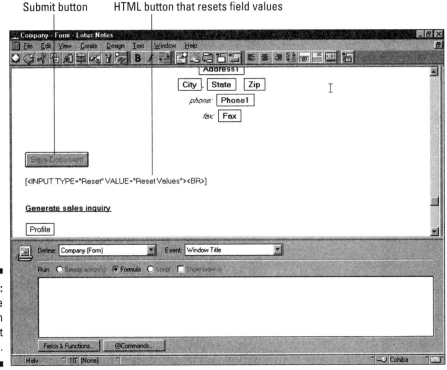

Submit button   HTML button that resets field values

Figure 18-5: The code behind an HTML reset button.

Figure 18-6:
The HTML
reset button
as seen
with a Web
browser.

Shoot the Messenger

The Domino default message, *Form processed,* that users see when they save a document is, frankly, boring. The saying "Don't shoot the messenger" (that's *you,* the developer, being the messenger of this boring message) doesn't apply here because, inasmuch as you are capable of changing the message, your users have full authority to "shoot the messenger" if it's boring!

Customizing the submit message

Got a little joke for you. What's the difference between a customized submit message and a bank robber caught red-handed? The bank robber will Return$$ and the customized submit message will use $$Return. Ha! I got a million of 'em!

Well, if that's a little obtuse, let me explain. If you want to customize the message users receive when they submit a document, which I strongly recommend that you do, create a special field named $$Return. The $$Return field is a calculated text field; its formula is the message you want to return to your users. For example, if you want the message to read, "Thank you for ordering with us. We greatly appreciate your business," type those words in the field's formula window. To create a $$Return field:

1. **Double-click the form to put the form in Edit mode.**

2. **Click the location in the form where you want to create the field.**

   You should put the field on its own line so it can remain hidden without interfering with the display of other fields.

3. **Choose Create⇨Field.**

   The Properties for Field InfoBox appears.

4. **Type $$Return in the Name text box.**

5. **Select Computed from the drop-down list.**

6. **In the formula window of the Design pane, type in the text that you want to appear in the submit message.**

   Be sure to enclose it in quotes (see Figure 18-7).

7. **Click the Hide tab in the InfoBox.**

   The Hide paragraph check boxes appear.

8. **Click all the check boxes except the Hide paragraph if formula is true check box.**

   You don't need to check the Hide paragraph if formula is true check box if you enable the other check boxes (see Figure 18-7).

Formatting the message

You can customize not only the *what* of the message that appears when users save a document but also the *how*. You can make it bold or italic or both, you can underline it or change its size, or you can do a combination of these things to it.

┌$$Return field   Select the check boxes to hide the field

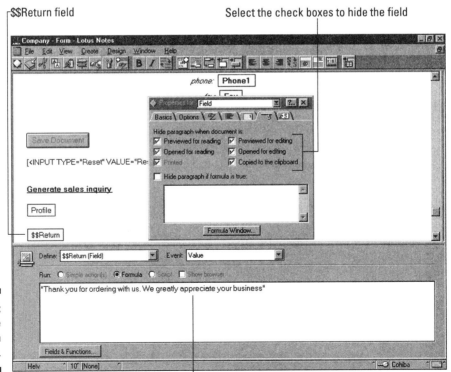

Figure 18-7:
Creating the
$$Return
field.

Message that appears when users save documents

✔ **Bold text:** Use the ⟨b⟩ HTML tag to bold text. Type the following line into the $$Return field's formula window of the Design pane to produce the text shown in Figure 18-8:

```
"<b>Thank you for ordering with us. We greatly
     appreciate your business.</b>"
```

✔ **Heading size:** You can specify any of the six levels of headings by using the ⟨h1⟩ through ⟨h6⟩ HTML tags. The different headings display text in different sizes, ⟨h1⟩ being the largest and ⟨h6⟩ being the smallest. Typing the following line into the $$Return field's formula window of the Design pane produces the text shown in Figure 18-9:

```
"<h2>Thank you for ordering with us. We greatly
     appreciate your business.</h2>"
```

✔ **Italic text:** Use the ⟨i⟩ HTML tag to italicize text. Typing the following line into the $$Return field's formula window of the Design pane produces the text shown in Figure 18-10:

```
"<h2><i>Thank you for ordering with us. We greatly
     appreciate your business.<i></h2>"
```

✔ **Underline text:** Use the ⟨u⟩ HTML tag to underline text. Typing the following line into the $$Return field's formula window of the Design pane produces the text shown in Figure 18-11:

```
"<h2><i>Thank you for ordering with us. We <u>greatly</
     u> appreciate your business.<i></h2>"
```

A generally accepted protocol on the Web is that text links are underlined. For this reason, you should avoid underlining text. You do not want to create a scenario where your users are getting confused by clicking on text that they think is a text link but is really just text you have formatted to be underlined.

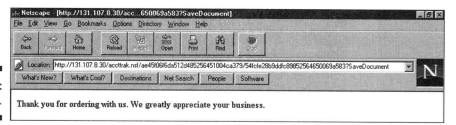

Figure 18-8:
Bold text.

Thank you for ordering with us. We greatly appreciate your business.

Thank you for ordering with us. We greatly appreciate your business.

Thank you for ordering with us. We greatly appreciate your business.

Thank you for ordering with us. We <u>greatly</u> appreciate your business.

Personalizing the message

You don't have to limit yourself to simple customization messages; you can personalize them. You can *concatenate* (or join together) the result of a formula with a text string. The following formula uses a user's first name when thanking her for her submission (for example, if Julianne Chan submits a document the message says, "Thank you for your submission, Julianne"):

```
"Thank you for your
submission,"+@if(@UserName="Anonymous";NULL;
        @Left(@UserName;" "))
```

Because most users access the database as Anonymous, the formula tests to make sure that if a user accesses the database as Anonymous, the formula simply reads "Thank you for your submission," when the user saves a document, instead of "Thank you for your submission, Anonymous," which is a bit impersonal.

Another nice thing you can do with the submission message is to include the date and time that the document was saved. Figure 18-12 shows the result of this formula:

```
"Your document was saved on "+@Text(@Now;"s0")+" at
        "+@Text(@Now;"s1")
```

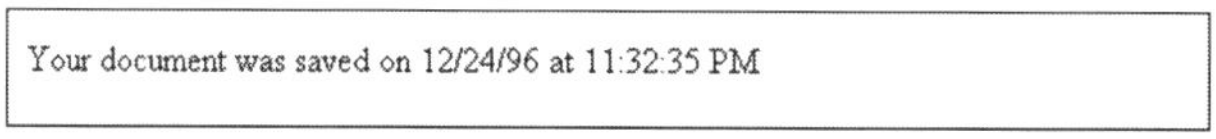

Figure 18-12:
A submission message telling the user when the document was saved.

Your document was saved on 12/24/96 at 11:32:35 PM

In this example, notice that if you mix text with dates (or for that matter mix text and numbers), you must use the @Text formula to convert the date to text. The @Now formula returns the current date and time. The s0 and s1 arguments return just the date and time portions, respectively, of the @Now formula.

Judging from the look of the time and date in Figure 18-12, somebody is making a last-minute submission to Santa's Domino Web site. Either that or the author is up too late doing screen captures for a book.

Linking to Another Page

You can combine text and formulas to customize the submission message, and you can format it to your liking — or, I should say, you can format it to *your customer's* liking, because, after all, you are trying to make your Domino Web site 100 percent customer focused. One more shortcoming of the default submit message must be addressed.

When users submit a document, the submission message appears on their screens, but what do they do then? They can press Esc to get back to a document, but how do they know that? Including "Press Esc to return to your document" is a bit clunky. You can skip the submission message and automatically navigate users to a view or document. Or, because Web browser users are accustomed to clicking images, buttons, or text links to do stuff on the Web, you can create links in the submission page that allow them to navigate to other pages. You have no reason, after all, to confuse people by expecting them to work differently at your Web site than they do at other places on the Web (that is, by requiring them to press a key on that often-seems-to-be obsolete thing called a "keyboard").

Skip the message

If you decide you don't want users to receive a submission message when they save documents, you can automatically navigate them to a document or view when they click the submit button. I cannot, however, discourage you enough from doing so; you should give users some indication when their documents save successfully.

Still, if you decide to automatically navigate them to a different document or view, specify the URL of the place you want to send them to in the $$Return field's formula window of the Design pane. Be sure to enclose the URL in brackets; otherwise, the Domino Web server doesn't convert the text to HTML. Also, be sure to enclose the URL and brackets with quotes; otherwise, you can't save the formula. Figure 18-13 shows an example of a formula that automatically navigates users to the North West view when they click the submit button.

If you specify a view name that contains a space in its URL, be sure to replace the space with a plus sign (+); otherwise users get an error when they click the submit button.

Figure 18-13:
Users are navigated to the North West view when they click the submit button.

Creating links

One thing you can do that your users should greatly appreciate is to create links in the submission page. Instead of leaving them out in the twilight zone to figure out what to do after the submission message jumps up and stares them in the face, create some intuitive links they can click to return to a view or document.

You create links the same way you do all the other customizations — by using the $$Return field. The only difference is the syntax you use to create the link. Typing the following syntax as the formula for the $$Return field causes the phrase *Click to open the North West view* to appear on the submission page. The phrase is underlined, indicating to users that it is a link. The link in this example opens the North West view in the `accttrak.nsf` database.

```
"<a href=http://131.107.8.30/accttrak.nsf/
north+west?OpenView>Click to open the North West view</a>"
```

Figure 18-14 shows how you can combine text and a number of links to create a great submission message.

Figure 18-15 shows the code behind the submission message in Figure 18-14. Some of the things contained in the code that I should point out:

- ✔ The Domino Web server ignores text in quotes following the REM command, as well as spaces in the code.

- ✔ Each HTML link is assigned to a temporary variable to make it a bit easier to understand the code and to perform necessary troubleshooting. The assignment symbol is a colon and equal sign (:=).

- ✔ Some of the HTML links include the split vertical bar (|) within the quotes to separate the links when users view them on a Web browser.

- ✔ The lines of text appear on different lines with the help of the <p> HTML tag, which represents paragraphs.

- ✔ Each line of code must be followed by a semicolon (;).

- ✔ The <b> HTML tag is used to bold the links.

- ✔ The last line of the code concatenates all the temporary variables; it's the line that controls what appears in the submission message.

Figure 18-14:
An award-winning submission message.

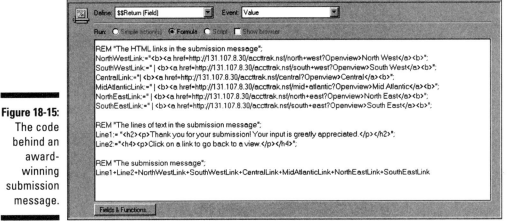

Figure 18-15:
The code
behind an
award-
winning
submission
message.

Within the figure:

```
Define: $$Return (Field)        Event: Value

Run:  ○ Simple action(s)  ● Formula  ○ Script  □ Show browser

REM "The HTML links in the submission message";
NorthWestLink:="<b><a href=http://131.107.8.30/accttrak.nsf/north+west?Openview>North West</a><b>";
SouthWestLink:=" | <b><a href=http://131.107.8.30/accttrak.nsf/south+west?Openview>South West</a><b>";
CentralLink:="| <b><a href=http://131.107.8.30/accttrak.nsf/central?Openview>Central</a><b>";
MidAtlanticLink:=" | <b><a href=http://131.107.8.30/accttrak.nsf/mid+atlantic?Openview>Mid Atlantic</a><b>";
NorthEastLink:=" | <b><a href=http://131.107.8.30/accttrak.nsf/north+east?Openview>North East</a><b>";
SouthEastLink:=" | <b><a href=http://131.107.8.30/accttrak.nsf/south+east?Openview>South East</a><b>";

REM "The lines of text in the submission message";
Line1:= "<h2><p>Thank you for your submission! Your input is greatly appreciated.</p></h2>";
Line2:="<h4><p>Click on a link to go back to a view.</p></h4>";

REM "The submission message";
Line1+Line2+NorthWestLink+SouthWestLink+CentralLink+MidAtlanticLink+NorthEastLink+SouthEastLink

Fields & Functions...
```

Part IV
Enhancing with Other Tools

In this part . . .

So you're surfing the Web and you see all these colorful, intense sites with lots of graphics, little wheels moving around on the pages, noises coming from your speakers, and things like that. That stuff is terribly advanced, you know. You have to be a real 10th-degree Webmaster with a black belt and everything before you can even *consider* doing the really cool stuff on your Web site.

Don't you believe it! True, extras like Java applets and graphics take some work, but you can use these and other elements with Domino while creating your site. Domino even comes with its own applications that can help you spruce up your Web pages. So what are you waiting for? Put on your black belt, get in the Lotus position, and read this part!

Chapter 19

Domino.Applications

*T*he Domino.Applications created by Lotus allow you to enhance and extend your Domino Web server. Presently, Lotus offers three applications in the Domino.Applications group:

✔ **Domino.Action:** Enables you to quickly create a Web site on your Domino Web server

✔ **Domino.Merchant:** Helps you build a powerful commerce site on your Domino Web server

✔ **Domino.Broadcast for PointCast:** Allows you to quickly disseminate time-critical information to people in your intranet (in conjunction with the PointCast, Inc., I-Server)

Domino.Broadcast for PointCast works only for people connected to your corporate intranet. Users with Web browsers cannot access this technology.

The Domino.Action software, which is actually two Lotus Notes template databases, comes free with Domino. One of the great things about it is that you don't need to have experience with HTML to create your Web site with the aid of Domino.Action. For that matter, you don't even need experience with Domino. If you know how to type and to click with a mouse, you can easily create a Web site with Domino.Action.

The other two applications, Domino.Merchant and Domino.Broadcast for PointCast, while equally valuable in their own right, do not come free with Domino and they require a little more knowledge or experience than just typing and clicking.

Domino.Action

Domino.Action, a separate program that ships with the Domino Web server, helps you create a Web presence quickly and smoothly and maintain it without difficulty. Domino.Action uses a template-based design process, which means you set the variable design elements before you start making your Domino Web site. When you create a site with Domino.Action, its content and design are consistent, regardless of how many different people are involved in creating and updating the site.

Domino.Action components

Domino.Action is composed of three components:

- **Library:** This Lotus Notes database stores the templates used to build your Web site's forms, subforms, views, fields, and other design elements. When you build your Web site, you determine from this database which design elements to use.

- **SiteCreator:** This Lotus Notes database is where you begin the design process. You create documents in the SiteCreator that specify what to include in the Web site, such as the site manager's name and e-mail address, graphics, company-specific information, and various site-specific areas — such as for a home page, policy and procedures, about the company, document library, FAQs, job opportunities, registration, and so on. You use the SiteCreator to control the appearance, organization, and content-approval process for each of these areas.

- **AppAssembler:** The AppAssembler combines the templates in the Library with the information you provide in SiteCreator, and actually builds the Web site.

Creating the required databases

In order to use Domino.Action, you must create the Library and SiteCreator Lotus Notes databases. You do both of these tasks through your Lotus Notes client.

You must have the full version of Lotus Notes, not the Desktop or Mail versions of Notes, to create the Library and SiteCreator databases.

Creating Library

To create the Domino.Action Library database, follow these steps:

1. **Launch the Lotus Notes client.**

   The Lotus Notes Workspace, which displays the Domino Web server's databases as rectangular icons, appears.

2. **Choose File➪Database➪New.**

   The New Database dialog box appears (see Figure 19-1).

3. **Choose the name of the server in which you want to store the database from the Server drop-down list box.**

4. **Type a name for the database in the Title text box.**

5. **Type an appropriate filename for the database in the File Name text box.**

   Use the .nsf extension when naming the Library database. Also, when you configure the site in the SiteCreator, the field that specifies the name of the Library database defaults to the name LibAct.nsf, so if you use a name other than that default when you create the Library database, be sure to make the change in the SiteCreator document.

6. **Choose the Domino.Action Library template from the scroll box below the Template Server button.**

7. **Click the OK button.**

   The newly created database appears on the Lotus Notes workspace.

Specify LibAct as Filename

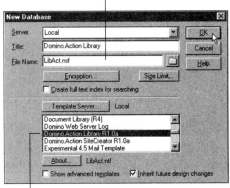

Figure 19-1:
Creating the
Domino.Action
Library
database.

Select the Library template

Creating SiteCreator

To create the Domino.Action SiteCreator database, follow these steps:

1. Launch the Lotus Notes client.

The Lotus Notes Workspace, which displays the Domino Web server's databases as rectangular icons, appears.

2. Choose File⇨Database⇨New.

The New Database dialog box appears (see Figure 19-2).

3. Type the name of the server on which you want to store the database in the Server text box.

You can also click the down-arrow button next to the text field and select the server from a drop-down list.

4. Type an appropriate name for the database in the Title text box.

5. Type an appropriate filename in the File Name text box.

Use the .nsf extension when naming the SiteCreator database. Also, if you used a filename other than the default LibAct.nsf when you created the Library database, be sure to type the same filename in this File Name text box. If you don't, the field that specifies the name of the Library database defaults to the name LibAct.nsf and you get an error.

6. Choose the Domino.Action SiteCreator template from the scroll box below the Template Server button.

7. Click the OK button.

The newly created database appears on the Lotus Notes workspace.

Figure 19-2:
Creating the
Domino.Action
SiteCreator
database.

Selected SiteCreator template

Configuring and Creating the Web Site

Your creation of the Library and SiteCreator databases must be complete before you begin the Web site configuration and creation process. If you don't have the two icons shown in Figure 19-3, you're not ready to configure and create your Web site. Complete the steps in the previous section (Domino.Action) before continuing with this section.

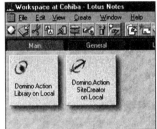

Figure 19-3:
The Library
and
SiteCreator
databases.

To configure and create the Web site, follow these steps:

1. **Launch the Lotus Notes client.**

   The Lotus Notes Workspace, which displays the Domino Web server's databases as rectangular icons, appears.

2. **Double-click the SiteCreator database icon to open the database.**

   The database opens, and the SiteCreator Overview appears (see Figure 19-4).

3. **Click the Configure Your Site graphic at the top of the screen.**

   The Step 1: Configure Your Site document appears (see Figure 19-5).

4. **Click the Configure Your Site button in the middle of the document.**

   The Configure Your Site profile appears (see Figure 19-6).

5. **Click the Edit button to put the profile in Edit mode, and then select the areas you want to include in your site.**

   These areas might include the site manager's name, the company name and address, the copyright message, images used in the site, the location of the site, and the location of the Library database.

6. **Click the Continue button at the bottom of the form when you're finished.**

   The Step 2: Design Your Site document appears (see Figure 19-7).

Click here

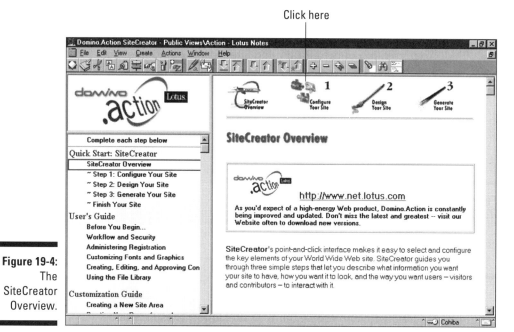

Figure 19-4:
The
SiteCreator
Overview.

Click here

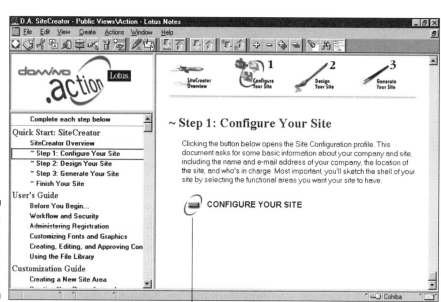

Figure 19-5:
The
Configure
Your Site
document.

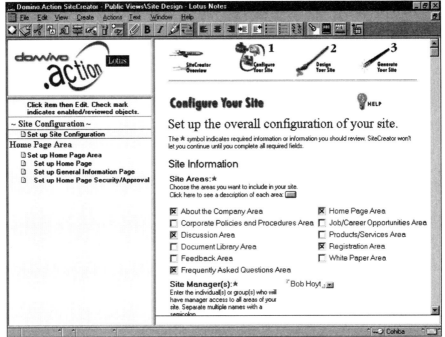

Figure 19-6:
The site configuration profile.

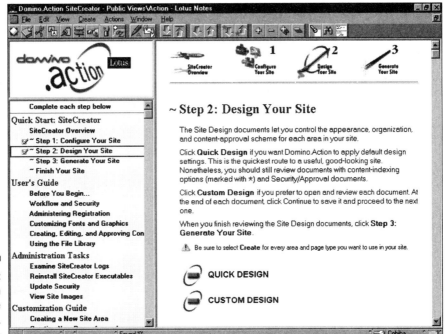

Figure 19-7:
The Design Your Site document.

7. Click either the Quick Design or the Custom Design button.

I recommend clicking the Quick Design button, because the purpose for using Domino.Action is quickness, ease, and consistency.

- **Quick Design:** Applies the default design settings to each document.
- **Custom Design:** Lets you review the design of each document.

8. Review the information indicated in the Design Your Site document.

To review part of the site, click on the object in the navigation (left-hand) pane and notice that the document representing the object is displayed in the view (right-hand) pane. For example, in Figure 19-8, "Set up Registration Area" is selected in the navigation pane and the "Set up Registration Area" document is displayed in the view pane. You must review all items marked with a star symbol to complete the design of your site.

9. Click the Generate Your Site graphic at the top of the document.

The Step 3: Generate Your Site document appears (see Figure 19-9).

Click here

Figure 19-8:
Review
necessary
information.

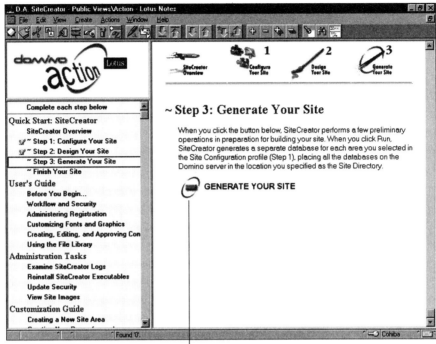

Figure 19-9:
The
Generate
Your Site
document.

Click here

10. Click the Generate Your Site button in the middle of the document.

After a few minutes, the Run AppAssembler document appears (see Figure 19-10).

11. Click the Run button.

The AppAssembler begins the process of creating a database for each of the areas you specified during the configuration step. Depending on how many databases AppAssembler needs to create, it can take as long as 45 minutes to complete the process.

Once the process is complete, you see the newly created databases that comprise your Domino Web site.

Click here

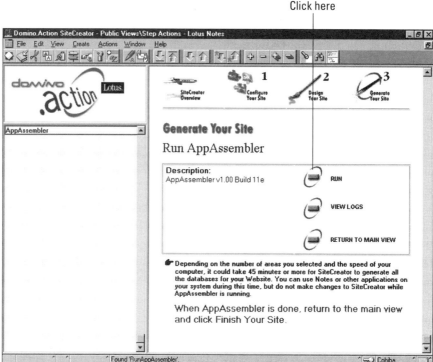

Figure 19-10:
The Run
App-
Assembler
document.

Domino.Merchant

Domino.Merchant helps you create an effective commerce site on your Domino Web server. Whether you want an information kiosk for marketing purposes or a high-end virtual store for selling products and services and accepting payment over the Internet, Domino.Merchant is a great tool you can use to accomplish your goals.

Domino.Merchant allows you to maintain a product catalog, register customers, accept orders, securely accept credit card payments, process the payments, deliver the ordered product, and keep a record of the transaction.

Creating the site

Domino.Merchant uses the SiteCreator to create the commerce site. The four basic components to SiteCreator are:

✔ **Store registration:** SiteCreator collects information, such as the company's name, and assigns a unique ID for secure transactions.

✔ **Layout configuration:** SiteCreator configures the site's design elements, such as home page, catalog, product information documents, shopping basket, and so on.

✔ **Store content creation:** SiteCreator sets up the catalog and specifies the approval process workflow for adding site content.

✔ **Customer information collection:** SiteCreator creates forms for registering and authenticating customers, and specifies a registration and validation process.

The consumer experience

Domino.Merchant uses the shopping-basket metaphor; users accumulate items in a virtual shopping basket as they go through your site. Before they check-out, users double-check to make sure that they have all the correct items, and then they submit the order.

After users submit their order, they also can specify their credit card number, and because the Domino Web server supports *SSL (Secure Socket Layer)* encryption, users can be sure that the credit card is encrypted for the entire time it takes the credit card information to reach the server.

Accepting payment and fulfilling orders

The payment functionality of Domino.Merchant enables the merchant to immediately validate the credit card transaction with a clearing agent, which means that the merchant can immediately offer the ordered product (assuming it is software, or information that the user can download) to the consumer.

Domino.Merchant also simplifies those scenarios in which the product can't be delivered electronically, like software can. For example, if a user orders a barber pole or something similar that must ship by mail or courier, the Domino Web server can handle the entire order-fulfillment process through *workflow,* meaning the server can notify the required order-processing people and then verify that the order was processed. The server can also archive the order in the event that future research to fulfill the order is necessary. The information can either be archived to a Lotus Notes database or to a corporate relational database (RDBMS).

Domino.Broadcast for PointCast

Domino.Broadcast for PointCast allows you to quickly disseminate time-critical information to people on your intranet. Instead of forcing users to rely on getting time-critical information on a Web site (which they may check only one or two times per day), or by e-mail (which they may check every hour or so), you can implement Domino.Broadcast for PointCast. Domino.Broadcast for PointCast enables you to send time-critical information that immediately appears on the computer screens of those using the corporate intranet to browse your Domino site.

Only people connected to your corporate intranet can benefit from Domino.Broadcast for PointCast.

PointCast is a popular news network that pulls information from various places on the Web and displays the information in tables and scrolling messages on-screen. The combination of the Domino Web server and the PointCast I-Server allows you to do the same thing with information that is stored on your Domino Web server (and also with information in other Web sites).

You can take advantage of the agent technology on the Domino Web server to send broadcasts on a schedule. For example, you can send a message at the end of every week telling your consultants to update their billable time reports. The message you send them can include a link to the report that you need them to complete.

If you have a daily news service pertaining to your industry and you want your sales reps to get breaking news as it breaks, the problem with sending the information to them via e-mail is that they may not view their e-mail until the end of the day. If you want to ensure that they get the information immediately, Domino.Broadcast for PointCast is the tool for you.

Chapter 20

HTML Help

In This Chapter

▶ Integrating HTML

▶ Formatting with HTML

▶ Adding links and images with HTML

▶ Using HTML in view columns

*H*ypertext *Markup Language (HTML)* is the language people use to create content on the World Wide Web. When you create elements such as views, forms, and documents on your Domino Web site, the server actually converts the elements to HTML so that Web browsers can interpret them.

So, if the Domino Web server automatically converts elements to HTML, why do you need to read an entire chapter on HTML? Because if you design your site strictly with the Lotus Notes functionality, you ever-so-slightly *limit* what you can design in the site. This chapter covers those areas in which you can integrate HTML to ever-so-slightly *enhance* your Domino Web site instead.

What Does HTML Look Like?

HTML uses tags to create and format Web page content. Figure 20-1 shows an example of the HTML code in a simple document. It gets a lot more complex-looking than this, though.

When viewing a page on a Web site, you can view the HTML code used to create that page. If you're using Netscape Navigator, choose View⇨Document Source to view a page's HTML code. If you're using Microsoft Internet Explorer, choose View⇨Source.

HTML tag that specifies the beginning of a hypertext document

Figure 20-1:
The HTML
code
behind a
simple Web
page.

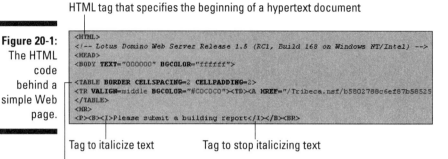

Tag to italicize text   Tag to stop italicizing text

Tag to create a table

The HTML code in the last line in Figure 20-1, `<P><B><I>Please submit a building report</I></B><BR>`, translates to plain English as follows:

- ✔ `<P>`: Start a new paragraph

- ✔ `<B>`: Bold the following text

- ✔ `<I>`: Italicize the following text

- ✔ `Please submit a building report`: Text to display via the Web browser

- ✔ `</B>`: Turn off the bold formatting so that text that follows isn't bold

- ✔ `</I>`: Turn off the italics formatting so that text that follows isn't italicized

Integrating HTML into Domino

When integrating HTML in a Domino Web site, you can't simply type an HTML tag and expect it to work. You have to tell the Domino Web server to interpret the HTML tag as an HTML tag instead of as text. For example, if you type `<I> Annual Report</I>` in a Lotus Notes form, the Domino Web server interprets the entire string, including the HTML tags, as text and displays "<I>Annual Report</I>" — instead of recognizing the HTML tags and displaying *Annual Report* italicized to the Web browser. You can get the Domino Web server to recognize the tags as HTML in either of two ways: enclosing the HTML code in brackets, or formatting the line of paragraph in which the HTML code appears with a Named Style called HTML. A *Named Style* is paragraph format style that can be reused throughout a database.

Enclosing HTML code in brackets

An easy way for you to present HTML in a way that the Domino Web server recognizes it is to enclose the HTML code in brackets. Figure 20-2 shows two lines of a form that is in Design mode. Notice that the text and tags are the same on both lines. Notice also that the second line is enclosed in square brackets; it is the one that works as expected.

Figure 20-2:
The right and the wrong way to integrate HTML into a Domino Web site.

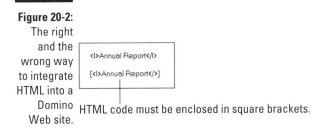

HTML code must be enclosed in square brackets.

Figure 20-3 shows the way the two lines appear to a Web browser. Notice that the Domino Web server recognizes the HTML tags in the second line and italicizes the text as you would expect.

Figure 20-3:
The result of the right and wrong ways to integrate HTML.

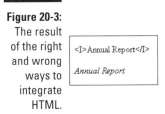

So, anytime you want the Domino Web server to recognize and convert an HTML tag correctly, be sure to enclose the code in square brackets — with one exception. When you're typing the HTML code into a form, you can choose an alternative to enclosing the code in brackets. You can format the line or paragraph in which the HTML line appears with the HTML Named Style.

Another way the server recognizes HTML

Enclosing HTML code in square brackets enables the Domino Web server to recognize the HTML code without a problem. If, however, you are typing multiple lines of HTML code into a form or are importing an existing HTML document into a Lotus Notes form, enclosing the code in brackets is time-consuming and cumbersome.

Another way you can integrate the HTML so that the Domino Web server recognizes it is to format the line or paragraph in which the HTML code appears with a Named Style called HTML. Before you can use the HTML Named Style to format a line or paragraph, you have to create it.

Creating the HTML Named Style

Creating the HTML Named Style is easy. Do the following:

1. **Launch the Lotus Notes client.**

   The Lotus Notes Workspace, which displays the Domino Web server's databases as rectangular icons, appears.

2. **Click the icon for the database where you want to create the HTML Named Style.**

3. **Choose View⇨Design.**

   The database opens. Refer to Chapter 6 if Design does not appear in the View menu.

4. **Click the Forms folder.**

   The names of the database's forms appear in the view pane.

5. **Double-click the name of any form.**

   The form appears in Edit mode. Because Named Styles can be used in all the forms in the database, it does not matter which form you open when creating the Named Style.

6. **Put the cursor on an unformatted line in the form.**

   Otherwise, the Named Style you create adopts the formatting of the line.

7. **Choose Text⇨Text Properties, or press Ctrl+K.**

   The Properties for Text InfoBox appears (see Figure 20-4).

8. **Click the Named Styles tab.**

   This tab looks like a luggage tag with the letter *S* on it.

Figure 20-4:
The Named
Styles tab
in the
Properties
for Text
InfoBox.

9. Click the Create Style button.

The Create Named Style dialog box appears (see Figure 20-5).

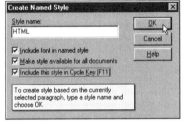

Figure 20-5:
The Create
Named
Style
dialog box.

10. Type HTML **in the Style name field.**

You must call the Named Style *HTML* — otherwise it has no effect.

11. Click the three check boxes in the dialog box.

The following list explains what each check box means:

- **Include font in named style:** Choosing this check box causes the font used to format the line in which you positioned the cursor when you started creating the Named Style to be adopted in the new HTML Named Style.

- **Make style available for all documents:** Choosing this check box allows you to use the Named Style on other documents in the database.

- **Include this style in Cycle Key (F11):** Choosing this check box includes the HTML Named Style in the Cycle List, so that you can simply press F11 to format a highlighted line or paragraph with the Named Style.

12. Click the OK button when you're finished.

Formatting with the HTML Named Style

After you create the HTML Named Style, you can use it to format lines and paragraphs. To format with the HTML Named Style, follow these steps:

1. **Place the cursor on the line, or highlight the entire paragraph, in which you want the Domino Web server to recognize the HTML code.**

2. **Press F11 until HTML appears in the status bar at the bottom of the screen, or click the Named Style section of the status bar and select HTML from the pop-up list.**

   Figure 20-6 shows the newly formatted line and the pop-up list that appears after you click the Named Style section of the status bar.

This line is formatted with the HTML Named Style.

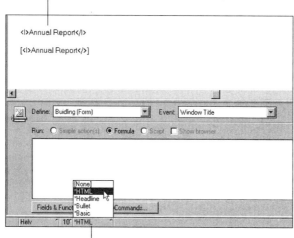

Figure 20-6:
Formatting a line with the HTML Named Style.

The Named Style is indicated in the status bar.

The result

Figure 20-6 shows HTML code that is not enclosed in square brackets but is formatted with the HTML Named Style (in the first line with the <I> code). Figure 20-7 demonstrates in a browser window the result of formatting a line with the HTML Named Style. The Domino Web server recognizes the HTML code in the first line just as it recognizes the HTML code in the second line, which is enclosed in square brackets.

Line of HTML code formatted with the HTML Named Style

Figure 20-7:
Both
methods
work!

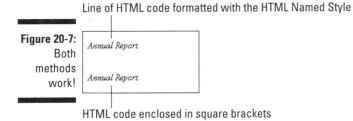

Annual Report

Annual Report

HTML code enclosed in square brackets

HTML Integration in Action

In forms, you can achieve some of the HTML effects demonstrated in this section, such as underlining, creating links, creating tables, and displaying images, with the standard Lotus Notes functionality. However, you need to know the HTML effects demonstrated in this section if you want to integrate them into columns or into the $$Return field. And keep in mind that, even if you are only incorporating HTML into forms, some of the effects demonstrated in the section, such as blinking text and a scrolling message in the status bar, can only be executed by using HTML tags.

Formatting text

Refer to these bullets for what HTML tags to use to generate the desired text format results:

- **Bold:** Use `<B>` to begin bolding and `</B>` to stop.
- **Underline:** Use `<U>` to begin underling and `</U>` to stop.
- **Italics:** Use `<I>` to begin italicizing and `</I>` to stop.
- **Paragraph:** Use `<P>` to begin a paragraph and `</P>` to end it.
- **Horizontal rule:** Use `<HR>` to create a horizontal rule.
- **Headings:** Use these sets of HTML tags to begin and end headings (in order from largest to smallest): `<H1>` and `</H1>`, `<H2>` and `</H2>`, `<H3>` and `</H3>`, `<H4>` and `</H4>`, `<H5>` and `</H5>`, or `<H6>` and `</H6>`.
- **Strikethrough:** Use `<Strike>` to begin strikethrough and `</Strike>` to end it.
- **Subscript:** Use `<Sub>` to begin subscript and `</Sub>` to end it.
- **Superscript:** Use `<Sup>` to begin superscript and `</Sup>` to end it.

Figure 20-8 shows examples of formatting with HTML on a form in Edit mode, viewed through the Lotus Notes client. Figure 20-9 shows how the formatting appears on a Web browser after Domino converts it to HTML.

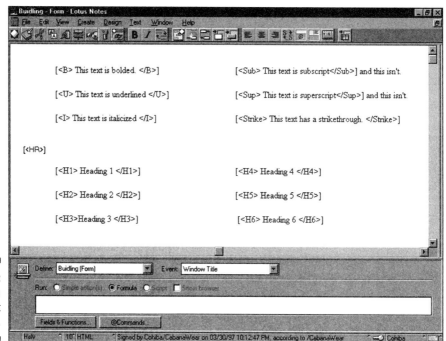

Figure 20-8:
HTML on a
form in Edit
mode.

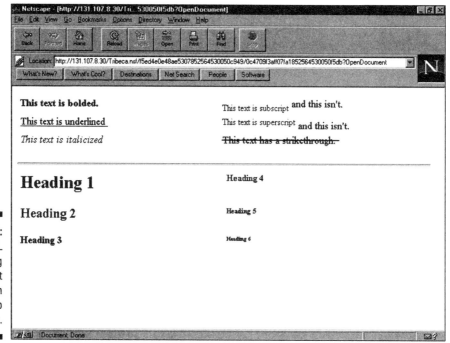

Figure 20-9:
HTML
formatting
as it
appears in
a Web
browser.

In addition to these tags, two other effects can't be achieved with the standard Lotus Notes functionality. You must use HTML to make text blink and to integrate links and images into your Domino Web pages. See the next two sections for more information.

Blinking text

One effect you can't achieve with the standard Lotus Notes functionality but must use HTML to get is *blinking text*. Use the <blink> HTML tag to get text to blink and </blink> to end the blinking. For example, if you type **The dog said [<blink>Bark, Bark, Bark</blink>] to the postal carrier**, the "Bark, Bark, Bark" portion of the sentence blinks on and off. (Notice that I put the HTML tags in brackets; see "Integrating HTML into Domino" earlier in this chapter for more about using this convention.)

I suggest that you refrain from using blinking text in your Web site, or at least that you use it in moderation. Why? Many Web surfers generally regard it as annoying rather than helpful or appreciated. Think of blinking text on the Web as being synonymous with scraping your fingernails across a chalkboard.

Integrating links and images

You can use HTML to create hypertext links and to display images, or to combine creating hypertext links and displaying images to give you an image that functions as a link.

Creating links

Here is an example of the syntax used to create a link:

```
[<A HREF="domino.lotus.com">]Go to the Domino
          Home Page[</A>]
```

This HTML code displays the underlined text "Go to the Domino Home Page"; the text is underlined, which to Web surfers indicates that the text is a hypertext link. The tag specifies that the browser is navigated to the domino.lotus.com site when users click the link.

Adding images

Here is an example of the syntax used to add an image:

```
[<img src = "/corporatelogo.gif">]
```

This example displays an image called `corporatelogo.gif`. Because no path is specified for the image, it must be located in the directory specified as the HTML directory field, which is located in the Mapping area of the HTTP Server section in the server document — which, in turn, is located in the server's Public Address Book (see Figure 20-10).

Location of images

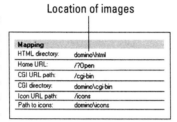

Figure 20-10:
Specify the
directory
where
images are
located.

Combining images with links

Standard practice for those who develop Web sites is to enable images to serve as links that do certain things when users click them. With HTML, the format for enabling images as links is:

```
[<A HREF="domino.lotus.com"><img src =
            "/corporatelogo.gif"></A>]
```

This line of HTML code displays the `corporatelogo.gif` file and enables it as a link that navigates users to the `domino.lotus.com` site when they click it.

The HTML Field

If you have an existing HTML document that you want to integrate into your Domino Web site, you don't have to paste it into a Lotus Notes form. You have another option.

You can create a field named *HTML* (and the field type can be either Editable or Computed) on a form and enter the name of the HTML file as the field value. Then whenever users with Web browsers open a document created using that form, all fields on the document, except HTML, are ignored. The HTML file specified in the field appears to the users who have the document in Read mode but not to those who have it in Edit mode.

The data type for the HTML field depends on the size of the HTML file you specify in the field value. Specify text data type if the HTML file is smaller than 15K and specify the rich-text data type if it is larger than 15K. Refer to Chapter 9 for more information on field data types.

HTML in Columns

Using HTML to format or add an image to a column can make things much easier on your site visitors when they try to quickly scan for information. You can control whether an icon appears based on whether certain values in a document are met. For example, you can have an icon appear if a document was created or modified a certain number of days ago, if it was created by a certain user, if it pertains to a certain department in your company, if a number field exceeds a certain value, and so on.

Figure 20-11 shows an example where the `closed.gif` image appears in the column if the value in a document's status field is set to Closed. If the value is anything other than Closed, the image doesn't appear.

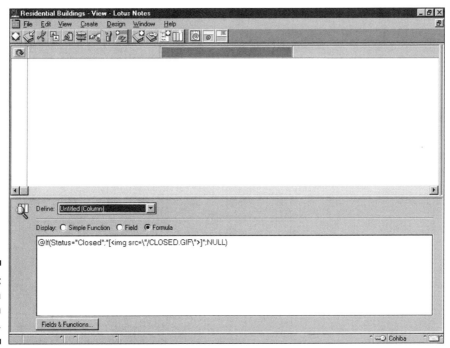

Figure 20-11:
HTML in a column formula.

The HTML code, which is enclosed in square brackets, must also be enclosed in quotes; otherwise the server tries to interpret the information enclosed in the brackets as a time value.

The HTML code that specifies the image in Figure 20-11 is:

```
[<img src = "/CLOSED.GIF">]
```

As I mentioned, the server tries to interpret this code as a time if you don't enclose it in quotes, so when you enclose it in quotes you get:

```
"[<img src = "/CLOSED.GIF">]"
```

A problem exists with the way that last formula is written. The server does not know how to interpret the different sets of quotes. Therefore, you must precede quotes that appear within quotes with a backslash (\). So, actually the correct formula is:

```
"[<img src = \"/CLOSED.GIF\">]"
```

Chapter 21

Coffee, Pictures, and More

· ·

In This Chapter

▶ JavaScript integration

▶ Multimedia integration

▶ Image integration

· ·

*I*f you want to spice up your Domino Web site, you're reading the right chapter. Using the tips and tricks in these pages, you can add images, sound, animated images, and programs that do things right before the eyes of visitors to your site.

You really should read the previous chapter (about HTML) just to make sure that you understand the HTML tag syntax necessary to implement some of these multimedia features into your Web site.

JavaScript

You can embed JavaScript in your Domino Web server documents. *JavaScript* is a powerful yet easy-to-use language (it doesn't need to be *compiled,* or translated into machine language) that you can include as part of an HTML document. Any JavaScript that you embed in a document loads when the Web browser opens the document. It can either execute automatically or execute when users click objects such as HTML buttons — you choose which way.

In order for the Domino Web server to interpret JavaScript as HTML code rather than as text, you must format the lines on which the code appears with the HTML Named Style. (See Chapter 20 for more information about this style and how to use it.)

The following example of JavaScript scrolls a message from right to left on the bottom of the screen. The script is embedded into a form as HTML. Figure 21-1 shows how the message appears on Web browsers.

```
<SCRIPT LANGUAGE="JavaScript">

  function scroll(temp)
  {
  /* Add more variables here to add more text  */
     var x1  = "This is an example of Java Script.";
     var x2  = " This message scrolls at the bottom of the
          screen.";

     var msg=x1+x2;
     var y = " ";
     var c  = 1;

     if (temp > 100)
     {
        temp--;
        var t="scroll(" + temp + ")";
        Delay=window.setTimeout(t,100);
     }

     else if (temp <= 100 && temp > 0)
     {
        for (c=0 ; c < temp ; c++)
        {
           y+=" ";
        }
        y+=msg;
        temp--;
        var t="scroll(" + temp + ")";
        window.status=y;
        Delay=window.setTimeout(t,100);
     }

     else if (temp <= 0)
     {
        if (-temp < msg.length)
        {
           y+=msg.substring(-temp,msg.length);
```

```
                temp--;
                var t="scroll(" + temp + ")";
                window.status=y;
                Delay=window.setTimeout(t,100);
            }
        else
            {
            window.status=" ";
            Delay=window.setTimeout("scroll(100)",25);
            }
        }
    }
}
</script>
<body
        onLoad="Loader=window.setTimeout('scroll(100)',600);">
```

Figure 21-1:
The
message
scrolls at
the bottom
of the
browser
screen.

> This is an example of JavaScript. This message scrolls at the bottom of the screen.

For more about JavaScript, pick up a copy of *JavaScript For Dummies* by Emily A. Vander Veer. That's another fine publication by the folks at IDG Books Worldwide, Inc.

Java Applets

Java applets are applications that you can insert in a Domino Web server document. Users must have browsers that support Java applets to take advantage of them. Think of Java applets as mini-programs that execute very quickly when users request them from a Web browser.

You use the `<applet>` HTML tag to embed Java applets into a Web page. This example runs a Java applet called Applebean:

```
[<applet codebase = "/Applebean" code = "Applebean.class"
          width=400 height=75 align=center></applet>]
```

Some of the key syntax attributes you should understand are:

- ✔ **Open bracket ([) and close bracket (]):** You must enclose HTML code in brackets so that the Domino Web server recognizes the code as HTML and converts it as expected.

- ✔ `<applet>` **and** `</applet>`: HTML tags that indicate the beginning and end of the applet's parameters.

- ✔ `codebase`: Indicates the location of the applet.

- ✔ `code`: Indicates the name of the applet.

- ✔ `width=`, `height=`, **and** `align=`: Formatting parameters for the applet.

Shockwave

The Domino Web server supports Shockwave applications. Shockwave is a technology developed by Macromedia. Shockwave applications display interactive multimedia presentations (which are created by using Macromedia Director) to Web browsers accessing your Web server. Users must have browsers that support Shockwave before they can take advantage of Shockwave applications on the Domino Web server.

You must use HTML to embed a Shockwave component into a Domino Web site. Here is an example of the syntax used to do this:

```
[<embed scr = "/green.dcr"></embed>]
```

In the preceding example, `green.dcr` is the Shockwave file, and it's located in the directory specified in the HTML directory field under the Mapping heading in the HTTP Server section of the server document (see Figure 21-2).

HTML directory field

Figure 21-2:
The HTML
directory
specified in
the server
document.

Mapping	
HTML directory:	domino\html
Home URL:	/?Open
CGI URL path:	/cgi-bin
CGI directory:	domino\cgi-bin
Icon URL path:	/icons
Path to icons:	domino\icons

In order to use Shockwave applications with the Domino Web server, you must make sure that the HTTPD.CNF file contains these lines:

```
AddType .dcr application/x-directory binary 1.0#Shockwave
        for Director
AddType .dir application/x-directory binary 1.0#Shockwave
        for Director
AddType .dxr application/x-directory binary 1.0#Shockwave
        for Director
```

You can open the file in any text editor to verify that it contains these lines. If the file does not contain them, simply type them in and save the file.

RealAudio

The Domino Web server supports RealAudio (developed by Progressive Networks), which allows users to hear audio in real-time — a fancy technical word for *immediately*. A user must have a plug-in application with your browser to take advantage of RealAudio.

You must use HTML to integrate RealAudio with a Domino Web site. Here is an example of the syntax necessary to associate a RealAudio file with an HTML button:

```
[<A HREF = "/playit.ram"><img scr = "/button.gif"></A>]
```

In the preceding example, playit.ram is the RealAudio file and button.gif is a graphic of a button. The files are located in the directory specified in the HTML directory field under the Mapping heading in the HTTP Server section of the server document.

In order to use RealAudio applications with the Domino Web server, you must make sure that the HTTPD.CNF file contains these lines:

```
AddType .ram audio/x-pn-realaudio binary 1.0
AddType .rpm audio/x-pn-realaudio-plugin binary 1.0
AddType .ra audio/x-pn-realaudio binary 1.0
```

You can open the file in any text editor to verify that it contains these lines. If the file does not contain them, simply type in the lines and save the file.

Animated GIFs

Animated GIFs are popping up (no pun intended) all over the Web. *Animated GIFs* are those images that seem to move — an image of a mail box with a letter popping in and out, for example, or an image of a spinning wheel, or an image of a character waving.

The Domino Web server supports animated GIFs. Here is an example of the syntax necessary to execute an animated GIF:

```
[<img src ="/dogwalk.gif">]
```

Because no directory is specified, the file is located in the directory specified in the server document's HTML directory field (by default, `domino\html`).

Generally speaking, it is a good practice to put your HTML files in the `domino\html` directory. That way you keep the files in one place and you don't have to type out the entire path every time you reference an HTML file. Also, putting HTML files in that directory is a generally accepted practice; if others take over for you as the Domino Web server administrator, they have a good idea of where those files are located.

Working with Images

Using images is an essential part of building a good Web site. Images add color and life to the often dry, boring text that makes up most Web sites. In addition to knowing how to implement images into design elements (HTML buttons, icons, navigators, and so on), you should be familiar with some of the Domino Web server's settings that are specific to images.

Type of images

The Domino Web server converts all images to one of two file formats: GIF or JPEG. These file formats are the formats most often used on Web sites and most often preferred by folks with Web browsers, because files in these formats are usually very small and don't take long to download. Using the server document in the Public Address Book, you determine which format the Domino Web server converts images to.

✔ **GIF (Graphics Interchange Format):** GIFs are 8 bits (which means the picture contains a maximum of 256 colors), and all Web browsers support them. Choose this image type if you want to ensure that everybody who accesses the server with a graphical browser can view the images. The tradeoff is that the image quality of GIFs is not as good as that of JPEGs.

✔ **JPEG (Joint Photographic Experts Group):** JPEGs are 24 bits (which means the picture contains millions of colors), and *not* all Web browsers support them. Choose this image type if you know that everybody who accesses the server has a browser that supports JPEGs (which is hard, and often impossible to determine, unless your site is available only on an intranet) because the image quality of JPEGs is far superior to that of GIFs.

Image setting in the server doc

You should be familiar with a number of fields in the server document under the Operational Information heading in the HTTP Server section, for the values you specify in these fields control how the Domino Web server works with graphics (see Figure 21-3).

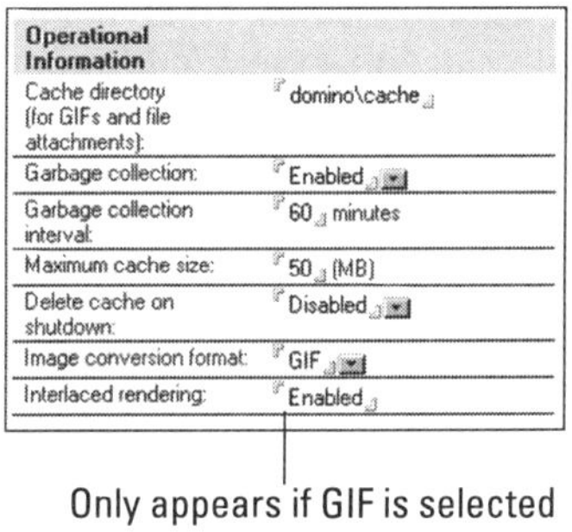

Figure 21-3: Image settings in the server document.

> Operational Information
>
> | | |
> |---|---|
> | Cache directory (for GIFs and file attachments): | domino\cache |
> | Garbage collection: | Enabled |
> | Garbage collection interval: | 60 minutes |
> | Maximum cache size: | 50 (MB) |
> | Delete cache on shutdown: | Disabled |
> | Image conversion format: | GIF |
> | Interlaced rendering: | Enabled |

Only appears if GIF is selected

✔ **Cache directory:** The default value is `domino\cache`. Click this field and type in the directory (relative to the Notes data directory, unless you type the entire directory path) on the Domino Web server in which image files and file attachments are cached. When a user requests a page that contains an image, the image is not only displayed but also is stored in this directory. The purpose of this functionality is to improve download performance when other users subsequently request the same image.

✔ **Garbage collection:** The default value is Enabled. Click the arrow to choose either the Enabled or Disabled settings. You use the Garbage collection function to specify whether you want Domino to periodically purge the cache of infrequently accessed files.

✔ **Garbage collection interval:** The default value is 60 minutes. Type in a number to specify how much time (in minutes) must pass before the garbage collection process purges infrequently accessed files from the cache.

✔ **Maximum cache size:** The default value is 50MB. Type a number in this field to specify the maximum size (in megabytes) of the cache. The garbage collection process executes automatically if the cache size reaches this specified maximum value.

✔ **Delete cache on shutdown:** The default value is `Disabled`. Click the arrow to choose either the Enabled or Disabled settings. You use these settings to specify whether you want the cache deleted when the Domino Web server is shut down.

✔ **Image Conversion format:** The default value is GIF. Click the arrow to choose either the GIF or JPEG setting. You use these setting to specify which image format you want the Domino Web server to convert images to.

✔ **Interlaced rendering:** This field appears only if you select GIF as the image conversion format. Click the arrow to choose either the Enabled or Disabled settings; the default value is `Enabled`. Web browsers typically display images top-to-bottom, one line at a time — and that can be time-consuming. Interlaced GIFs display differently; specifically, every eighth row displays, then every fourth row displays, and so on, until the entire image displays. Interlaced rendering is somewhat more user-friendly than top-to-bottom rendering because users' eyes tend to "fill in the blanks" as the image gradually fills out, so the image seems to display faster.

✔ **Progressive rendering:** This field appears only if you select JPEG as the image conversion format (see Figure 21-4). Click the arrow to choose either the Enabled or Disabled settings; the default value is `Enabled`. Web browsers typically display images top-to-bottom, one line at a time; yes, rather time consuming, isn't it? Progressive JPEGs display in several passes, the image becoming clearer with each pass, until the image displays in its full depth and richness. Progressive rendering is a little more user-friendly than top-to-bottom rendering because the users can recognize the image even before it displays completely.

✔ **JPEG image quality:** This field appears only if you select JPEG as the image conversion format. The default value is 75, but you can type a number between 5 and 100 in this field. The larger the value, the higher the quality of the image but the slower it displays. The smaller the value, the faster the image displays but the lower its quality.

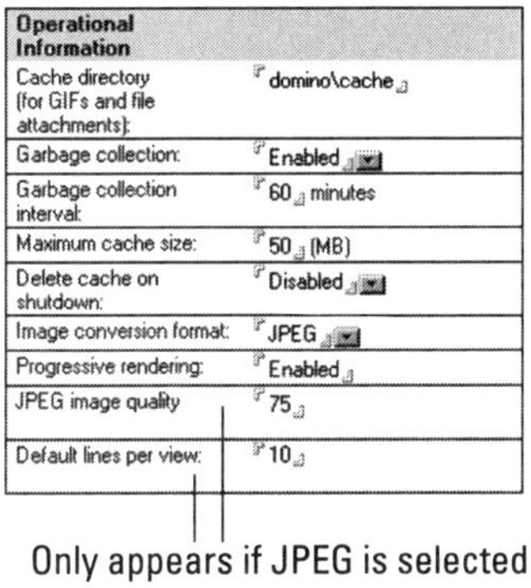

Figure 21-4: JPEG options.

Only appears if JPEG is selected

Part V
The Part of Tens

The 5th Wave   By Rich Tennant

"SINCE WE BEGAN ON-LINE SHOPPING, I JUST DON'T KNOW WHERE THE MONEY'S GOING."

In this part . . .

Everybody can use a helping hand — even those of us who are wise enough to choose Lotus Domino as our Web server of choice. When you can't figure out just what's gone wrong on your Domino Web site, pick up this book and take a look at the chapters in this part. Can't figure out why your users are complaining of unopenable documents? Check out the chapter on error messages. Need some other Domino-specific sources? Take a look at the chapter on getting more information. Hey, this is a full-service book!

Chapter 22
Ten Error Messages

▶ Common error messages

▶ Troubleshooting tips

*A*s a developer, your goal is for your users to have error-free interaction on your Domino Web site. Your users can get a number of common error messages if you don't take some precautions when you develop your site. In many chapters of this book, I point out how Web browsers don't interact with your site the same way that Notes clients do. If you're migrating or expanding from a scenario in which your users access your server only via Lotus Notes clients to one in which they access the server with Web browsers, you should beware of some things that work in Notes but cause errors in Web browsers.

Even though this chapter is in the Part of Tens, it contains 11 tips for handling error messages; consider the extra chapter a freebie — something really rare these days! Each of the 11 error messages described in this chapter begins with a designation of what category the error falls in — namely, Error 401, Error 404, or Error 500. For example, the `Unauthorized Exception` error categorized under `Error 401` is returned to the browser as `Error 401 Unauthorized Exception`. Each message is covered in the appropriate section of this chapter — Error 401, Error 404, and Error 500 — and each error description includes its cause and solution.

Error 401

An Error 401 error indicates an error regarding a user's access to execute a certain command or navigate to a certain view in the Domino Web site.

HTTP Web Server: Lotus Notes Exception — You are not authorized to perform that operation

Users get this error when they try to access a database with which they can't authenticate. Users must *authenticate* with a database by providing a name and password to Domino if they want to perform a task that requires a higher access level than the Anonymous user has in the Access Control List (ACL). For example, if Anonymous is limited to the No Access level in the ACL, users must authenticate to open the database. If Anonymous has Reader access in the ACL, users must authenticate if they want to create a document. Users get this error if they don't provide a name listed in the database's ACL or fail to provide a valid password.

You prevent this error from occurring for your users via a two-step process. First, you either add users' names or add a group in the Domino Web server's Public Address Book that includes the users' names to the ACL. Second, you must have each user add his or her password in the proper Person document of the Public Address Book.

Follow these steps to add a user's name and assign access in the database's ACL:

1. **Launch the Lotus Notes client.**

   The Lotus Notes Workspace, which displays the Domino Web server's databases as rectangular icons, appears.

2. **Click the icon for the database to which you want to add a name or group to the ACL.**

3. **Choose File⇨Database⇨Access Control.**

   The Access Control List dialog box appears (see Figure 22-1).

4. **Click the Add button.**

   The Add User dialog box appears.

5. **Type a name or group into the Add user dialog box and click OK.**

   The Access Control List dialog box appears again, and the name or group is now in the list of groups and users.

6. **Choose an access level from the Access drop-down list.**

7. **Click OK.**

Levels of access

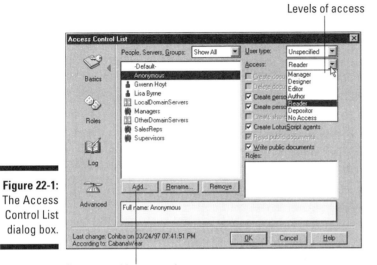

Figure 22-1:
The Access
Control List
dialog box.

Button to add users and groups

You can add a password to the person document in the Public Address Book
by following these steps:

1. Launch the Lotus Notes client.

The Lotus Notes Workspace, which displays the Domino Web server's
databases as rectangular icons, appears.

2. Click the icon for the Public Address Book.

3. Choose View➪People.

The Public Address Book opens, displaying all the person documents in
the database.

4. Double-click a name.

The person document opens in Read mode.

5. Put the person document in Edit mode by pressing Ctrl+E or by clicking the Edit Person action button.

The person document changes from Read mode to Edit mode.

6. Add a password to the HTTP field.

The HTTP field is in the Name section (see Figure 22-2). As soon as you
save or recalculate the document, the password is encrypted so that
other users (and you — so don't forget it) cannot see it.

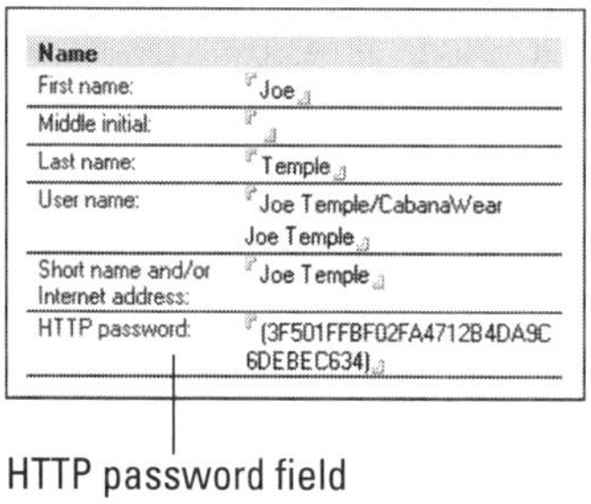

Figure 22-2:
Specify a
password in
the person
document.

HTTP password field

7. Press Ctrl+S to save the document.

Unauthorized Exception

Users get this error if they try to access a database with which they can't authenticate and, instead of typing a name and password to authenticate with the Domino Web server, they attempt to circumvent the authorization process by clicking the Cancel button in the authorization dialog box.

The solution to this error is identical to the solution to the preceding error message, HTTP Web Server: Lotus Notes Exception - You are not authorized to perform that operation. You prevent this error from occurring for your users via a two-step process. First, you either add users' names or add a group in the Domino Web server's Public Address Book that includes the users' names to the ACL. Second, you must have each user add his or her password in the proper Person document of the Public Address Book.

Error 404

An Error 404 message indicates an error in which the information requested by the user does not exist.

Not found — file doesn't exist or is read protected [even tried multi]

Users get this error when they try to open a view (by clicking on a text link, action button, navigator hotspot, or by typing a Domino-specific URL) when the database name isn't included in the URL, the database name is misspelled, or the database name doesn't include an extension.

Double-check the existence and spelling of the database name when you specify a Domino-specific URL as the formula behind a text link, action button, or navigator hotspot. If your users get the error because they frequently type an incorrect ?OpenView URL, you should consider engineering the database in such a way that users click a button or link rather than typing in a URL when they make a request to open a view. See Chapter 5 for more information on correct URL syntax.

HTTP Web Server: Lotus Notes Exception — File does not exist

People using Web browsers get this error when they execute the ?SearchSite URL on a database that isn't a search site database. The purpose of the ?SearchSite URL is for searching the Domino Web server's search site database, which groups together databases on the server.

If your users commonly get this error because they specify the name of the wrong database when typing the ?SearchSite URL, you should consider designing the database in such a way that they click instead of type to execute a search.

See Chapter 14 for ideas of how to set up a search site of a single database or a search site of a group of databases.

Figure 22-3 shows the ?SearchSite URL being executed on the `accttrak.nsf` database, which isn't a search site database. Figure 22-4 shows the result of the search. Notice that, although the search found four documents, Domino can't display them. If the user tries to click the open and closed parentheses characters, he or she gets the "HTTP Web Server . . ." error message.

Figure 22-3:
A site search executed on the wrong database.

Location: http://131.107.8.30/accttrak.nsf/$SearchForm?SearchSite

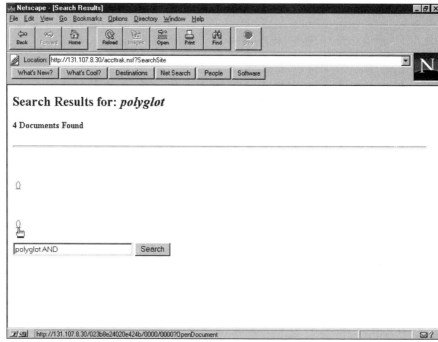

Figure 22-4:
The result
of the
erroneous
site search.

Error 500

An Error 500 error indicates an error in which the server doesn't support the user's request.

HTTP Web Server: Lotus Notes Exception — Database is not full-text indexed

To understand this error, you should know that a Full Text Index is a collection of all the words in a database, for the purpose of searching. Users get this error if they try to execute a search on a database that does not have a Full Text Index. To prevent this error, you can create a Full Text Index for the database. Refer to Chapter 14 for guidance on creating a Full Text index.

HTTP Web Server: Unknown Command Exception

Users get this error when they try to search or open a view that has a space in its name and they fail to replace the space with a plus sign (+). The URL shown in Figure 22-5 produces this error. The URL in Figure 22-6 doesn't produce this error, though, because it properly includes the plus sign (+) to replace the space in the view name.

Unfortunately, this limitation is inherent in Domino, so you as a developer can't do anything about this. You can, however, put a search or open action button on the Web page to keep users from needing to type the URL. If you like that idea, turn to Chapters 11 and 14 for more information.

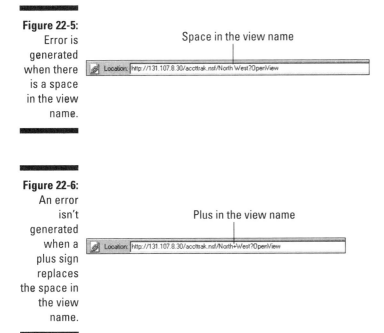

Figure 22-5:
Error is generated when there is a space in the view name.

Space in the view name

Location: http://131.107.8.30/accttrak.nsf/North West?OpenView

Figure 22-6:
An error isn't generated when a plus sign replaces the space in the view name.

Plus in the view name

Location: http://131.107.8.30/accttrak.nsf/North+West?OpenView

HTTP Web Server: Invalid URL Exception

Users get this error when they type a URL that doesn't include all the necessary components. For example, you get this error if you execute a ?SearchView or ?OpenView URL that doesn't include the name of a view.

Double-check the syntax of your URLs to make sure you entered them into the Domino site correctly. If your users often get the error because they incorrectly type the URL, consider engineering the database so that they click an action button or link instead of type a URL to make an open-view request. See Chapter 11 on how to create an action button or link to a view.

HTTP Web Server: Illegal Arguments Exception

Users get this error when they try to open a view that doesn't exist, or a view with a misspelled name, or a private view.

To prevent this error, double-check the syntax of your URLs, and if your users get the error commonly because they incorrectly type the URL, consider engineering the database so that they click a link or button rather than type to make a request to open a view. See Chapter 11 on how to create a link or button to a view.

So that users don't get this error when they try to open a private view, make sure that all of your views are shared. Unfortunately, if you created a view as private, you have to re-create it as shared; it's not an option that you can change after creating the view. Figure 22-7 shows the Shared check box that must be selected in the Create View InfoBox when you create a view. You need to check this box, because by default it isn't checked. Refer to Chapter 10 for more information on creating views.

HTTP Web Server: Lotus Notes Exception — Invalid or nonexistent document

Users get this error if they try to execute an agent for which you didn't enable the Shared Agent check box when you created it. When you create agents, make sure that you check the Shared Agent check box (see Figure 22-8), because by default it isn't selected. It's easy to forget to check that box. Unfortunately, after you create the agent, you can't change the Shared Agent attribute. To avoid your users getting this error when they try to execute the agent, you must re-create the agent. Refer to Chapter 13 for more information on agents.

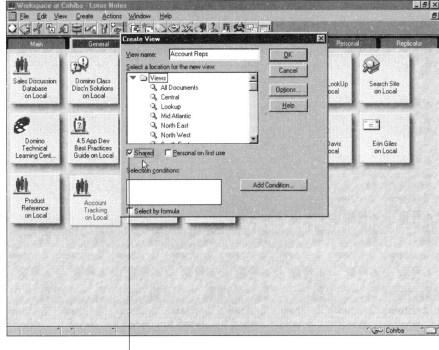

Shared check box

Figure 22-7:
Click the
Shared
check box
to make
sure your
views are
shared.

Shared check box

Figure 22-8:
Be sure to
check the
Shared
Agent
check box
when
creating
agents.

Shared Agent check box

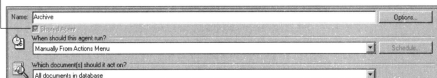

HTTP Web Server: Lotus Notes Exception — Unsupported trigger and search type for agent being run in the background

Users get this error when they try to execute an agent that you've set up in one of two ways. If you chose If Documents Have Been Pasted for the When should this agent run? setting when you created the agent (see Figure 22-9), people using a Web browser to access the site get the error when they execute the agent. Browser users also get the error if they execute an agent in which during setup you chose Selected documents from the Which document(s) should it act on? setting (see Figure 22-10). Web browsers, unfortunately, don't support these options. To prevent this error from occurring, be sure to avoid specifying either of these options when you create or edit agents.

Figure 22-9:
Agents
can't be
triggered to
run when
documents
are pasted.

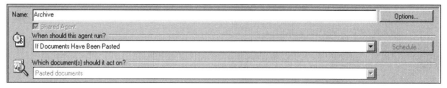

Figure 22-10:
Agents
can't run on
selected
documents.

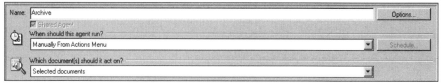

HTTP Web Server: Lotus Notes Exception — This database has local access protection and you are not authorized to access it locally

Users get this error when they try to open a database that has been encrypted with a Notes User ID. The error is generated because no such thing as a Notes User ID exists in the realm of Domino, so the Domino Web server can't decrypt the database for the Web browser. To prevent the error from being generated, you must decrypt the database using the same ID with which you encrypted it. Follow these steps:

1. **Launch the Lotus Notes client.**

   The Lotus Notes Workspace, which displays the Domino Web server's databases as rectangular icons, appears.

2. Click the icon for the database you want to decrypt.

3. Choose File⇨Database⇨Properties.

If the Properties for Database InfoBox appears, skip to Step 10. If you get the error dialog box shown in Figure 22-11, continue with Step 4.

Figure 22-11:
The error if the wrong ID is selected.

Lotus Notes

⚠ This database has local access protection and you are not authorized to access it locally

OK

4. Click the OK button in the error dialog box.

5. Choose File⇨Tools⇨Switch ID.

The Choose User ID to Switch To dialog box appears.

6. Click the ID that the database was encrypted with.

I am sorry to inform you at this point that you must know the ID used to encrypt the database; otherwise the database can't be decrypted.

7. Click the Open button.

The Enter Password dialog box appears.

8. Type the password and click OK.

You return to the main Domino window.

9. Choose File⇨Database⇨Properties.

The Properties for Database InfoBox appears.

10. Click the Encryption button.

The Encryption dialog box appears.

11. Click the Do not locally encrypt this database radio button, and then click OK.

A dialog box message tells you that your request to decrypt the database is being carried out.

12. Click OK in the dialog box.

13. Repeat Steps 5 – 8 to change back to the original ID.

Now the database is decrypted, so users with Web browsers can access it.

Chapter 23

Ten Web Sites where You Can Get More Info

. . . .

In This Chapter

▶ Access reference material

▶ Participate in discussion threads

▶ Download Domino Web server

▶ Search KnowledgeBase

▶ Get HTML information

▶ Get Java information

. . . .

*T*his book is intended to be your initial step in building and understanding a Domino Web site. A number of sites on the Web offer information that can help you build an award-winning site. Most of the sites belong to Lotus sites, but some of them belong to other vendors and organizations.

domino.lotus.com

If you could pick only one Web site from which to get additional Domino information, `domino.lotus.com` would be your best choice. This site contains more Domino information than any other site and gives you the most up-to-date information. You can download Domino at this site, and you can download sample applications and templates. As I mentioned, this is the most up-to-date site because Lotus constantly adds information, so you should visit it often to check for new free downloads.

You can read about industry awards Domino has received, news stories about Domino, competitive briefs, *FAQs* (an Internet-coined acronym for *Frequently Asked Questions*), and Domino release notes. More content is added all the time, so you may find yourself visiting often. You can usually find presentations given by product developers at industry shows such as the Lotusphere, which is Lotus' huge show held in Florida every January. Lotus is also taking advantage of the wonderful communication medium the Internet offers by allowing you to submit bugs (I mean, report undocumented features, of course) that you find in Domino.

Two of the most important things that the `domino.lotus.com` site offers is a means for people to post their Web sites that they develop and manage with Domino, and a discussion forum in which users can participate. Well, it's probably not so great to you that you can post your Domino site, but seeing the sites that others have posted can certainly help you see what others are doing with their Domino Web sites, and steal — I mean *borrow* — their ideas (with their permission, of course).

Once you get involved with the design of your Domino Web site, I can't encourage you strongly enough to visit the discussion forum as often as possible. I try to go to the forum every day to see what types of things people are trying to do with their sites, what recommendations they are making, what questions they are asking, and most importantly, what the Lotus developers are saying in their responses to the questions. That's right — Lotus developers actually answer people's questions, unlike the developers from most software companies these days.

www.lotus.com

The `www.lotus.com` site is the main Web site for Lotus Development Corporation. Like all the other Lotus Web sites, it is built on and runs on a Domino Web server. It contains over 8,000 pages from more than 80 Lotus Notes databases throughout the world, thereby demonstrating the unique distributive and collaborative environment that you can create when you build and run your Web site on a Domino Web server.

Although I would start by visiting the `domino.lotus.com` site first, I would visit `www.lotus.com` site next in a quest for Domino-specific information. And I would go to the latter site first if I want to access information on Business Partners (independent consulting and training companies that have a relationship with Lotus and provide services and products that utilize and enhance Lotus technologies), LotusScript, or some other topic that, although not specific to Domino, could still help me regarding my use of Domino. The site offers a wide range of stuff such as downloads, discussion areas, reference materials, software/operating system testing results, and services offered by Lotus. Much of the information is categorized in separate directories on the site.

The `www.lotus.com/solutions` directory offers you success stories and a look at the solutions that Lotus Business Partners have developed. If you're in the market for hiring a consulting company to do some work for you, you can see what many of the different Lotus Business Partners have to offer.

The directory also includes a special section called Notes@Work, which focuses on business and commerce solutions with Lotus products, especially Domino and Lotus Notes.

The `www.lotus.com/internet` directory includes product demonstrations, Domino customer success stories, pricing information, performance testing information, and a calendar of events held throughout the world where you can see Domino showcased.

The `www.lotus.com/devtools` directory contains information specific to developers. You can find a great deal of documents written by Lotus product managers and developers focusing on the technical aspects of the products. The directory offers two helpful sections called, respectively, Tips & Techniques and Tip of the week. One of the most useful elements in this directory is the IBM Redbooks. You can download the very well written and helpful books, which are in Adobe Acrobat file format. Redbooks, including the official *Developer's Handbook*, cover topics such as how to develop with LotusScript.

The `www.lotus.com/notes` directory offers much reference material specific to Lotus Notes. You can find the Return on Investment (ROI) Study on using Lotus Notes. In fact, from this directory you can download software and access more reference material than you could possibly read.

www.internet.ibm.com

This site offers information that goes beyond the scope of just the Domino Web server. As a matter of fact, if you click most of the Domino-related links, such as the link to download Domino, you are actually navigated to the official Domino site (`domino.lotus.com`). From the `www.internet.ibm.com` site, you can get a lot of high-level information about the Internet, especially about commerce on the Internet. The information is grouped into directories.

The `www.internet.ibm.com/solutions` directory offers information on IBM's Internet software solutions, industry solutions, cross-industry solutions, and integrated solutions. You can learn what technology is hot and, from the customer testimonials, how the technology is being implemented. Although the subjects are diverse, you won't be disappointed with this directory, especially if you are interested in commerce over the Internet.

The `www.internet.ibm.com/news` directory has links to IBM's Internet-related press releases and news stories. You can view the top stories by month or by category. The categories that you might find most interesting are Internet/intranet, Lotus, Business Solutions, Commerce, Web Servers, and Security. This directory is a good place to look if you want to find out how other companies, possibly even your competitors, are using the Internet.

The www.internet.ibm.com/partners directory contains information on companies that develop Internet solutions with Domino and other IBM Internet products. IBM's Value Added Reseller (VAR) and Business Enterprise Solutions Teams (BESTeams) directories can be found here. This directory is the place to look if you are interested in talking with a consulting company who can build an Internet solution, or if you are interested in getting an idea of how top-notch consulting companies are building Internet solutions.

A number of other directories on this site are worth checking out. Don't forget to take a look at www.ibm.com.

orionweb.lotus.com

The orionweb.lotus.com site allows you to search through Lotus' vast library of technical information. If you need to find out about a particular error message, or if you want to find out how to design something on your Domino Web site, you can come to this site and perform a search. Figure 23-1 shows the standard search form you get when you specify the URL orionweb.lotus.com/basic.html. To execute a search:

1. **In the Select Datasource(s) scroll box, choose Support Technical Information and Support File Library.**

2. **Choose Notes from the Select Product Group(s) scroll box.**

3. **Type the word or phrase you want to search for in the Ask Your Question text box.**

   The search engine works best if you type a sentence explaining what you are searching for. For example, "How to create a keyword field."

4. **Choose a language from the Document Language scroll box.**

   If you choose English, only those documents on your topic and written in English return to you at the end of the search.

5. **Choose a number in the Return documents scroll box.**

   This tells the search engine how many documents you want returned from the search. The choices are in five-document increments.

6. **Click the radio button of your choice in the Sort Results by section.**

   You have three choices of how you want the search results sorted: by Relevance, Date, or Product Area.

7. **Click the Search button.**

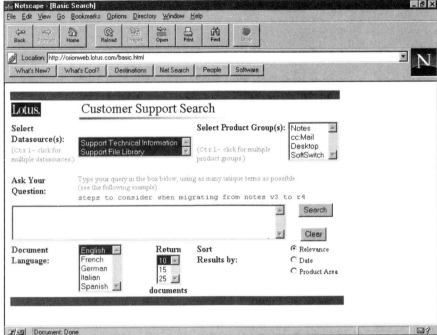

Figure 23-1:
The search
form for
orionweb.
lotus.com.

www.support.lotus.com

This site contains technical support information for all Lotus products.
Although the information herein is not Domino-specific, it is useful enough
to make it worth visiting periodically. It has a product discussion area and a
FAQ area. You can learn about the various technical support offerings, and
you can get telephone numbers for Lotus technical support. This site has a
good collection of software programs that you can download. As a matter of
fact, I find that it has a more comprehensive offering of downloadable
programs that most other Lotus sites do.

You can also go to www.support.lotus.com/feedback/feedback.htm if
you want to submit a product suggestion to Lotus. Lotus welcomes new
product suggestions, new functionality suggestions for existing products,
and specific suggestions on improving functionality for existing products.

www.notes.net

Iris Associates, Inc., which was founded in 1984 and became a wholly owned subsidiary of Lotus Development Corporation in 1994, is the developer of Lotus Notes. The `www.notes.net` site belongs to Iris Associates, and it's a great site. You can access step-by-step guides and technical papers on Domino, and you can download a 90-day trial version of the software. After you finish reading *Lotus Domino For Dummies*, you can read the equivalent of *Lotus Domino For Astrophysicists* by downloading the document *Architectural Overview of the Domino Web Server*.

Another nice part of the site is the Notes Café, which is an open discussion area where you can exchange ideas with management and core developers at Iris.

Although the Internet Cookbook seems a bit out-of-date — which is not too hard within an industry where technology becomes obsolete in a matter of months — you can access it at `www.notes.net/cookbook.nsf`. I mention this not because I think you should read out-of-date material, but because I am sure it will be updated by the time you read this.

www.net.lotus.com

Once you read Chapter 19, which covers Domino.Applications, you are ready to pay the `www.net.lotus.com` Web site a visit. It focuses on the Domino.Applications products Domino.Merchant, Domino.Action, and Domino.Broadcast for PointCast. This site is to Domino.Applications what `domino.lotus.com` is to Domino; that is, it is *the* unofficial official site for Domino Applications. It is the first place you should go for the most comprehensive and up-to-date information on Domino.Applications.

www.w3.org

The World Wide Web Consortium (W3C) was founded in 1994 "to develop common standards for the evolution" of the Web. The consortium is jointly hosted by the Massachusetts Institute of Technology Laboratory for Computer Science (MIT/LCS), a group in Europe, and a group in Asia. W3C's membership consists of more than 165 companies and organizations that are leaders in the areas of hardware, software, telecommunications, academics, and government.

Think of W3C as sort of the carrier of the World Wide Web torch. If you want vendor-independent information on where the Web is coming from, where it is headed, and what is new with it, or if you want Web architectural or security information, info about HTML, and so on, this is the site to check out. The W3C is working to promote standards among the major players in the Web, so you'll find unbiased (that is, vendor-independent) information intended for Web users and developers, sample applications that demonstrate Web technology, and a reference on code implementation at the site.

java.sun.com

This site should be your number-one source of information on Java. You find reference material, success stories, and information on what's new with Java, and you can see demos of Java applets here.

If you're a hard-core developer, you'll like how you can get all sorts of information on Java, JavaBeans, Java applets, Java Security, and Java so on. You can download the Java Development Kit (JDK) and you can see a tutorial on Java from this site.

kona.lotus.com

After you investigate the previous nine sites (only because they are more relevant to the subject matter of this book), I recommend you check this one out. Although its subject matter doesn't relate directly to Domino Web server, it gives you an idea of what the future holds if you develop an intranet solution (and Internet, although to a lesser degree, because an intranet consists of internal employees sharing resources) with the Domino Web server.

Kona is a code name for Java applets that Lotus is developing. The individual applets perform spreadsheet, word processor, schedule, calendar, to-do, or presentation graphics tasks. Each applet is task-focused, compact, fast and — since it is developed with Java — cross-platform. Even without a spreadsheet program installed on a computer, a Web browser user can execute the spreadsheet Kona applet to quickly perform a spreadsheet task such as adding a column of numbers.

The `kona.lotus.com` Web site has technical and strategical information about the Kona applets. You can also view a demo and read press releases regarding the technology. The site is new, so it's only going to get more comprehensive. It's a window to the future — check it out!

Chapter 24

Top Ten Reasons to Use Domino

*Y*ou may decide to build your Web site on a Domino Web server for any number of reasons, some good, some bad. If you're cost conscious, you may choose Domino because it's the least expensive way to create a full-featured, robust, and scalable intranet site. If you have a lot of Lotus Notes expertise, you may decide that learning how to build a site will take less time if you use Domino. Or if your boss has told you that you are going to use Domino and that's that, you may simply have no say in the matter.

Whatever your reason, I can tell you that, based on my experience with different Web servers, building your Web site on a Domino Web server is a good choice. I want to share with you ten reasons why I think so.

Security

The security model you can take advantage of when developing and maintaining your Domino Web site is very comprehensive.

You can grant or deny different levels of access to different users or groups of users. You can grant or deny users access to the Domino Web server. For those users to whom you grant access to the server, you can grant or deny access to certain databases. For those users to whom you grant access to a database, you can grant or deny access to individual documents. For those users to whom you grant access to a document, you can grant or deny access to individual sections or fields.

Not only can you grant or deny users access to a particular database, but you can specify what they can do in that database. You can determine whether users can read, create, edit, or delete documents. The security model is dynamic, which means that if you give someone just the ability to read documents, you can later give her the ability to read and create documents.

Here's another Domino security bonus: Consider a scenario in which a document is Editable during a review process but is submitted as soon as it is 30 days old. It makes sense that the document be Editable during the review process, but as soon as the clock strikes midnight on the 30th day, you want the document's security access to automatically change so that nobody can edit it. You don't want it to be necessary for somebody to remember the document's expiration, manually go into the server, and change security for the document.

Also, using SSL (Secure Sockets Layer) encryption, you can encrypt information as it transmits to the Domino Web server. Domino Web server's support of SSL should make your customers much more comfortable about submitting their credit card numbers to your Web site.

Ability to Quickly Create a Web Presence

Domino enables you to create your Internet or intranet site easily and quickly. Domino.Action, which ships with Domino, is a tool you use to build a Web site even if you have absolutely no Web or Lotus Notes development experience. All you need is a mouse for clicking buttons and boxes and a keyboard for typing information such as your company name, your company address, and any other information you want to communicate to site visitors.

Domino.Action builds a site using a library of templates (a Lotus Notes database that you create based on the `LibAct.ntf` template file) and the configuration selections you make. Domino.Action builds the site based on templates, which means that the design and content of your site is consistent no matter how geographically dispersed are the people responsible for its content and design.

Most Web servers require you to keep individual HTML files on the server's hard drive. A Domino Web site pulls all its design and content from Lotus Notes databases (although if you want, you can certainly reference HTML files on the server's hard drive, as well). You can manage the site much easier because all the information about design and content about your site is stored in a single Lotus Notes database or a group of Lotus Notes databases. On most Web servers, if you move a group of HTML files from one directory to another, you either have to change all the links that referred to them as being in that original place, or redirect the URLs to another location, which complicates the design of the site. Also, when HTML files are stored on a server's hard drive, determining which files are old and okay to remove is hard. Storing all the documents on the Domino Web server in one database makes determining what you can remove from the site considerably easier.

Say No to HTML . . .

Hypertext Markup Language (HTML) is the language you use to create documents that users can view with their Web browsers. It's a relatively easy-to-understand language (compared to other software programming languages), but it nonetheless takes some time to learn.

You don't have to know a single bit of HTML to develop a Domino Web site. The Domino Web server automatically converts all your design work and content creation to HTML when users with Web browsers request a look at the information.

While you're designing the Domino Web site, you can format everything by clicking SmartIcons with your mouse and by making selections from the resulting menus. The Domino Web server automatically adds the sometimes cryptic HTML formatting tags. When you create site content, you type documents in plain English and the Domino Web server translates them to HTML.

. . . Or Say Yes to HTML

You say you're an HTML guru who has spent years developing your craft? No problem. You can integrate HTML into Domino if you want. Actually, even if you know HTML, I'm sure you'll find yourself clicking with your mouse and typing plain English, and letting the Domino Web server handle the conversion. But, there are certain things, like getting text to blink, that you must use HTML to accomplish. Also, the ability to integrate HTML is useful when you add graphics to view columns and when you format the submission page that users get when they submit a document. And, if you have created a site with HTML, you can import the existing files into a Lotus Notes database or simply put them on the Domino Web server's hard drive and access them via URLs.

In addition to integrating HTML, the Domino Web server also supports the integration of Java applets, JavaScript, Perl scripts, ActiveX, OLE, Animated GIFs, RealAudio, Shockwave, GIF files, and JPEG files.

Your site must have a visual identity if you want people to remember it and enjoy coming back to it. Your ability to integrate images into your Web site is paramount to its success. Using the Domino Web server, you can fully integrate images into your Web site, and you can specify regions of images as hotspots. When users click a hotspot that you create, they navigate to other areas of the Domino Web site or to others areas of the Web itself, or they execute a command or process on the server.

Backend Power

The term *backend* in computer lingo means, "stuff that happens behind the curtain." It describes the things that happen on the server. Meanwhile, the term *front end* refers to things that happen pretty much before your eyes, as on the client PC or Web browser used to access the Domino Web site.

Your Domino Web server offers considerable backend power. It can route mail, replicate databases, index databases so that they can be searched, and most importantly, automatically execute processes or agents. (Examples of *processes* are the automatic archiving of documents when they are 30 days old, and the automatic sending of an e-mail notification to an account rep when one of his accounts has a payment that becomes past due.) And you control these powerful functions of Domino.

The Domino Web server's agent technology is the heart and brains of its ability to handle workflow. For example, if you have a project-approval process that requires several different people to sign off in succession for a project, don't physically carry the document from person to person or manually e-mail it to each person (which introduces the possibility of e-mailing it to the wrong person). Just make the server handle the routing of the information by creating a workflow agent. All any one person needs to do is give it a stamp of approval; the Domino Web server handles the process of getting the electronic document to the next person in the approval succession.

Distributed Design and Content

The Domino Web server separates design from content. You can assign responsibility for the design (views, forms, action buttons, fields, and so on) of a Domino Web site to some people and responsibility for its content (the documents) to others. That's an important characteristic in environments in which the practical solution is to have Information Services employees responsible for designing a Web site and maintaining that design, and to have managers and product developers responsible for filling the Web site with the information that they deem most pertinent. Of course, users with Web browsers also create content; it's not just the managers and product developers determining content.

The Domino Web server can replicate the Web site's design to people, no matter where they are; so people in Boston and Seattle can work on the design of the same Web site. But Domino's inherent design freedom does even more. If you put the design of the Web site on a laptop, people can even work on the design while they're traveling on a plane.

The Domino Web server also can replicate the Web site's content. If your Domino Web site is located in New York, you can have people creating site content from Milan, Sydney, a plane, a boat, or a train.

Compound Document Support

You can store a wide array of information in the documents on your Domino Web server, not just text. You can have text, formatted text, numbers, time, objects, voice, video, scanned images, and relational data stored in your Domino Web site.

If you want an application that includes compound documents, try out a Human Resource intranet site. As job candidates submit their résumés, you can scan these résumés into the Domino Web site as individual documents so that hiring managers can view them. Or you can perform an OCR (Optical Character Recognition) process on them so that each word they contain becomes searchable. Rather than scrolling through a view on the Domino Web site one résumé at a time, hiring managers can execute a search for some key words and then scroll through just the documents that match the criteria.

File Attachment Support

Server users can upload and download files from your Domino Web site without your having to set up an FTP server. (File Transfer Protocol, or *FTP*, is an Internet protocol for transferring files.) Note that users must have a Web browser that supports attaching files before they can upload files to a Domino Web site.

Users can attach any file to a document in your Domino Web server, regardless of the type. If they can see the files on their hard drives, they can attach them to documents.

Sometimes you may need to distribute important information that isn't suited for the graphical viewing nature of Web documents. Say, for example, that you have a large spreadsheet that you simply wanted to make available to employees. In such a case, converting it to HTML so that users can view it through their Web browsers would not make sense. With Domino, you can attach such a file to a document on your Web site.

If security is a concern, you can make it so that users can download files from your Web site only after submitting a registration. If your Domino Web site is a commerce site, you can make it so that only people who have submitted payment information can download files. Note that payment information submitted to Domino is validated *immediately;* many servers accept payment information, grant user access to content, and then validate that information at a later date.

A common example of when uploading files comes in handy is when you upload budget projections that you have requested from different employees. You can have the employees create a document on the Domino Web server and then attach their Microsoft Excel or Lotus 1-2-3 file. Or you may attach a word processor file to a document on the Domino Web server and then ask certain employees to detach the file, make updates in the word processing program, and attach the file back to the original document on the Domino Web server.

If you do not want to detach files from documents on the Domino Web site to your hard drive, you can view attached files with the appropriate viewer, assuming your Web browser supports that viewer.

Access to Your E-Mail and Calendar

If you're a Lotus Notes mail user, you can view your e-mail and calendar with a Web browser. You aren't required to have your Notes ID with you. All you need to do is find a machine that has a Web browser, access the Domino Web server your mail files are on, open your mail database (which you can do only after you specify your name and password, of course), and work with it as if you were sitting in front of your computer back in the office.

Beginning in version 4.5, your Lotus Notes mail database also includes your calendar, which means you can view your calendar from the Web browser just as if you were sitting in front of your computer in the office.

If you don't have a Lotus Notes client or Lotus Notes ID but would like to use the powerful Lotus Notes mail program, you can do so by paying a reduced license fee and creating a mail database and person document on the Domino Web server.

Access to Relational Data

Many companies have spent thousands, if not millions, of dollars creating and maintaining their relational databases (RDBMs). These high-end transactional systems are the power behind the ordering and fulfillment process that goes on when you order from a clothing catalog, the power behind the debit and record process that goes on when you make a withdrawal from a bank's ATM machine, and the power behind the reporting and research process that goes on when you call your credit card company to get your outstanding balance.

Many companies rely heavily on these RDBM systems. The problem with these systems is that they are centrally located and sharing or viewing their information is no simple matter when you're working remotely.

The Domino Web server, in conjunction with software that transfers information back and forth with the machine that holds the relational data, can display the information on your Web site. So, people working remotely with just a Web browser and modem can access the information stored in the relational database, and can use their Web browsers in creating documents that can be transferred to the relational database.

When dealing with enterprise data of this nature, security must be an absolute top priority. The Domino Web server can ensure that only a specific individual or group of individuals can access the information through a Web browser. And, just as it can with any database, it can also ensure than only certain people can create, edit, and delete information.

Index

• D •

• *Q* •

• *R* •

• T •

• U •

• *X* •

• *Y* •